MARK WAID · PETER KRAUSE

IRREDEEMABLE

VOLUME 1

IRREDEEMA

ROSS RICHIE
chief executive officer

ANDREW COSBY
chief creative officer

MARK WAID
editor-in-chief

ADAM FORTIER
vice president,
publishing

CHIP MOSHER
marketing director

MATT GAGNON
managing editor

IRREDEEMABLE – July 2009 published by BOOM! Studios. Irredeemable is copyright © 2009 Boom Studios. BOOM! Studios™ and the BOOM! logo are trademarks of Boom Entertainment, Inc., registered in various countries and categories. All rights reserved. The characters and events depicted herein are fictional. Any similarity to actual persons, demons, anti-Christs, aliens, vampires, face-suckers or political figures, whether living, dead or undead, or to any actual or supernatural events is coincidental and unintentional. So don't come whining to us. Office of publication: 6310 San Vicente Blvd Ste 404, Los Angeles, CA 90048. Printed in Canada.

FIRST EDITION: JULY 2009
10 9 8 7 6 5 4 3 2 1

BLE

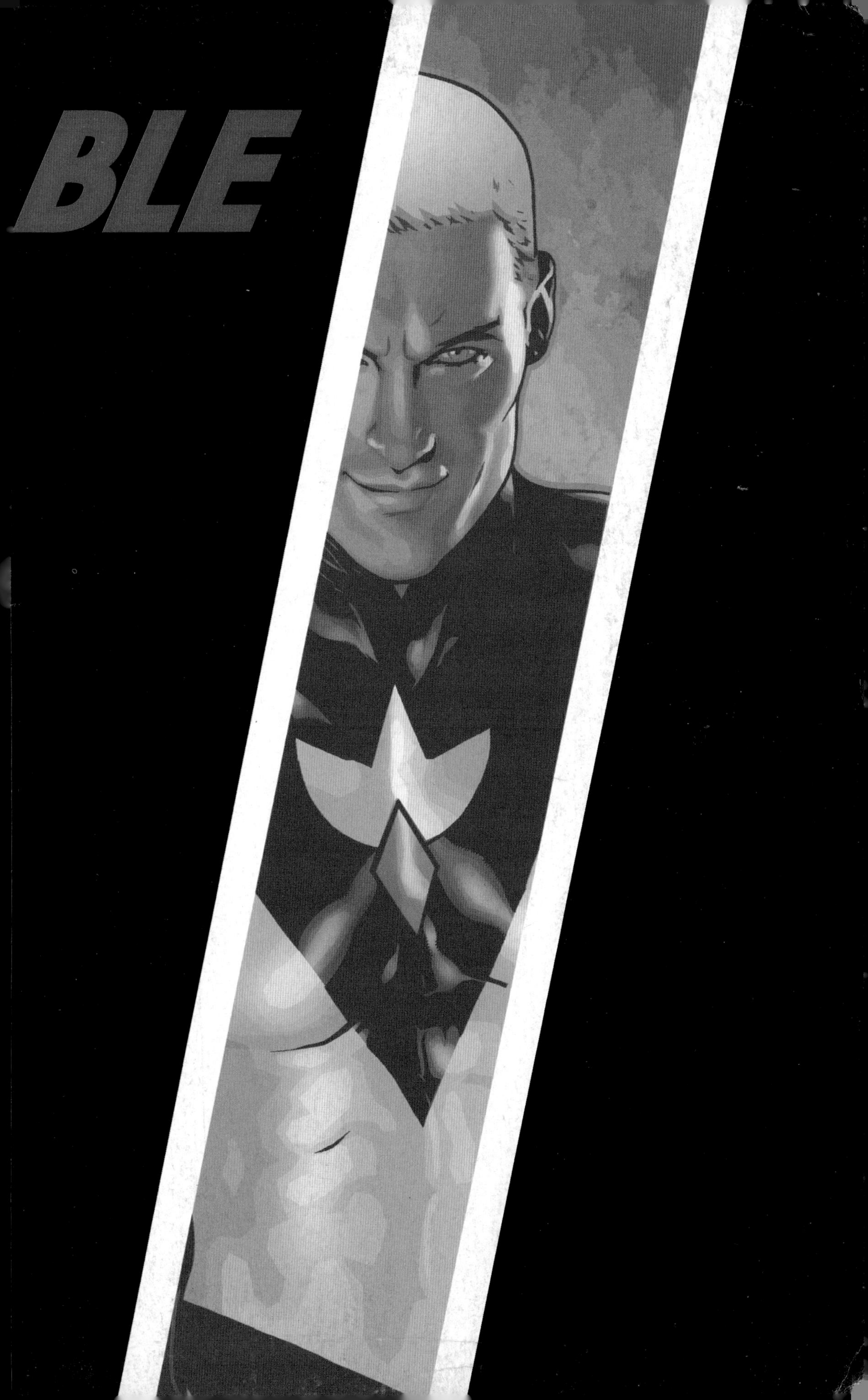

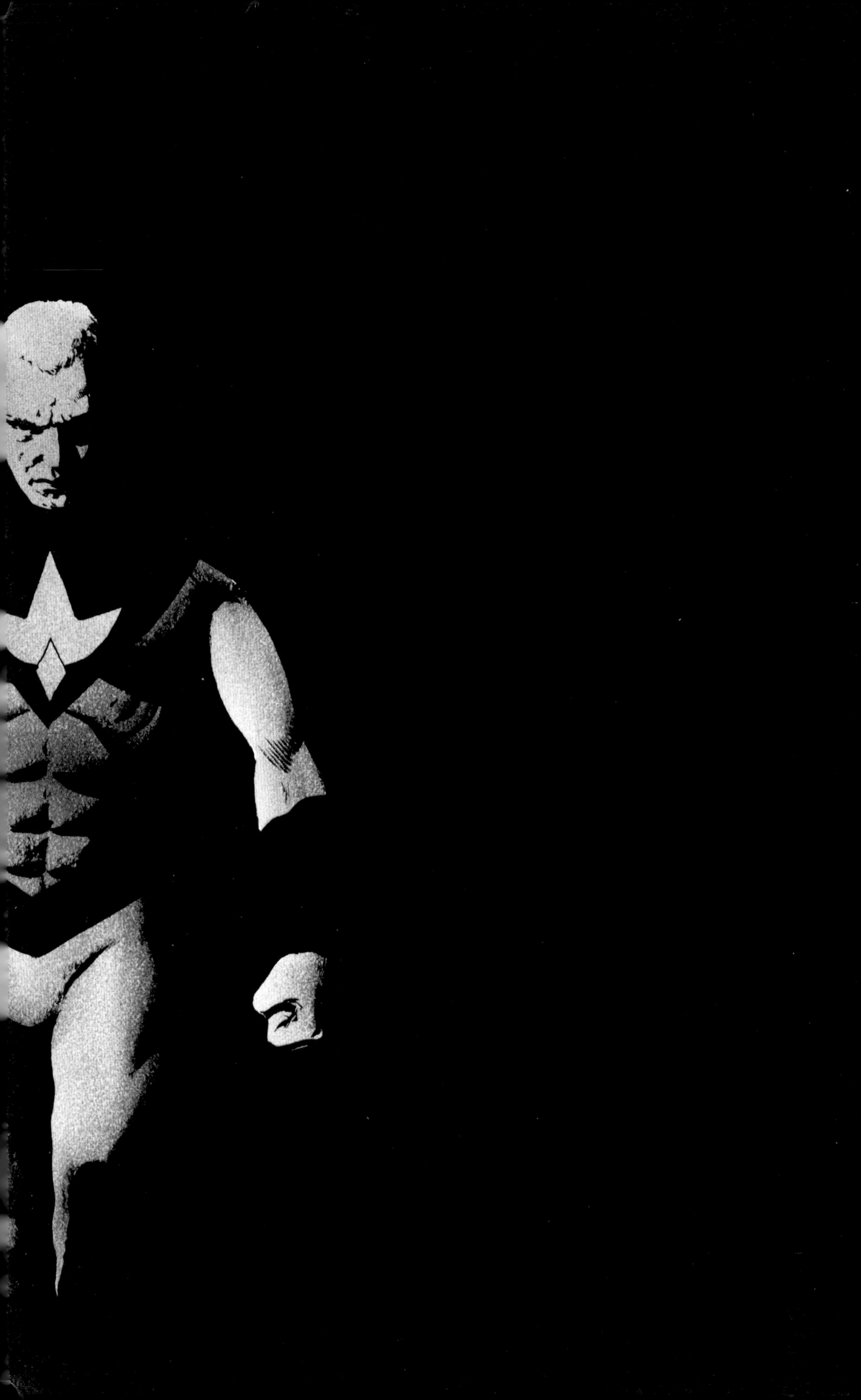

CREATED & WRITTEN BY: **MARK WAID**
ARTIST: **PETER KRAUSE**

COLORIST: **ANDREW DALHOUSE**
LETTERER: **ED DUKESHIRE**
EDITOR: **MATT GAGNON**

COVER: **JOHN CASSADAY**
colors / **LAURA MARTIN**

PLUTONIAN CHARACTER DESIGN: **PAUL AZACETA**

TRADE DESIGN: **ERIKA TERRIQUEZ**

INTRODUCTION

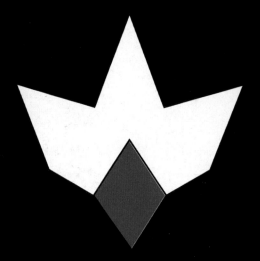

In superhero comics, pretty much everyone who's called upon to put on a cape is, at heart, emotionally equipped for the job.

I reject that premise.

IRREDEEMABLE is an idea that's been kicking around in my head for a long, long time. You saw flashes of it in KINGDOM COME and in EMPIRE—but the first was about the ethical price of heroism and the second was about a world where heroism just flat-out didn't exist. IRREDEEMABLE is, in a way, the third and most complex chapter on the cost of superheroics—a pulp adventure tale of horror about how the lessons we learn about right and wrong as children can become warped and twisted when challenged by the realities of the adult world. IRREDEEMABLE is the story of a man who was the greatest and most beloved superhero of all time...

...and how he became the world's greatest supervillain.

No one simply turns "evil" one day. Villainy isn't a light switch. The road to darkness is filled with moments of betrayal, of loss, of disappointment, and of superhuman weakness. In the case of the Plutonian, there were sidekicks who sold his secrets. There were friends who preyed too often on his selflessness and enemies who showed him unsettling truths about himself. And those were the good days.

IRREDEEMABLE takes us down that Conradian path of transformation in horrifying detail, as illustrated with grim poignancy by the unbelievably talented Peter Krause and narrated by the Plutonian's former allies—a team of heroes on the run from the world's most powerful and angry being, racing desperately through time and space to learn the Plutonian's secrets just as he knows all of theirs. How did he come to this? What became of the hope and promise once inside him? What happens to the world when its savior betrays it?

What makes a hero IRREDEEMABLE?

Mark Waid
Los Angeles
January 2009

CHAPTER 1

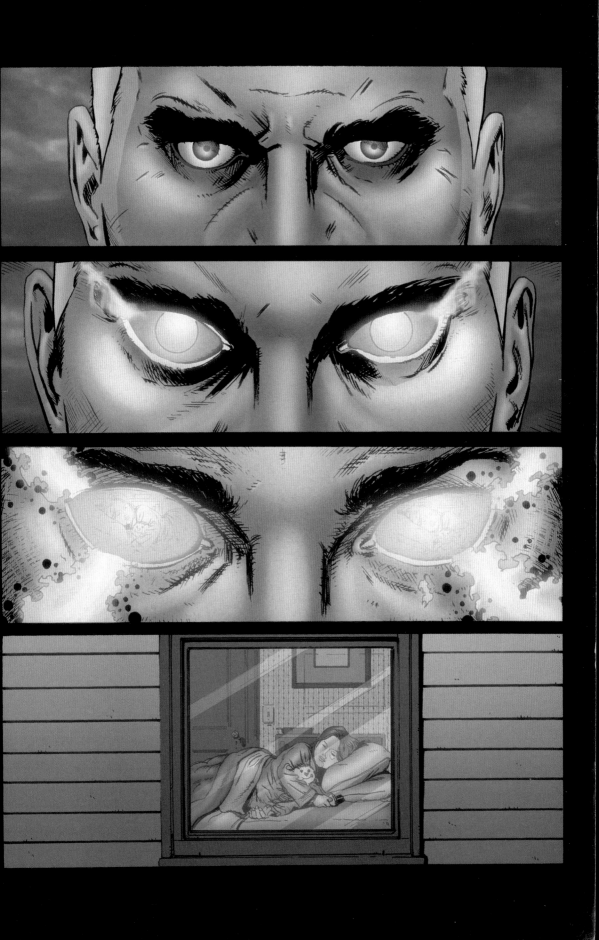

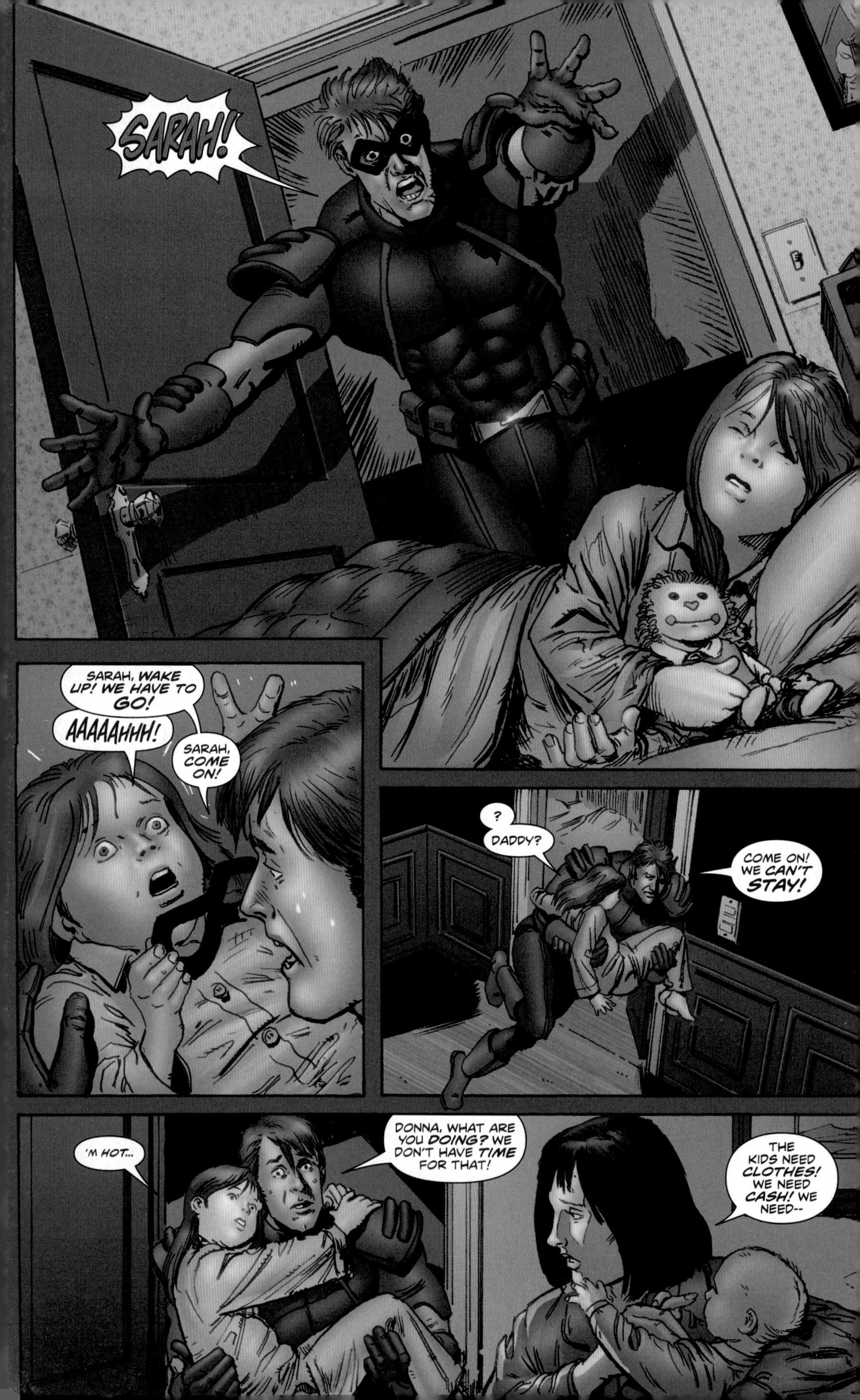
SARAH!
SARAH, WAKE UP! WE HAVE TO GO!
AAAAAHHH!
SARAH, COME ON!
?
DADDY?
COME ON! WE CAN'T STAY!
'M HOT...
DONNA, WHAT ARE YOU DOING? WE DON'T HAVE TIME FOR THAT!
THE KIDS NEED CLOTHES! WE NEED CASH! WE NEED--

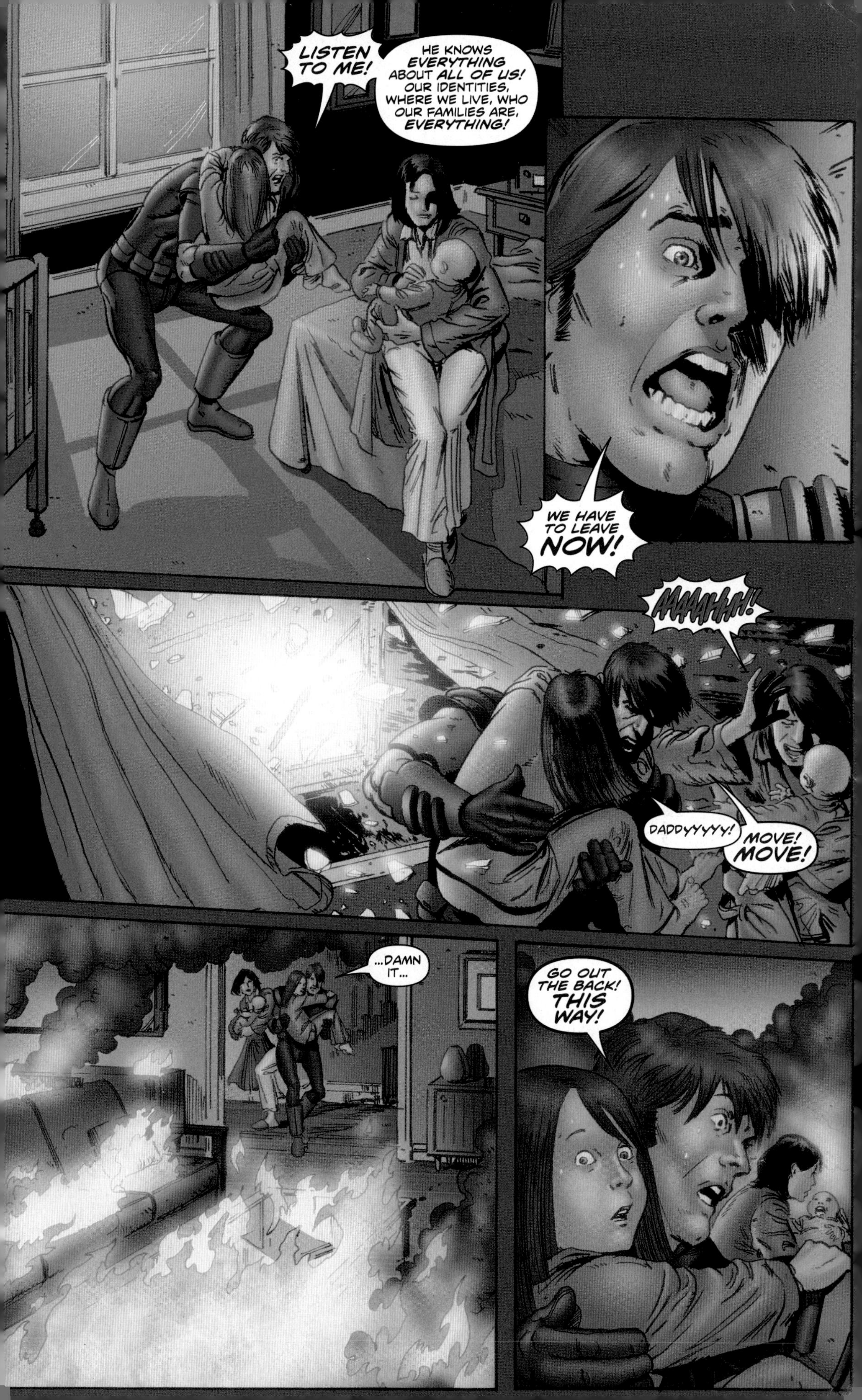
LISTEN TO ME!
HE KNOWS EVERYTHING ABOUT ALL OF US! OUR IDENTITIES, WHERE WE LIVE, WHO OUR FAMILIES ARE, EVERYTHING!
WE HAVE TO LEAVE NOW!
AAAAAHHH!!
DADDYYYYY!
MOVE! MOVE!
...DAMN IT...
GO OUT THE BACK! THIS WAY!

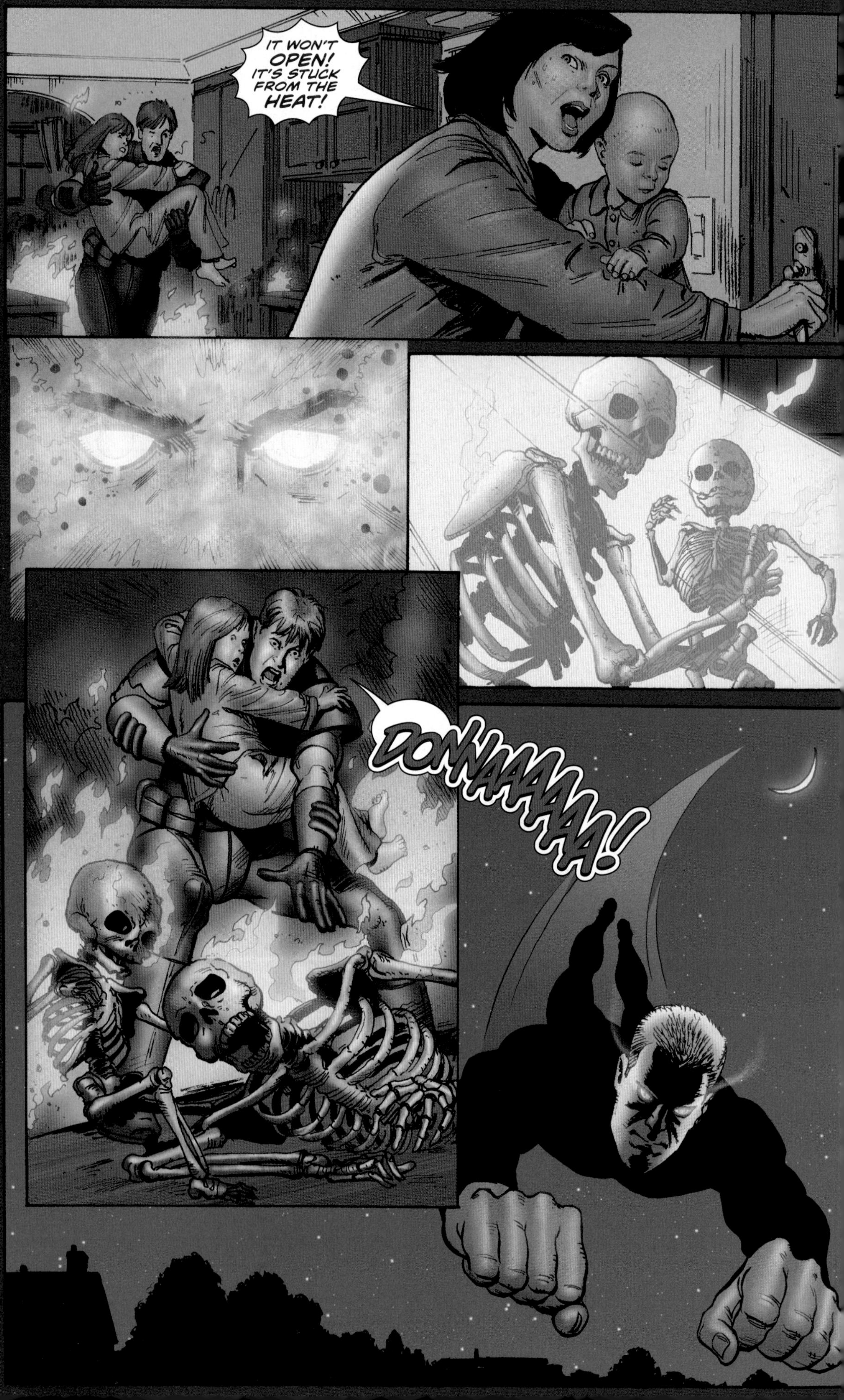
IT WON'T OPEN! IT'S STUCK FROM THE HEAT!
DONNAAAAAAA!

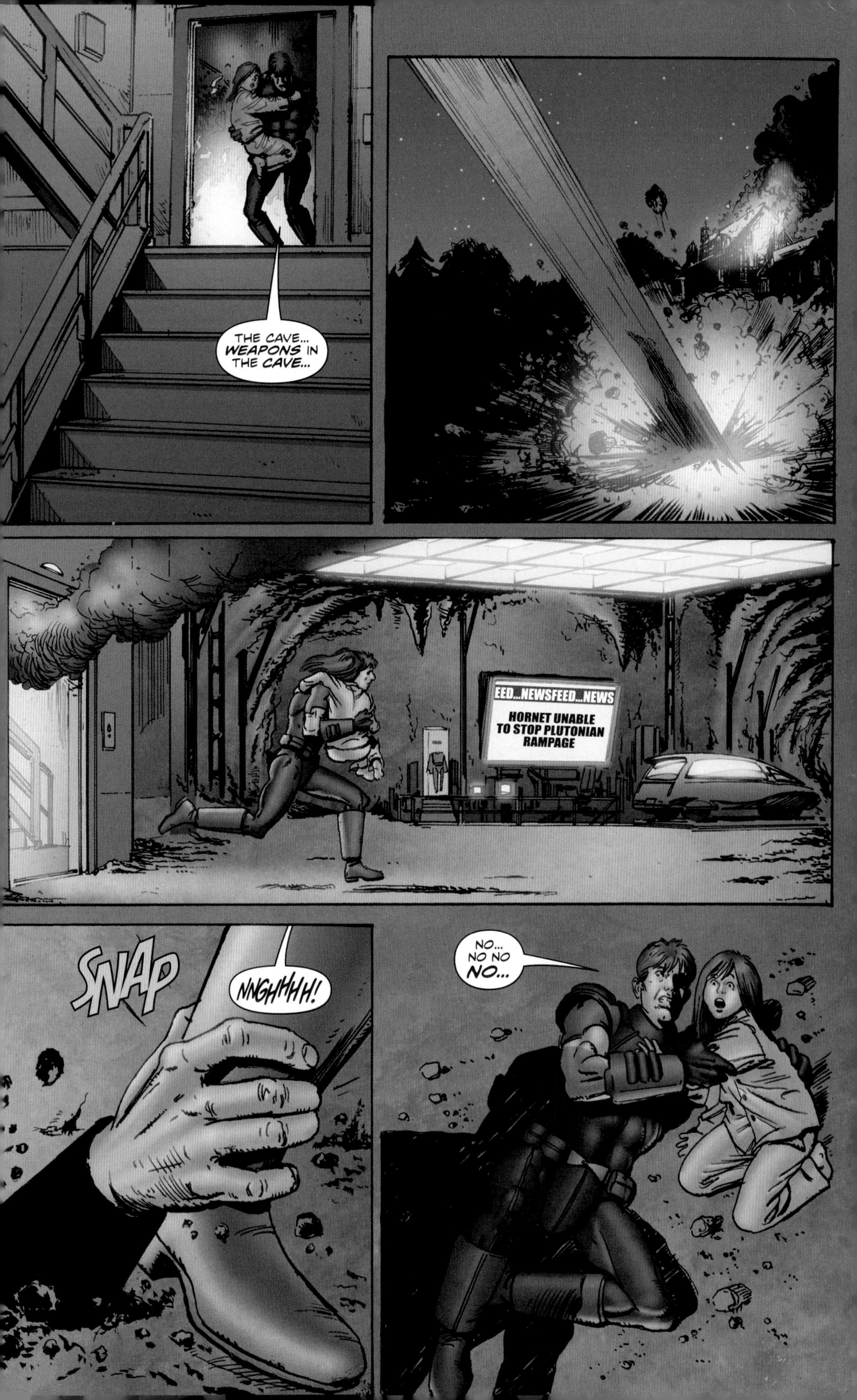
THE CAVE... WEAPONS IN THE CAVE...
EED...NEWSFEED...NEWS
HORNET UNABLE TO STOP PLUTONIAN RAMPAGE
SNAP
NNGHHHH!
NO... NO NO NO...

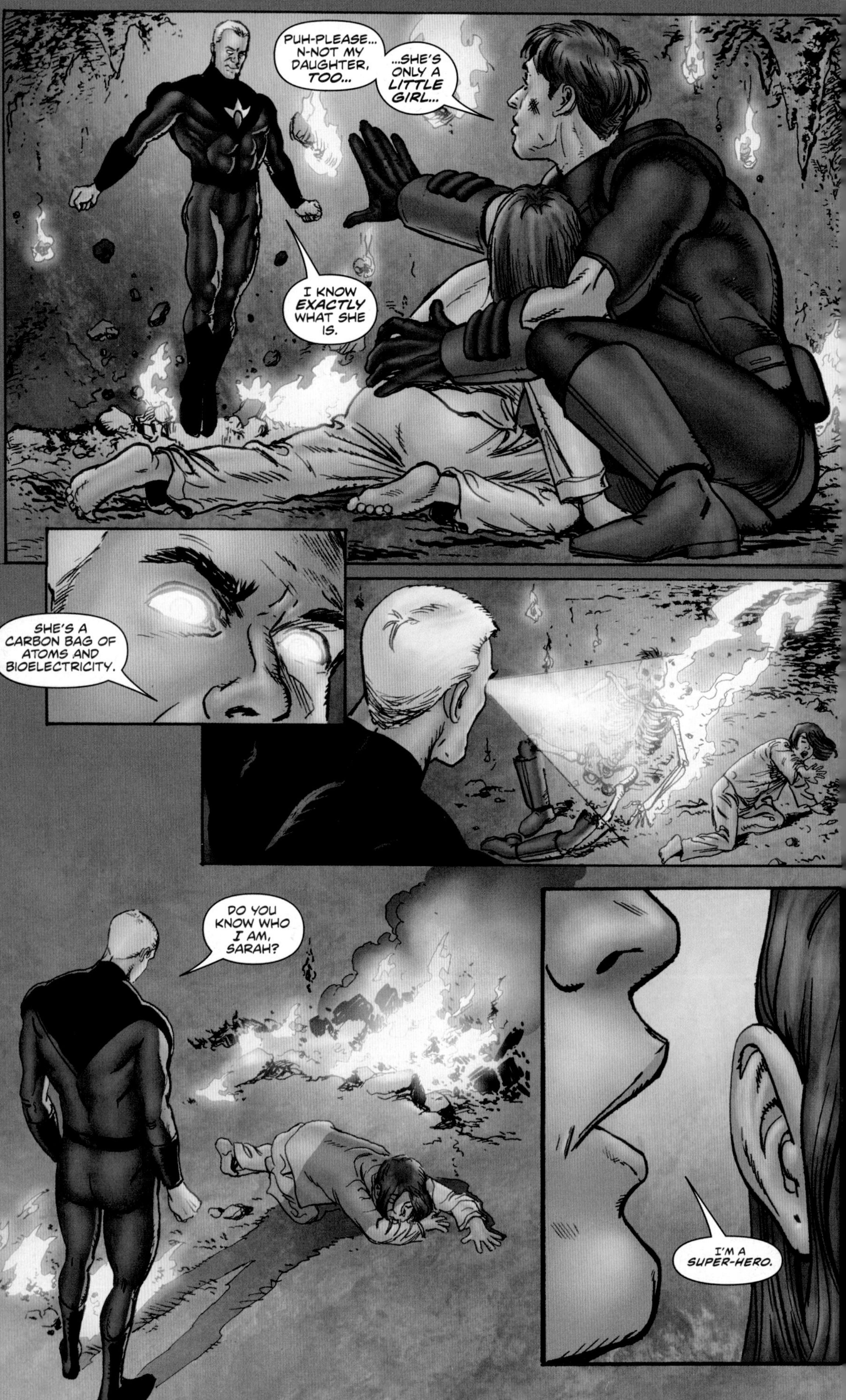
PUH-PLEASE... N-NOT MY DAUGHTER, TOO...
...SHE'S ONLY A LITTLE GIRL...
I KNOW EXACTLY WHAT SHE IS.
SHE'S A CARBON BAG OF ATOMS AND BIOELECTRICITY.
DO YOU KNOW WHO I AM, SARAH?
I'M A SUPER-HERO.

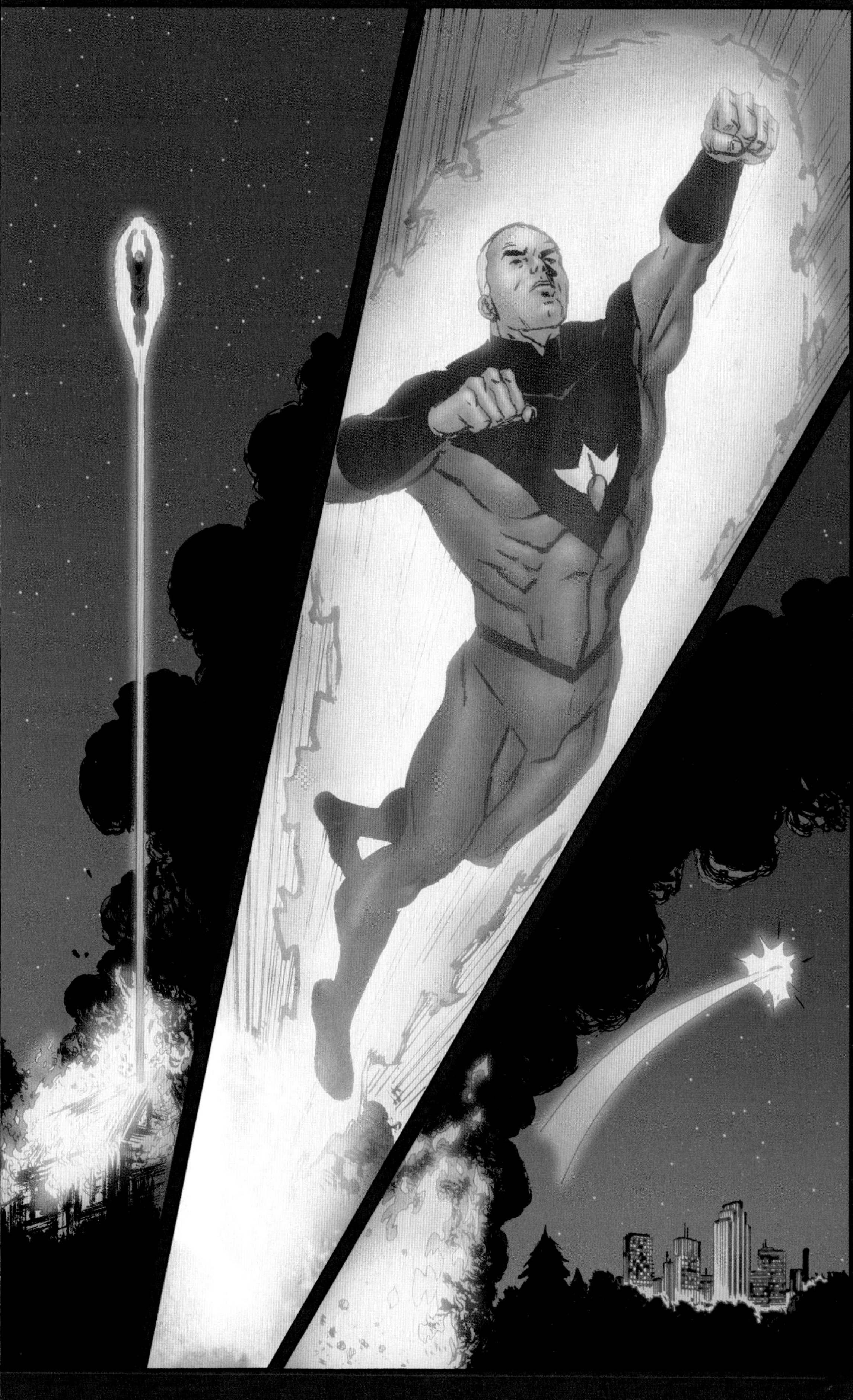

ONE WEEK LATER

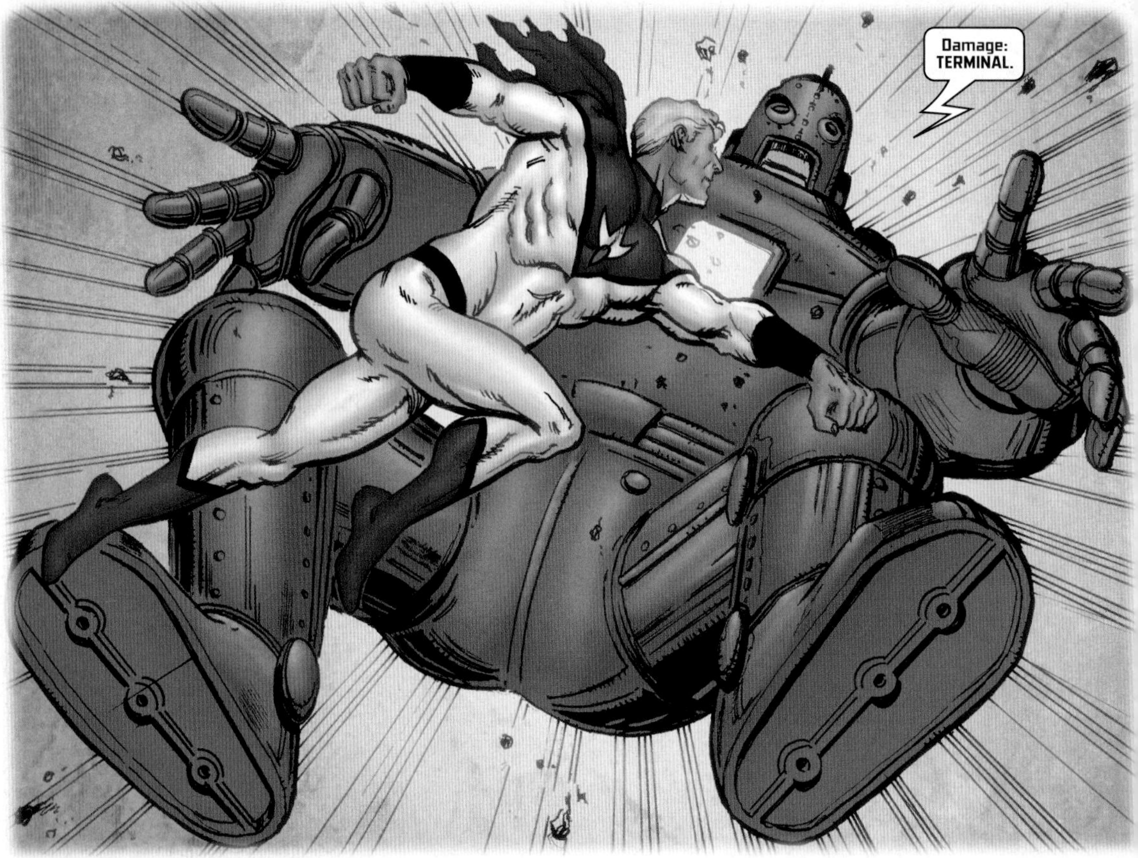
Damage: TERMINAL.

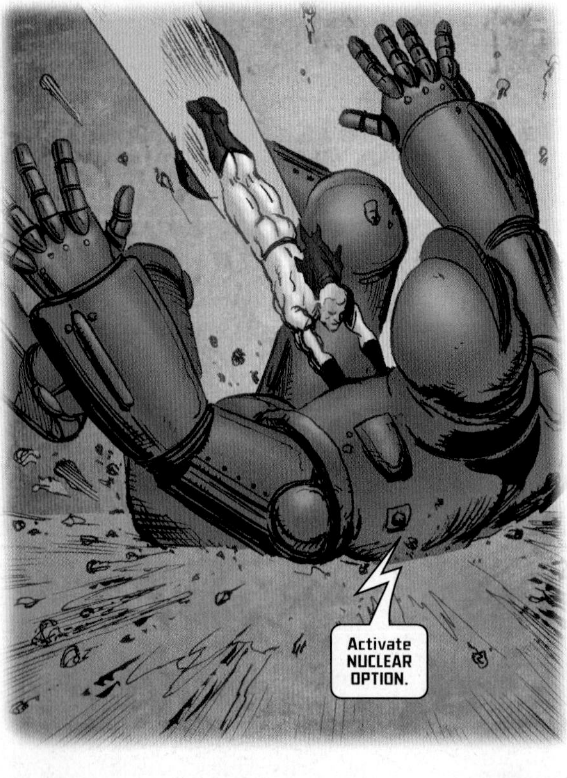
Activate NUCLEAR OPTION.

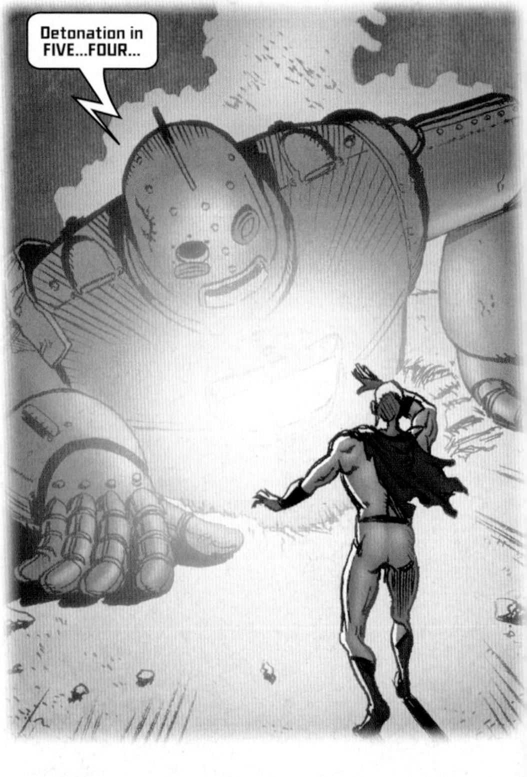
Detonation in FIVE...FOUR...

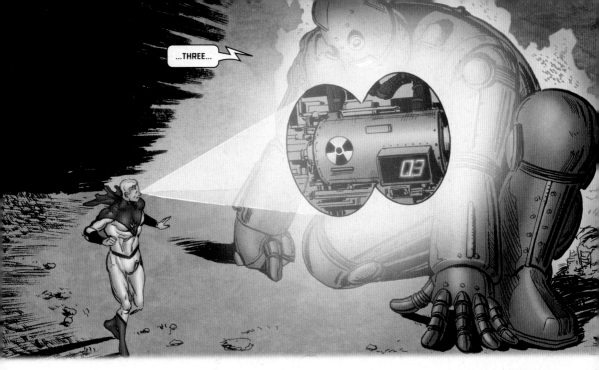

...THREE...

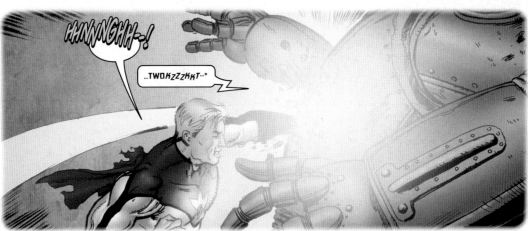

HHNNNGHH--!

..TWOKZZZKKT..*

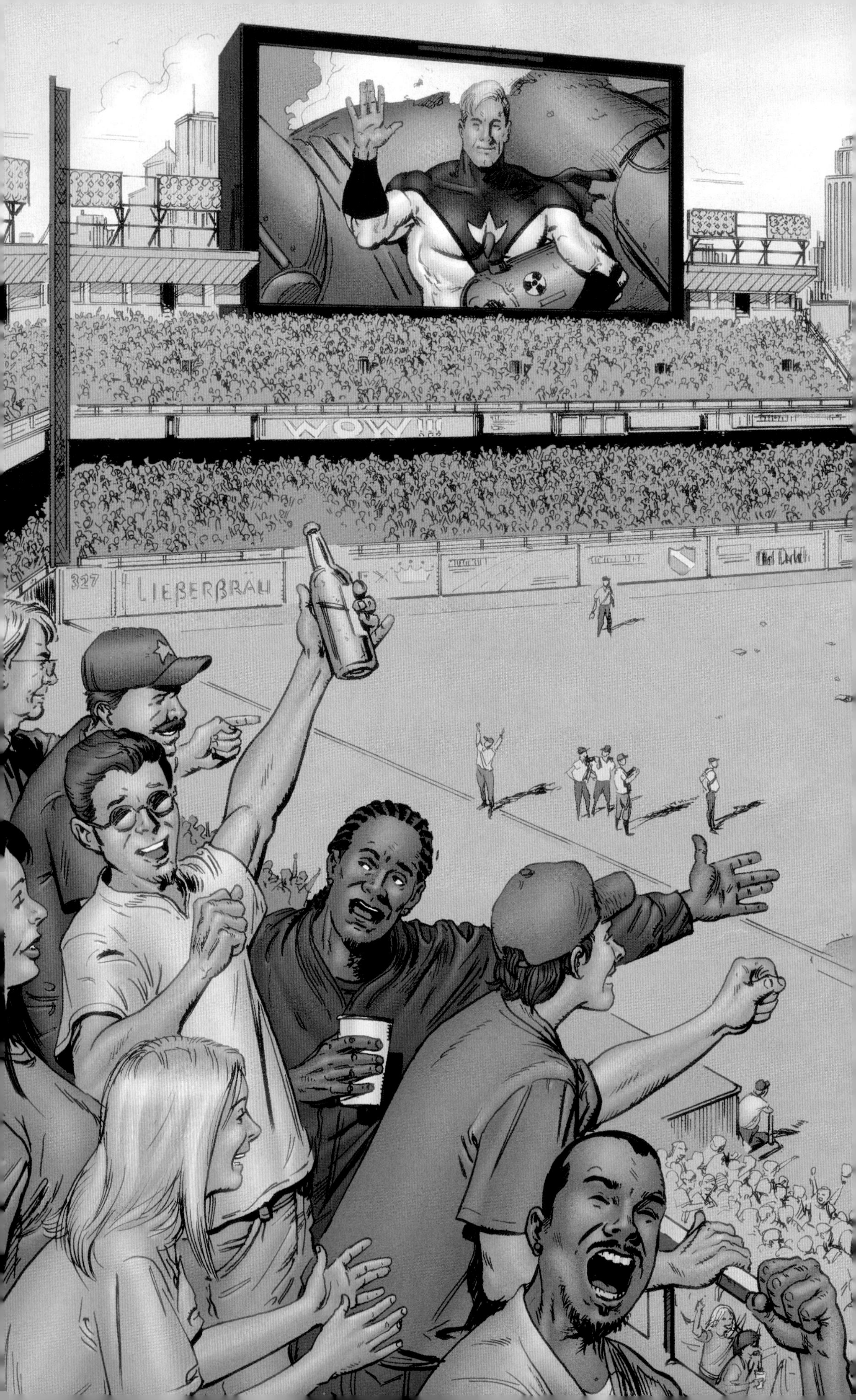
WOW!!
327
LIEßERßRAU

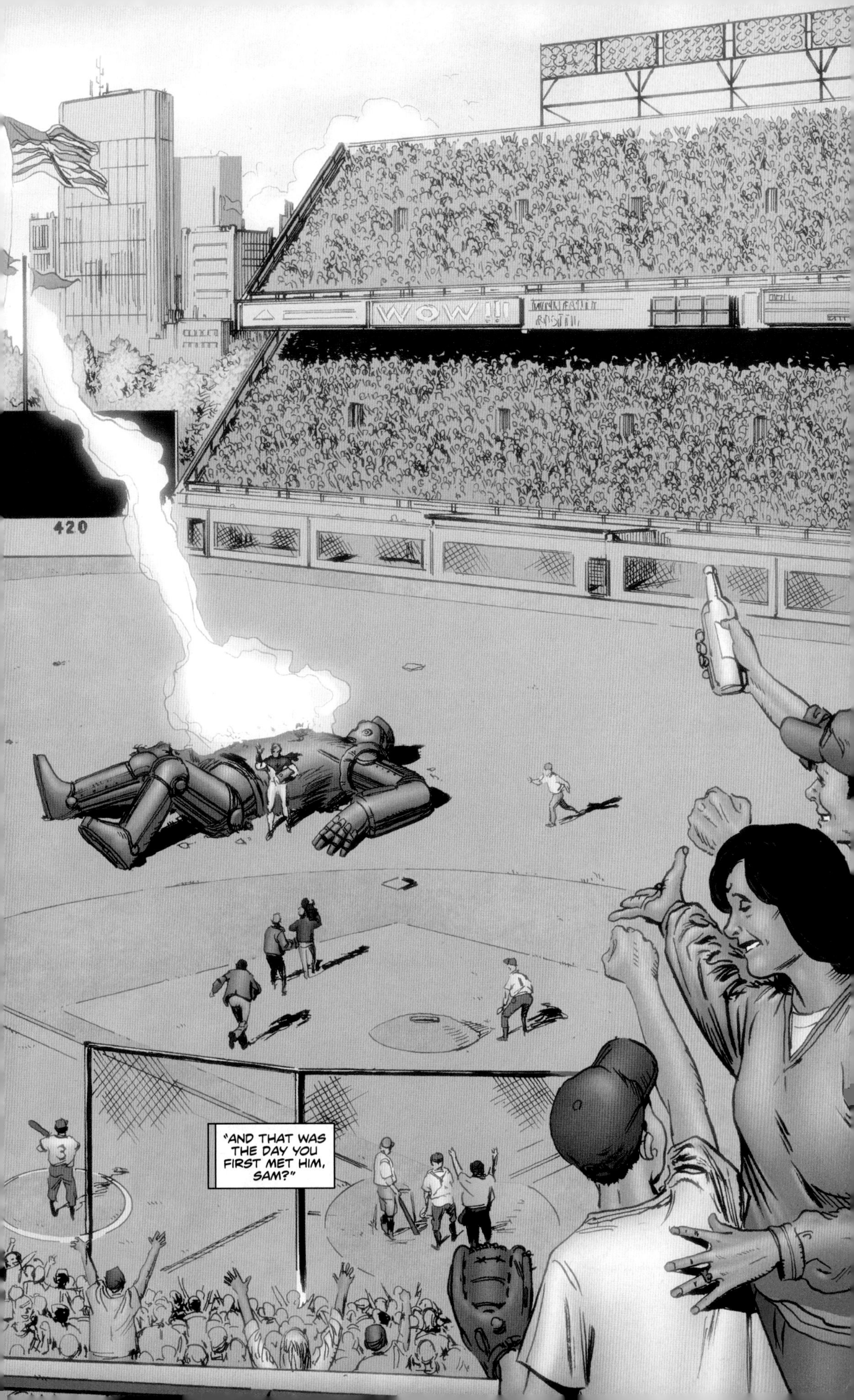
WOW !!!
420
3
"AND THAT WAS THE DAY YOU FIRST MET HIM, SAM?"

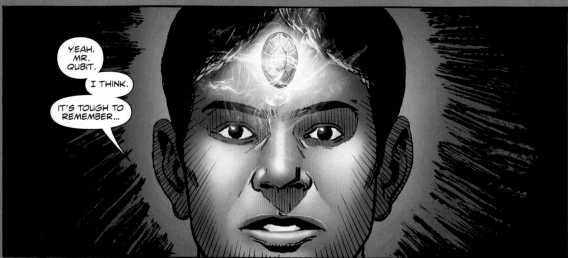

YEAH, MR. QUBIT.

I THINK.

IT'S TOUGH TO REMEMBER...

IT'S SO VERY TERRIBLY IMPORTANT, SAM.

PLEASE TRY. TRY AS HARD AS YOU CAN.

UMMM... SCYLLA WAS...THERE, RIGHT...?

"SCYLLA AND CHARYBDIS..."

"...AND VOLT AND...SOMEONE ELSE..."

"GILGAMOS. AND GILGAMOS BROUGHT YOU, HE SAYS."

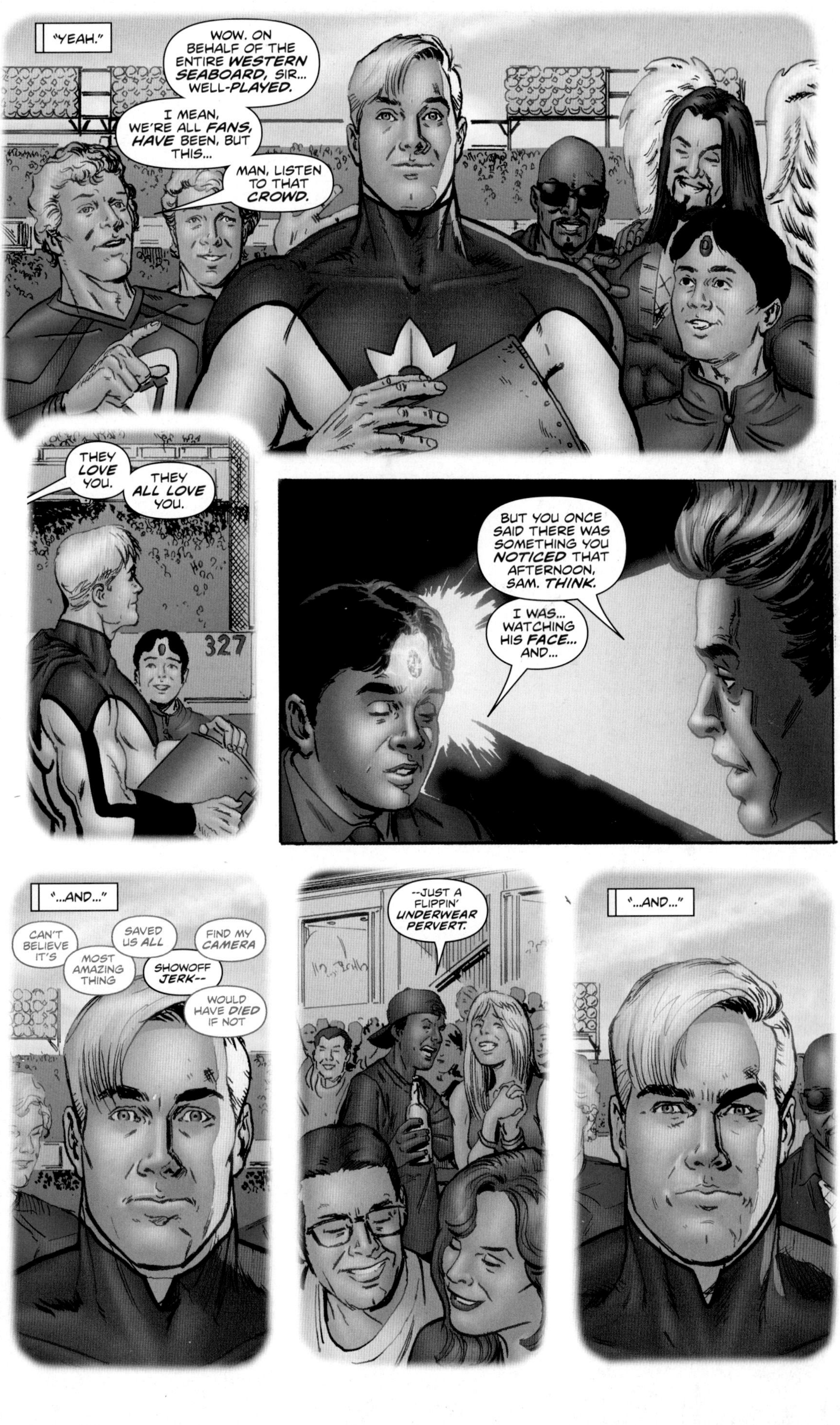
"YEAH."
WOW. ON BEHALF OF THE ENTIRE WESTERN SEABOARD, SIR... WELL-PLAYED.
I MEAN, WE'RE ALL FANS, HAVE BEEN, BUT THIS...
MAN, LISTEN TO THAT CROWD.
THEY LOVE YOU.
THEY ALL LOVE YOU.
327
BUT YOU ONCE SAID THERE WAS SOMETHING YOU NOTICED THAT AFTERNOON, SAM. THINK.
I WAS... WATCHING HIS FACE... AND...
"...AND..."
CAN'T BELIEVE IT'S
MOST AMAZING THING
SAVED US ALL
SHOWOFF JERK--
FIND MY CAMERA
WOULD HAVE DIED IF NOT
--JUST A FLIPPIN' UNDERWEAR PERVERT.
"...AND..."

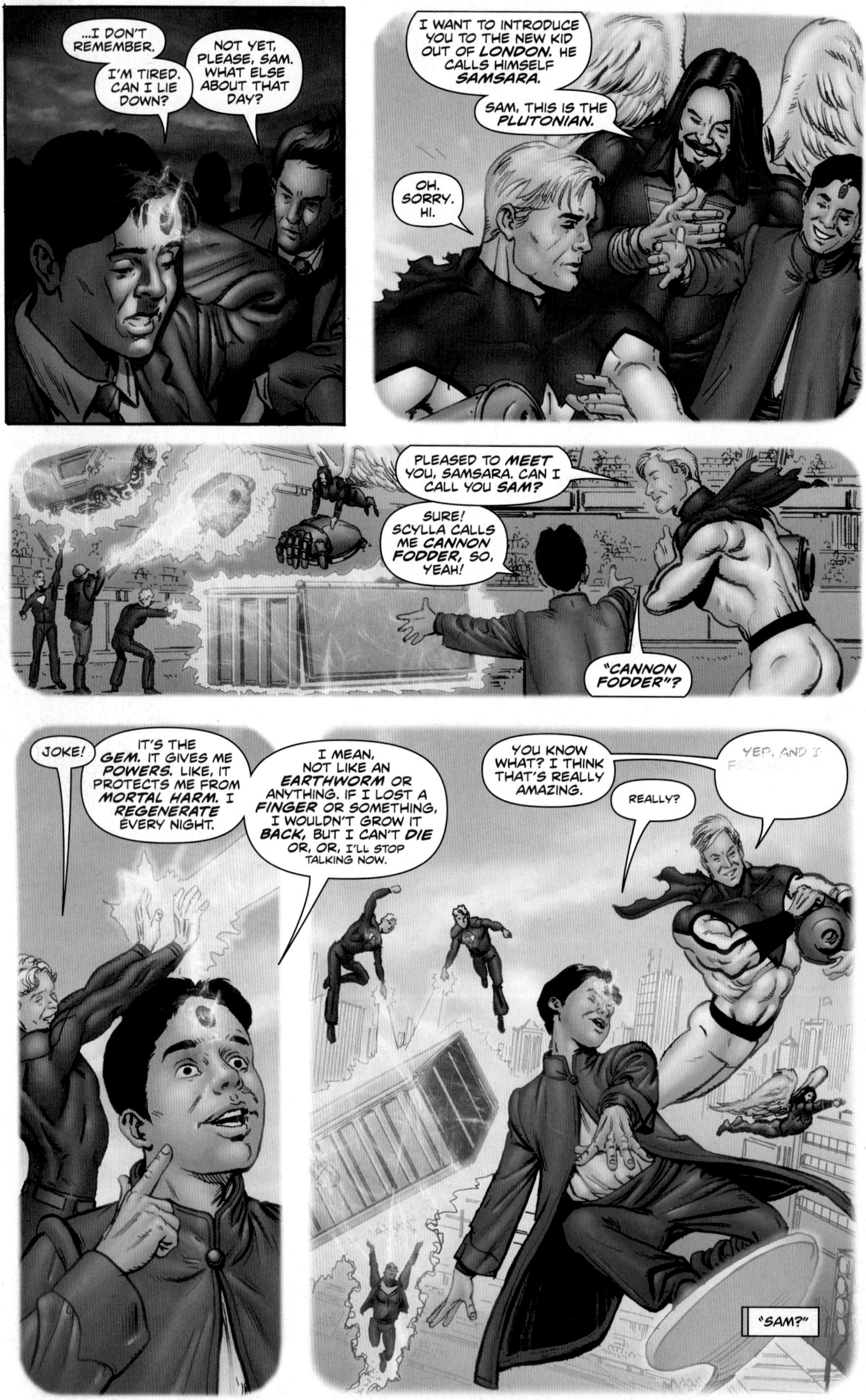
...I DON'T REMEMBER.
I'M TIRED. CAN I LIE DOWN?
NOT YET, PLEASE, SAM. WHAT ELSE ABOUT THAT DAY?
I WANT TO INTRODUCE YOU TO THE NEW KID OUT OF LONDON. HE CALLS HIMSELF SAMSARA.
SAM, THIS IS THE PLUTONIAN.
OH. SORRY. HI.
PLEASED TO MEET YOU, SAMSARA. CAN I CALL YOU SAM?
SURE! SCYLLA CALLS ME CANNON FODDER, SO, YEAH!
"CANNON FODDER"?
JOKE!
IT'S THE GEM. IT GIVES ME POWERS. LIKE, IT PROTECTS ME FROM MORTAL HARM. I REGENERATE EVERY NIGHT.
I MEAN, NOT LIKE AN EARTHWORM OR ANYTHING. IF I LOST A FINGER OR SOMETHING, I WOULDN'T GROW IT BACK, BUT I CAN'T DIE OR, OR, I'LL STOP TALKING NOW.
YOU KNOW WHAT? I THINK THAT'S REALLY AMAZING.
REALLY?
YEP. AND I
"SAM?"

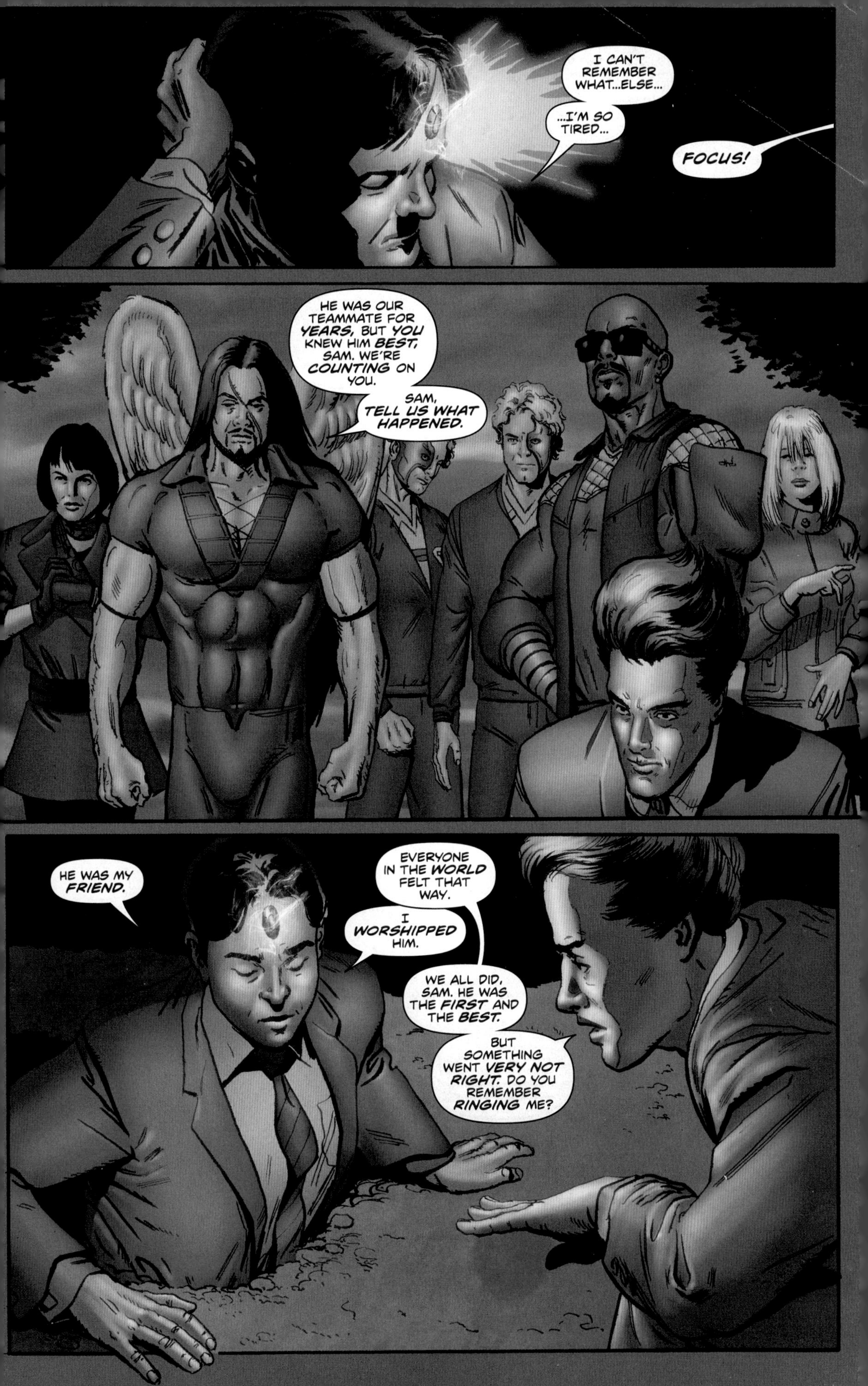
I CAN'T REMEMBER WHAT...ELSE...
...I'M SO TIRED...
FOCUS!
HE WAS OUR TEAMMATE FOR YEARS, BUT YOU KNEW HIM BEST, SAM. WE'RE COUNTING ON YOU.
SAM, TELL US WHAT HAPPENED.
HE WAS MY FRIEND.
EVERYONE IN THE WORLD FELT THAT WAY.
I WORSHIPPED HIM.
WE ALL DID, SAM. HE WAS THE FIRST AND THE BEST.
BUT SOMETHING WENT VERY NOT RIGHT. DO YOU REMEMBER RINGING ME?

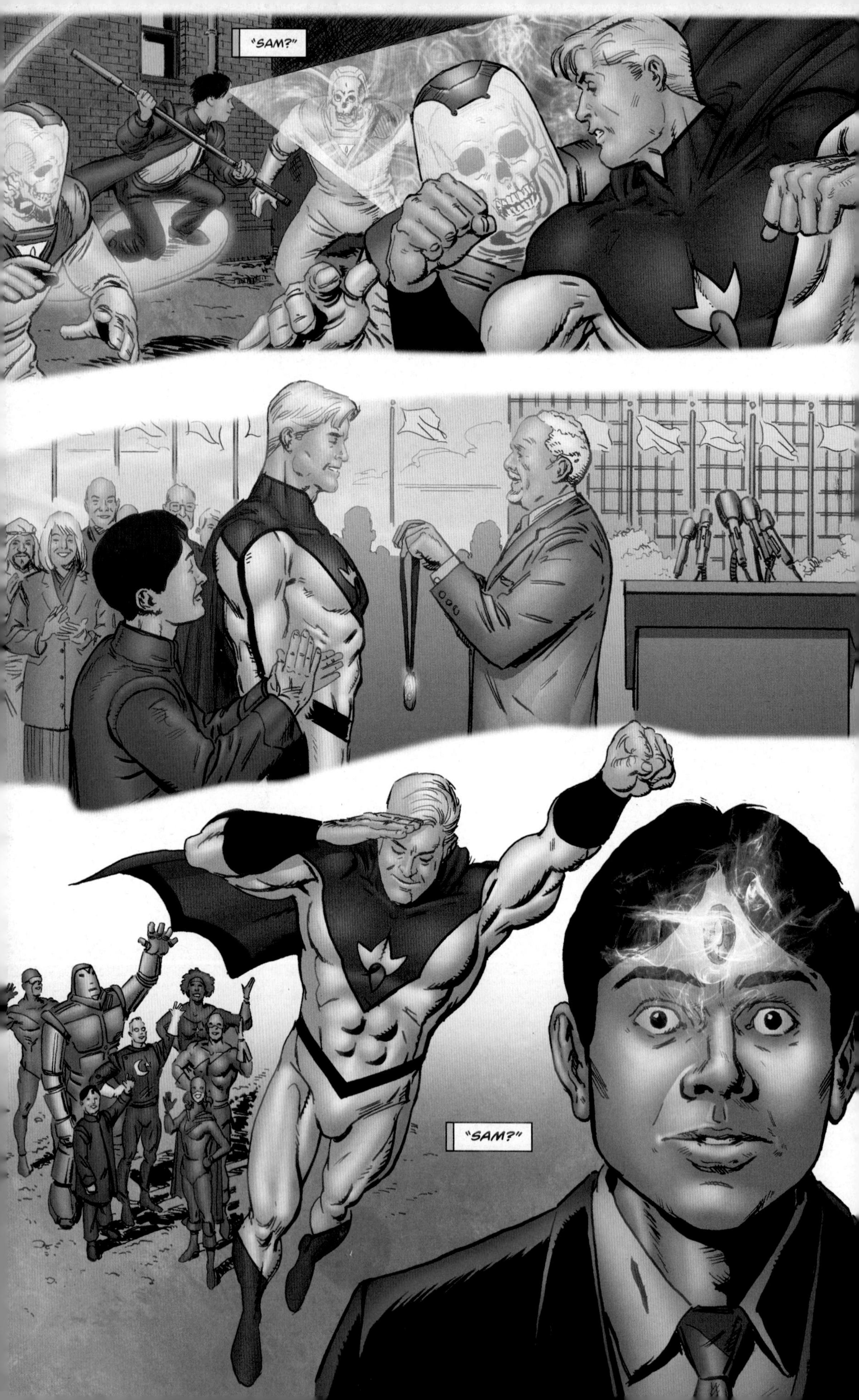
"SAM?"
"SAM?"

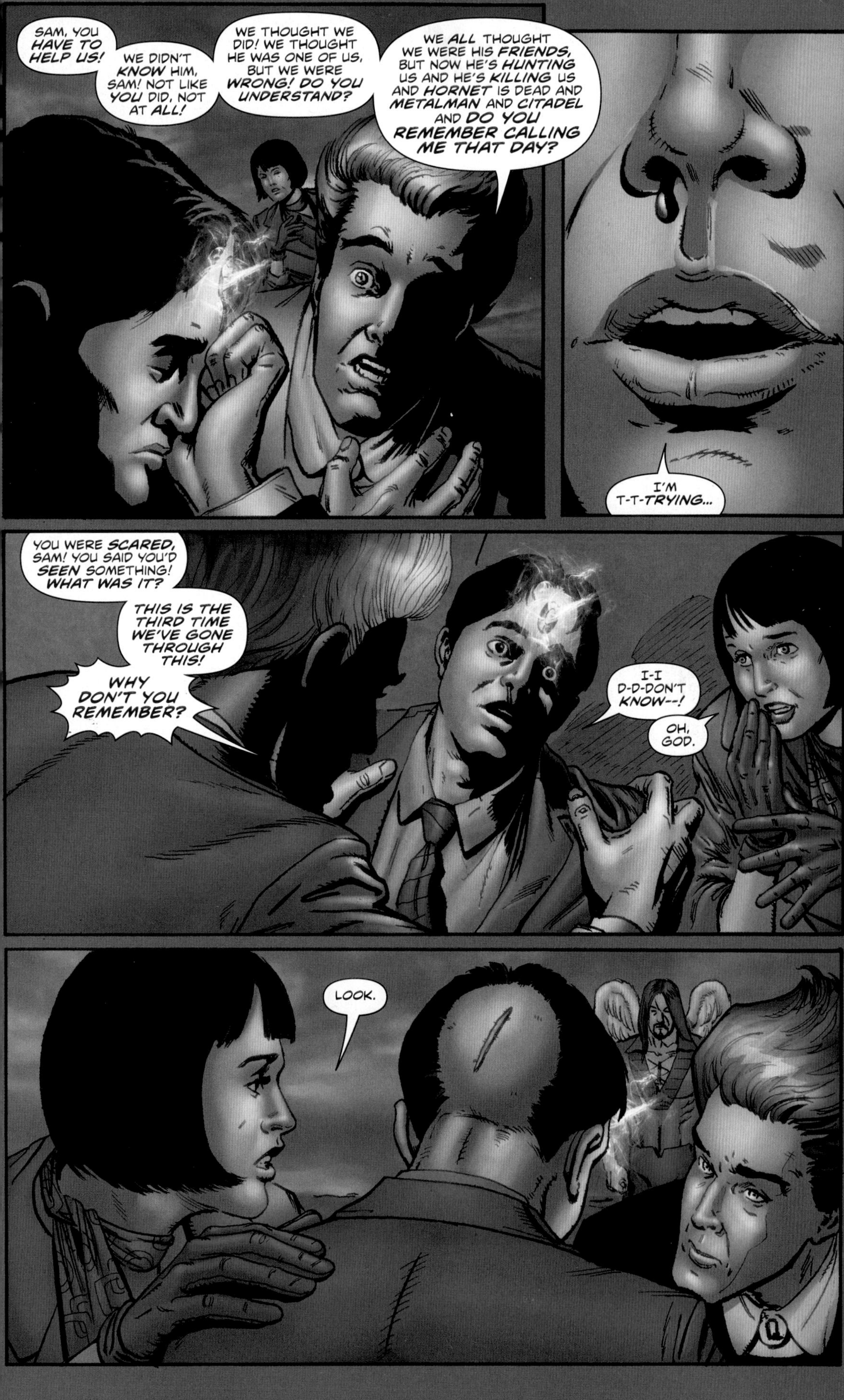
SAM, YOU HAVE TO HELP US!
WE DIDN'T KNOW HIM, SAM! NOT LIKE YOU DID, NOT AT ALL!
WE THOUGHT WE DID! WE THOUGHT HE WAS ONE OF US, BUT WE WERE WRONG! DO YOU UNDERSTAND?
WE ALL THOUGHT WE WERE HIS FRIENDS, BUT NOW HE'S HUNTING US AND HE'S KILLING US AND HORNET IS DEAD AND METALMAN AND CITADEL AND DO YOU REMEMBER CALLING ME THAT DAY?
I'M T-T-TRYING...
YOU WERE SCARED, SAM! YOU SAID YOU'D SEEN SOMETHING! WHAT WAS IT?
THIS IS THE THIRD TIME WE'VE GONE THROUGH THIS!
WHY DON'T YOU REMEMBER?
I-I D-D-DON'T KNOW--!
OH, GOD.
LOOK.

I DON'T...

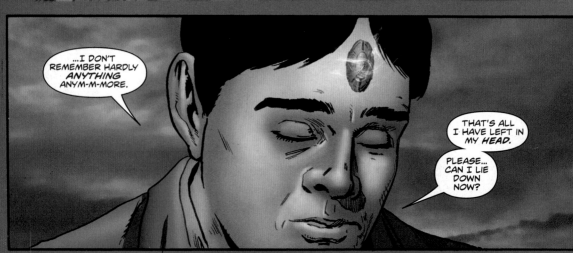

...I DON'T REMEMBER HARDLY *ANYTHING* ANYM-M-MORE.

THAT'S ALL I HAVE LEFT IN MY *HEAD.*

PLEASE... CAN I LIE DOWN NOW?

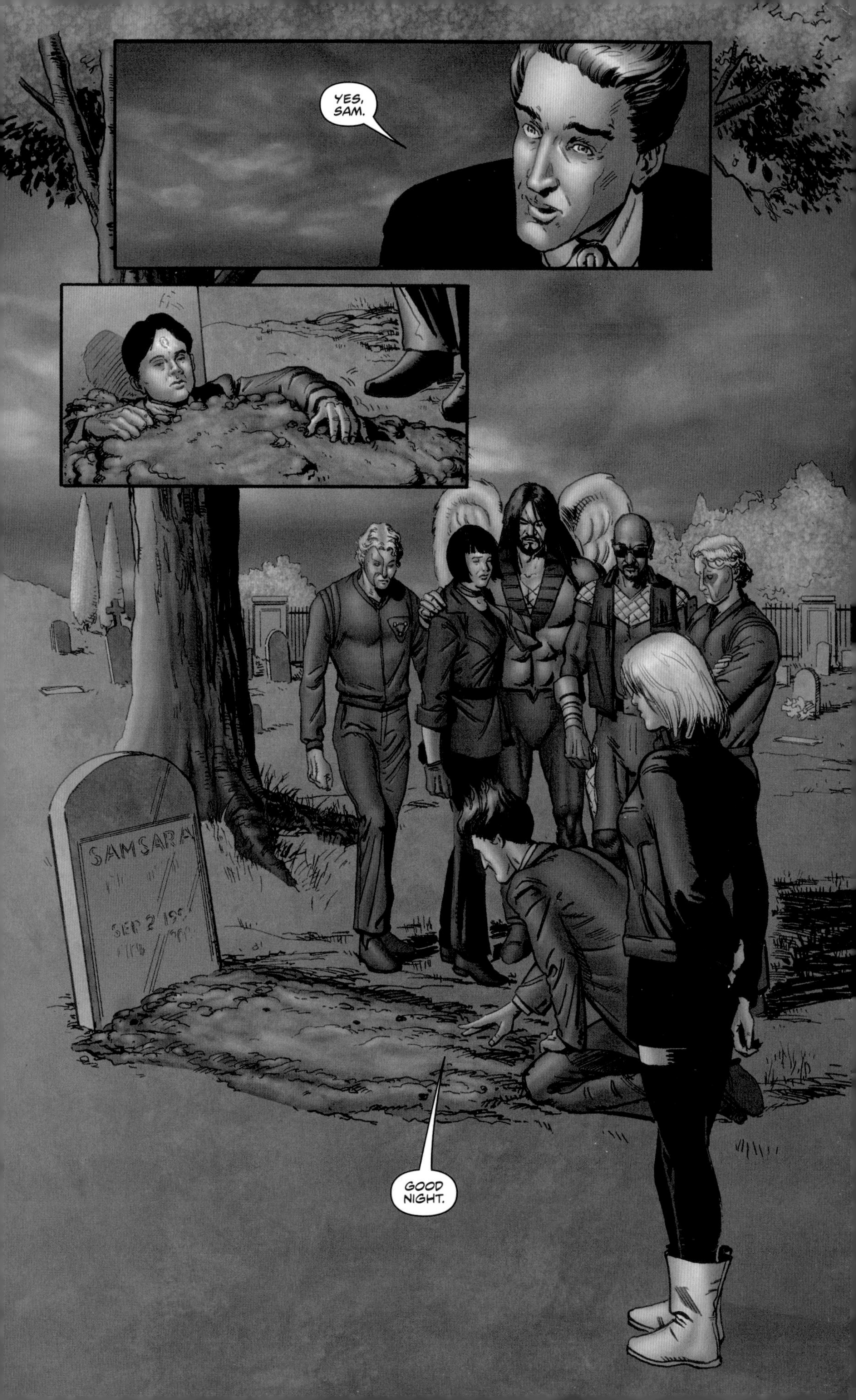
YES, SAM.
SAMSARA
GOOD NIGHT.

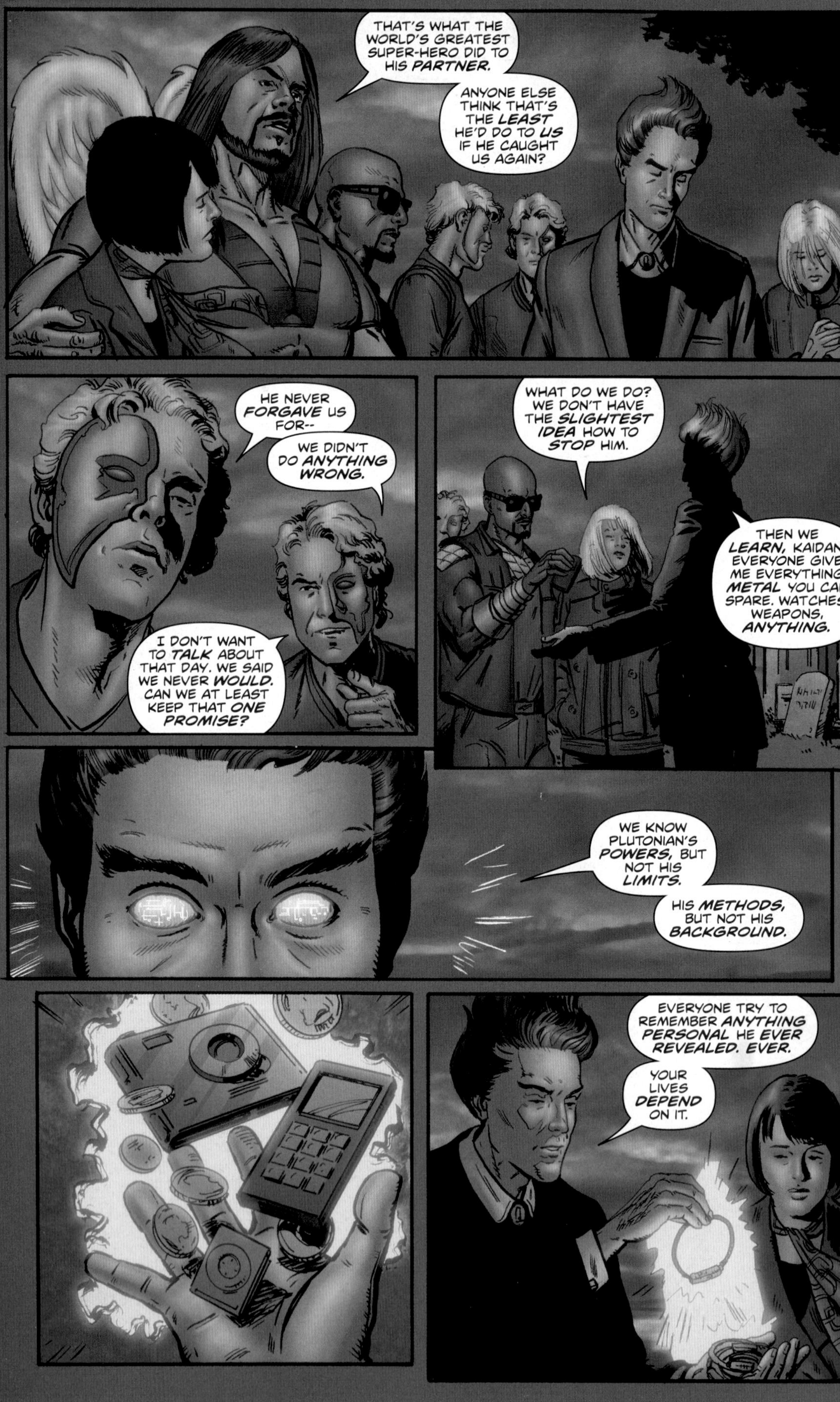
THAT'S WHAT THE WORLD'S GREATEST SUPER-HERO DID TO HIS PARTNER.
ANYONE ELSE THINK THAT'S THE LEAST HE'D DO TO US IF HE CAUGHT US AGAIN?
HE NEVER FORGAVE US FOR--
WE DIDN'T DO ANYTHING WRONG.
I DON'T WANT TO TALK ABOUT THAT DAY. WE SAID WE NEVER WOULD. CAN WE AT LEAST KEEP THAT ONE PROMISE?
WHAT DO WE DO? WE DON'T HAVE THE SLIGHTEST IDEA HOW TO STOP HIM.
THEN WE LEARN, KAIDAN. EVERYONE GIVE ME EVERYTHING METAL YOU CAN SPARE. WATCHES, WEAPONS, ANYTHING.
WE KNOW PLUTONIAN'S POWERS, BUT NOT HIS LIMITS.
HIS METHODS, BUT NOT HIS BACKGROUND.
EVERYONE TRY TO REMEMBER ANYTHING PERSONAL HE EVER REVEALED. EVER.
YOUR LIVES DEPEND ON IT.

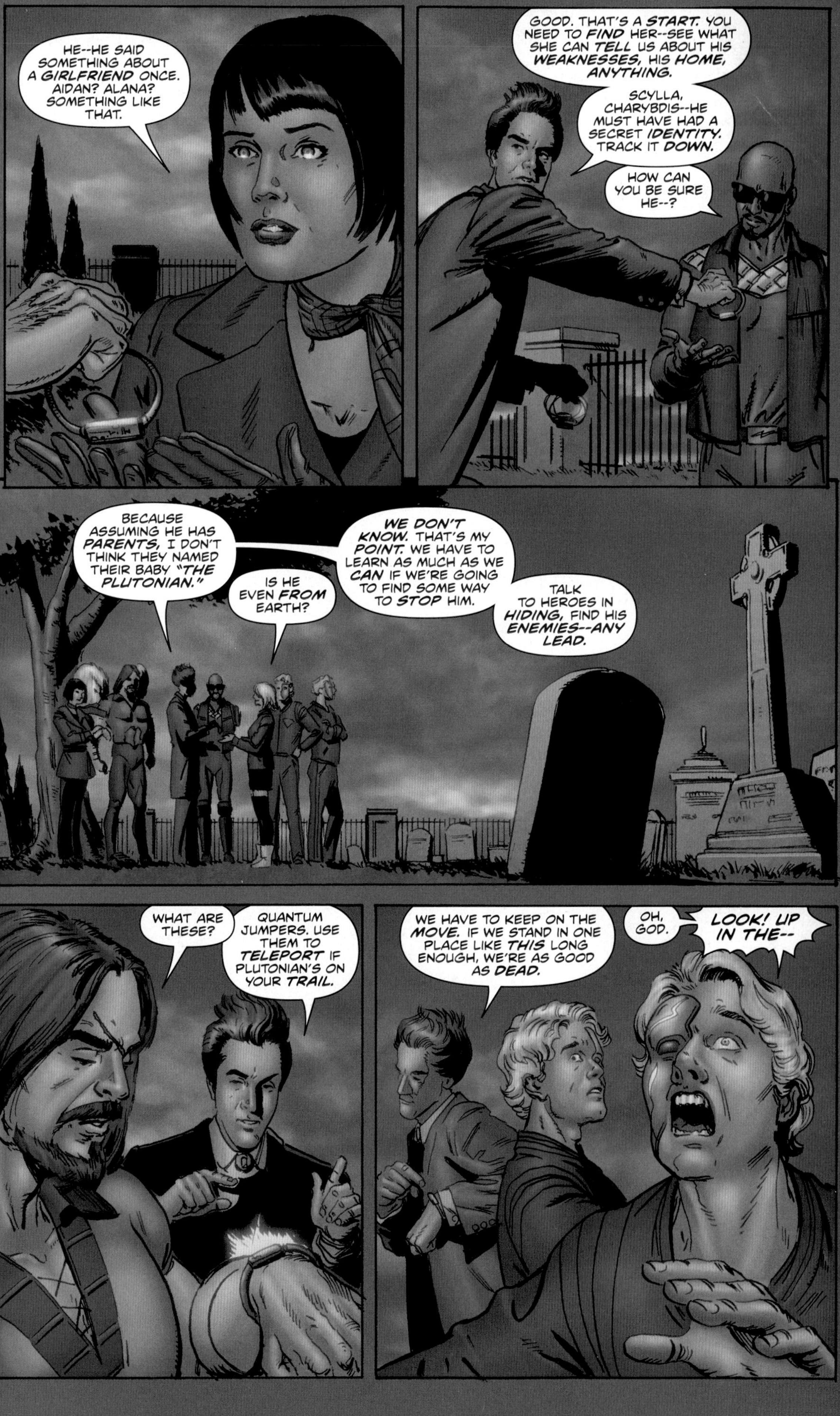
HE--HE SAID SOMETHING ABOUT A GIRLFRIEND ONCE. AIDAN? ALANA? SOMETHING LIKE THAT.
GOOD. THAT'S A START. YOU NEED TO FIND HER--SEE WHAT SHE CAN TELL US ABOUT HIS WEAKNESSES, HIS HOME, ANYTHING.
SCYLLA, CHARYBDIS--HE MUST HAVE HAD A SECRET IDENTITY. TRACK IT DOWN.
HOW CAN YOU BE SURE HE--?
BECAUSE ASSUMING HE HAS PARENTS, I DON'T THINK THEY NAMED THEIR BABY "THE PLUTONIAN."
IS HE EVEN FROM EARTH?
WE DON'T KNOW. THAT'S MY POINT. WE HAVE TO LEARN AS MUCH AS WE CAN IF WE'RE GOING TO FIND SOME WAY TO STOP HIM.
TALK TO HEROES IN HIDING, FIND HIS ENEMIES--ANY LEAD.
WHAT ARE THESE?
QUANTUM JUMPERS. USE THEM TO TELEPORT IF PLUTONIAN'S ON YOUR TRAIL.
WE HAVE TO KEEP ON THE MOVE. IF WE STAND IN ONE PLACE LIKE THIS LONG ENOUGH, WE'RE AS GOOD AS DEAD.
OH, GOD.
LOOK! UP IN THE--

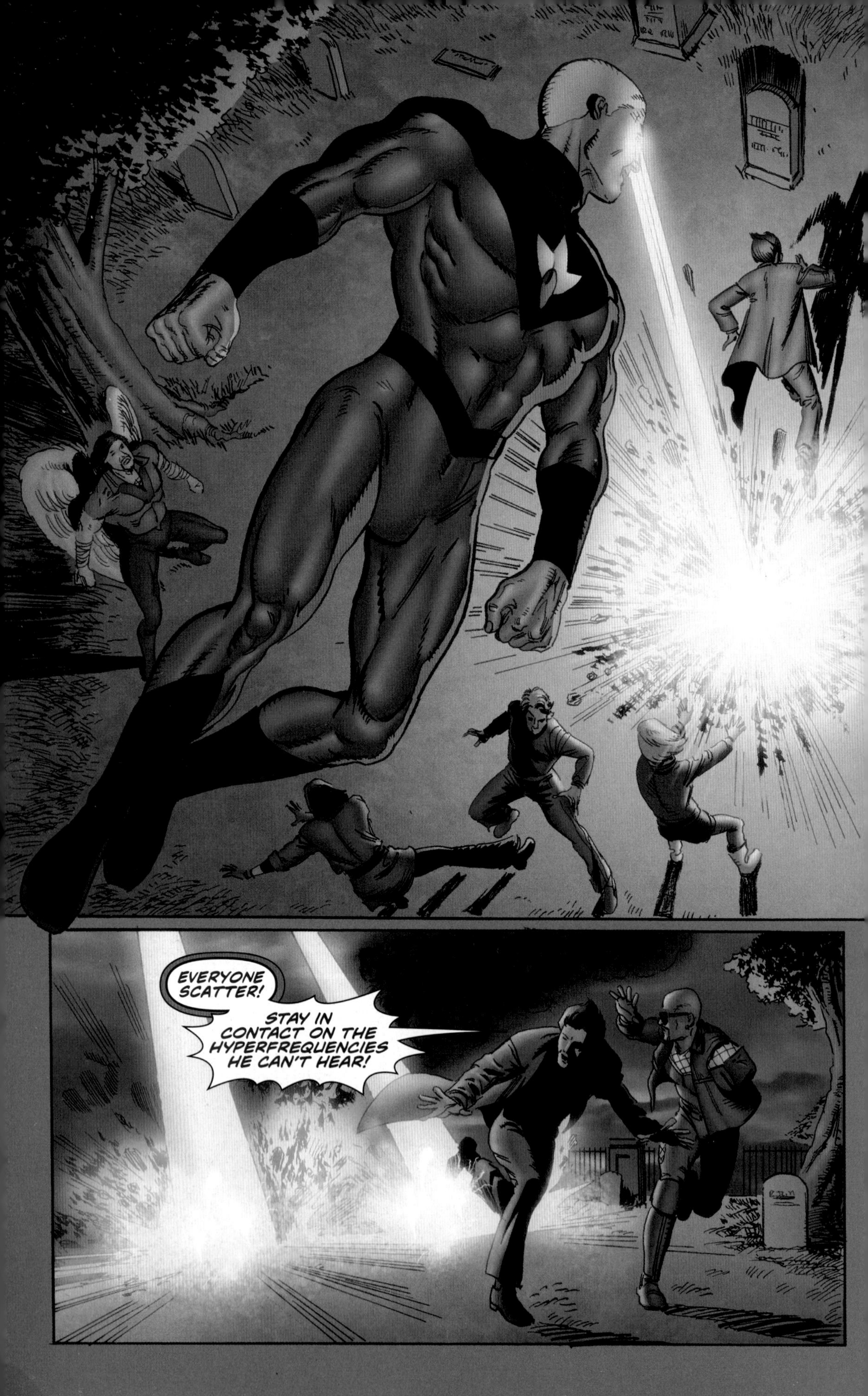
EVERYONE SCATTER!
STAY IN CONTACT ON THE HYPERFREQUENCIES HE CAN'T HEAR!

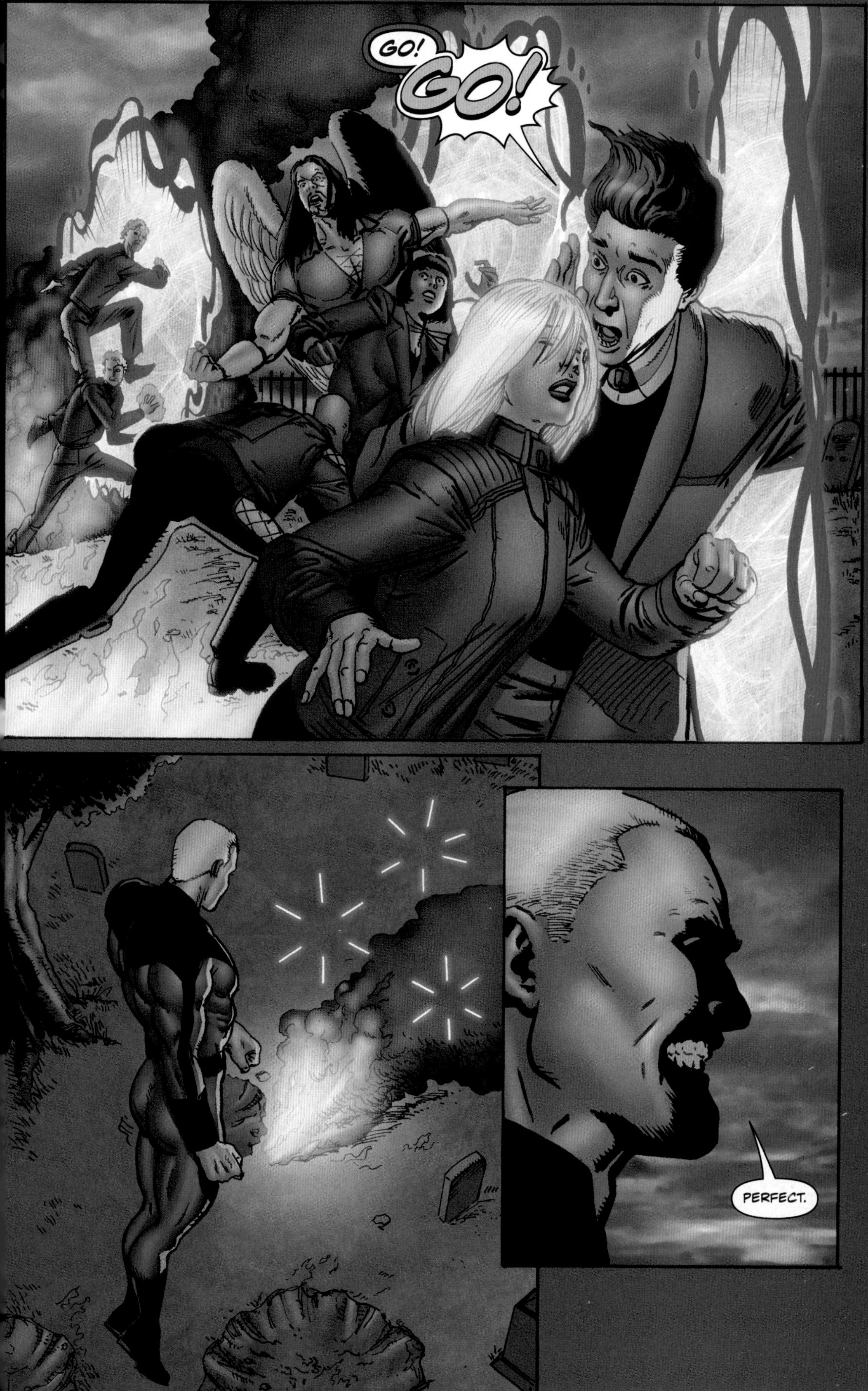
GO! GO!
PERFECT.

CHAPTER 2

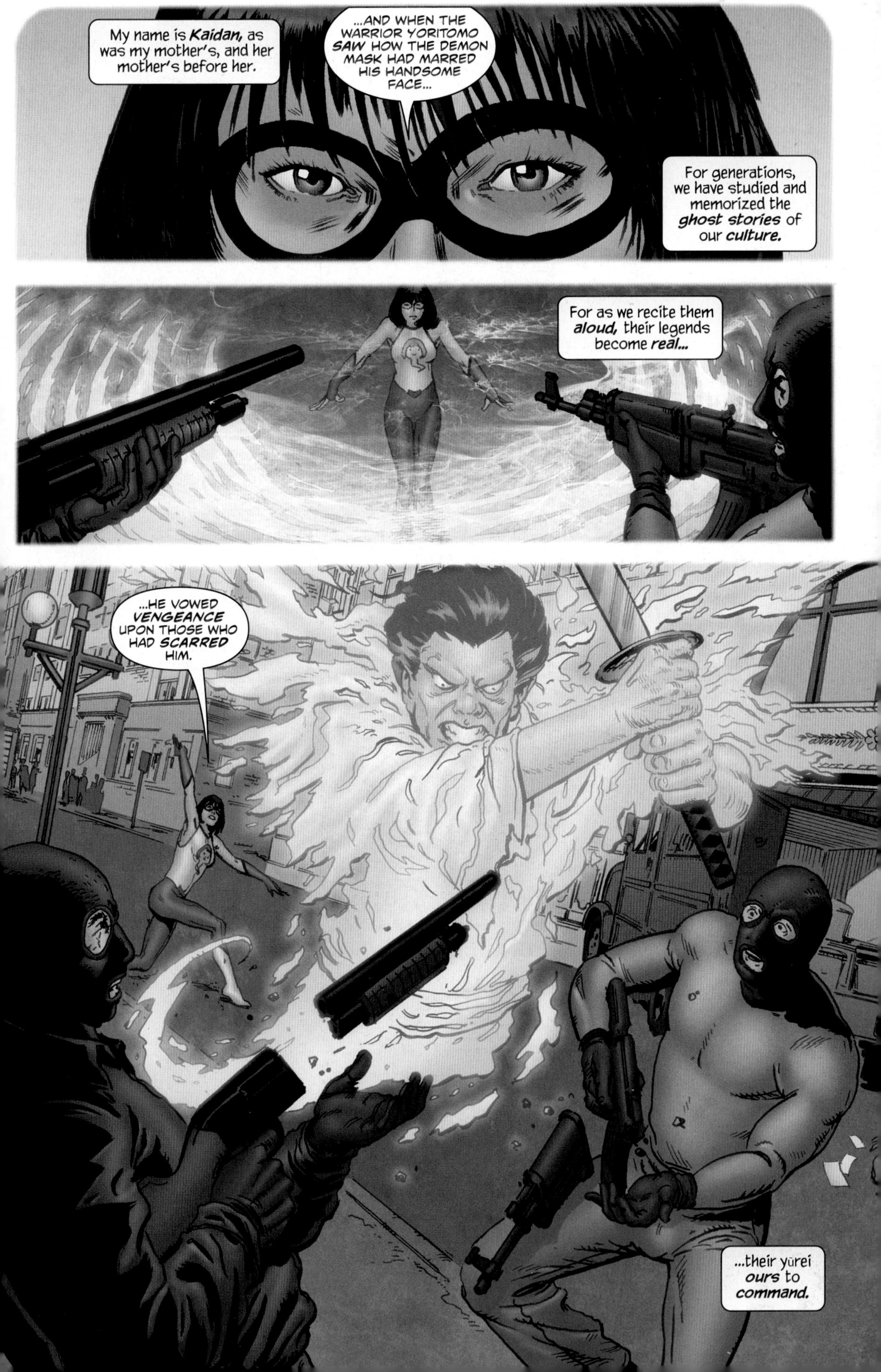

My name is Kaidan, as was my mother's, and her mother's before her.
...AND WHEN THE WARRIOR YORITOMO SAW HOW THE DEMON MASK HAD MARRED HIS HANDSOME FACE...
For generations, we have studied and memorized the ghost stories of our culture.
For as we recite them aloud, their legends become real...
...HE VOWED VENGEANCE UPON THOSE WHO HAD SCARRED HIM.
...their yūrei ours to command.

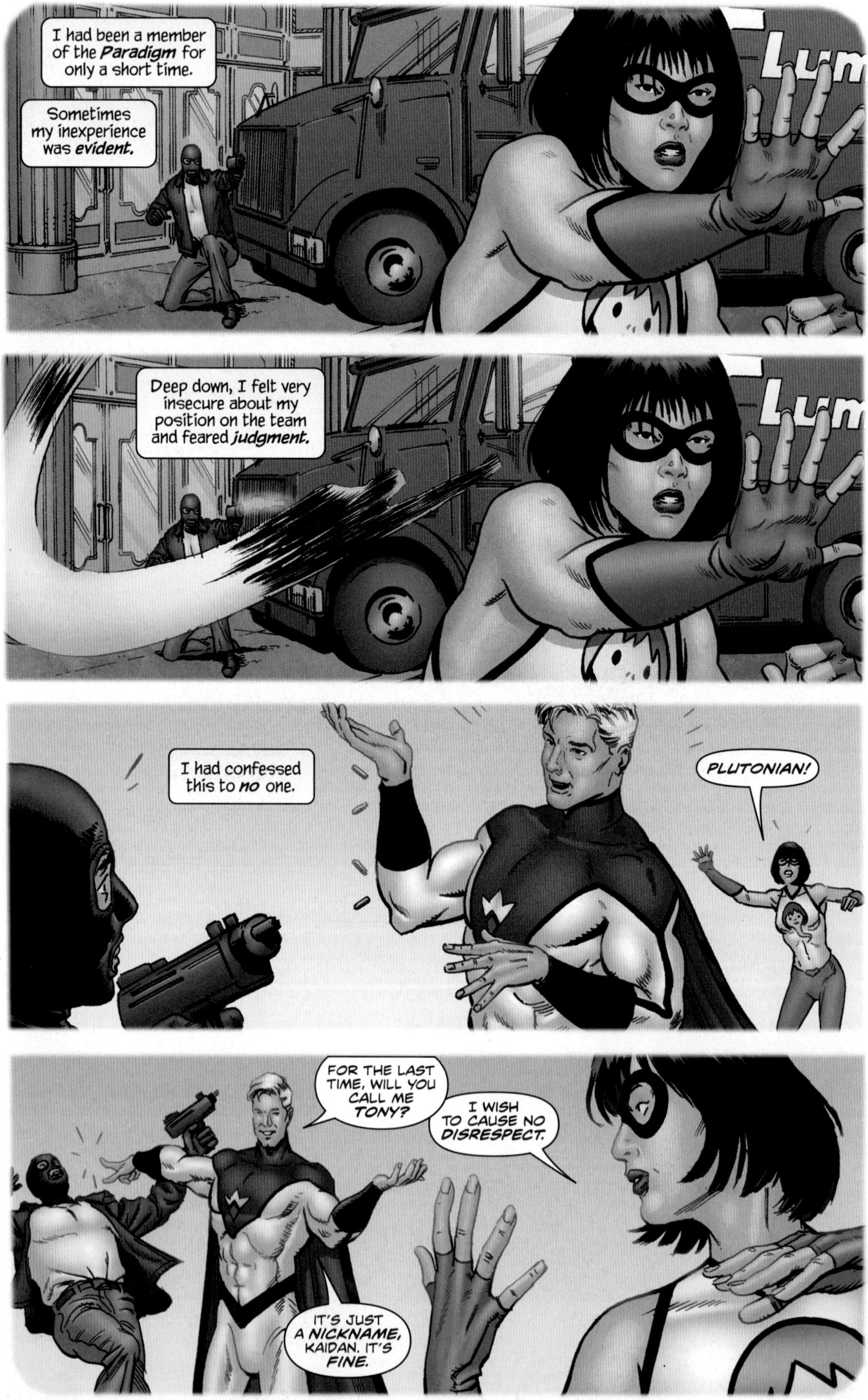
I had been a member of the *Paradigm* for only a short time.
Sometimes my inexperience was ***evident.***
Lum
Deep down, I felt very insecure about my position on the team and feared ***judgment.***
I had confessed this to ***no*** one.
PLUTONIAN!
FOR THE LAST TIME, WILL YOU CALL ME *TONY?*
I WISH TO CAUSE NO *DISRESPECT.*
IT'S JUST A ***NICKNAME,*** KAIDAN. IT'S ***FINE.***

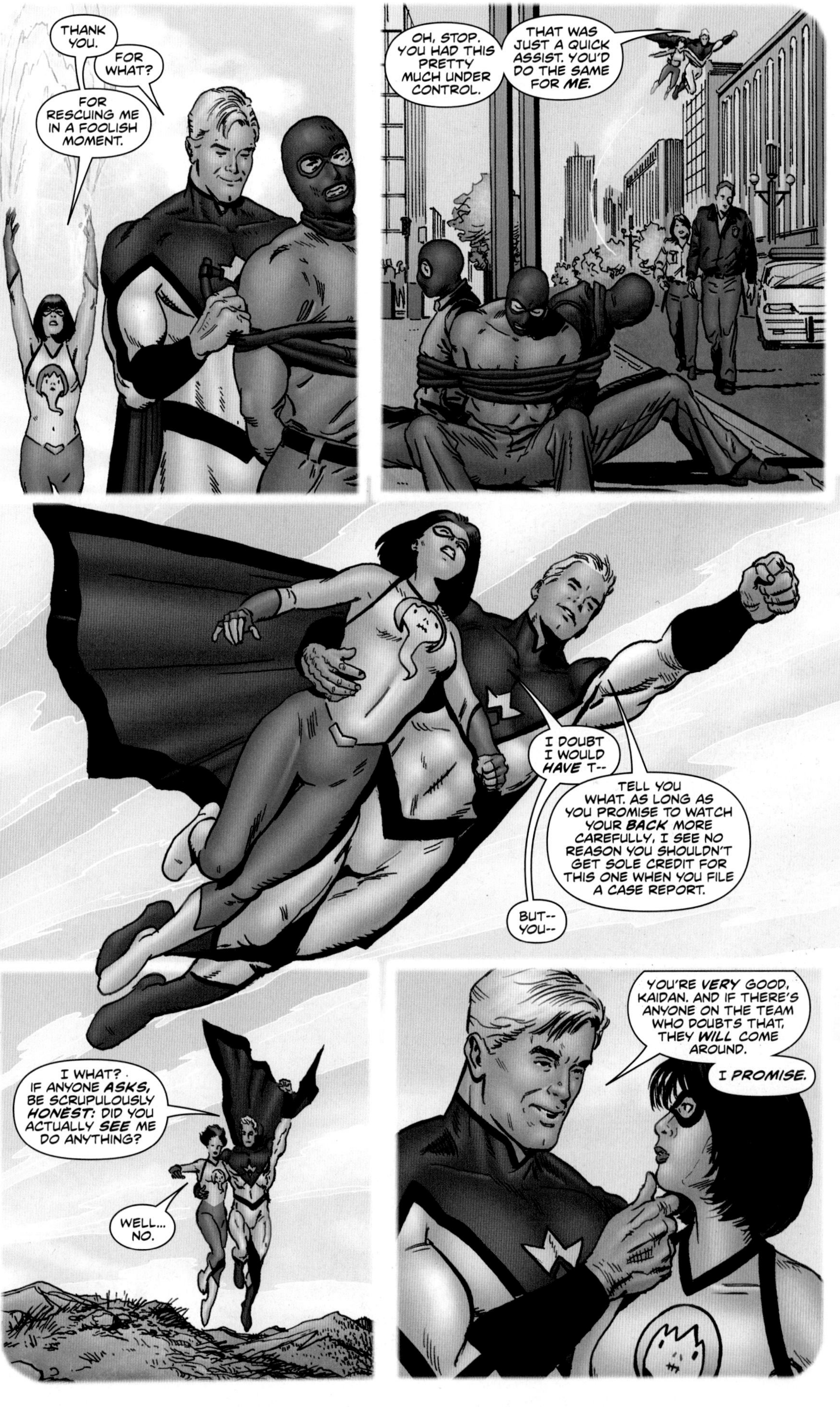
THANK YOU.
FOR WHAT?
FOR RESCUING ME IN A FOOLISH MOMENT.
OH, STOP. YOU HAD THIS PRETTY MUCH UNDER CONTROL.
THAT WAS JUST A QUICK ASSIST. YOU'D DO THE SAME FOR ME.
I DOUBT I WOULD HAVE T--
TELL YOU WHAT. AS LONG AS YOU PROMISE TO WATCH YOUR BACK MORE CAREFULLY, I SEE NO REASON YOU SHOULDN'T GET SOLE CREDIT FOR THIS ONE WHEN YOU FILE A CASE REPORT.
BUT-- YOU--
I WHAT? IF ANYONE ASKS, BE SCRUPULOUSLY HONEST: DID YOU ACTUALLY SEE ME DO ANYTHING?
WELL... NO.
YOU'RE VERY GOOD, KAIDAN. AND IF THERE'S ANYONE ON THE TEAM WHO DOUBTS THAT, THEY WILL COME AROUND.
I PROMISE.

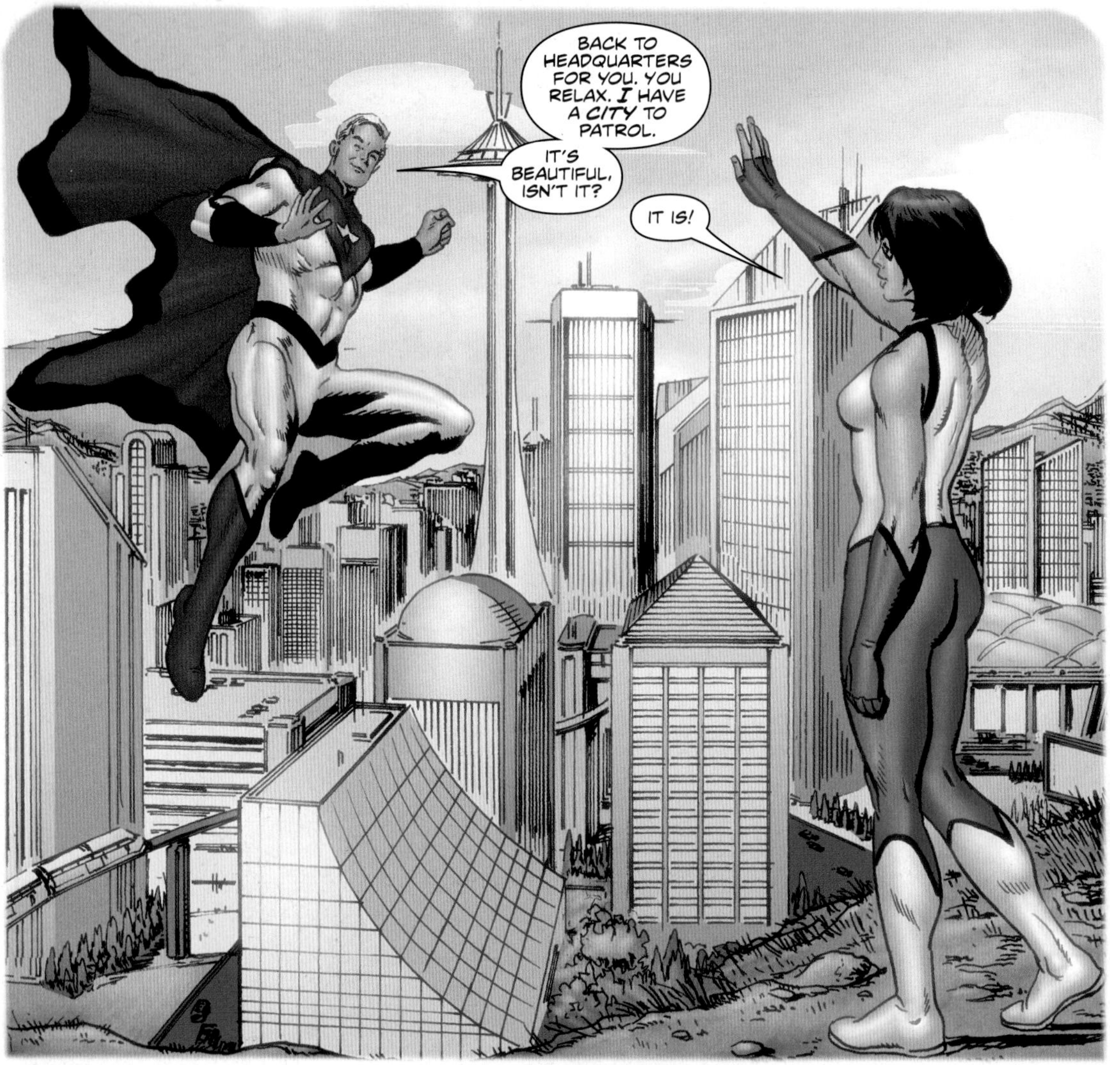
BACK TO HEADQUARTERS FOR YOU. YOU RELAX. I HAVE A CITY TO PATROL.
IT'S BEAUTIFUL, ISN'T IT?
IT IS!
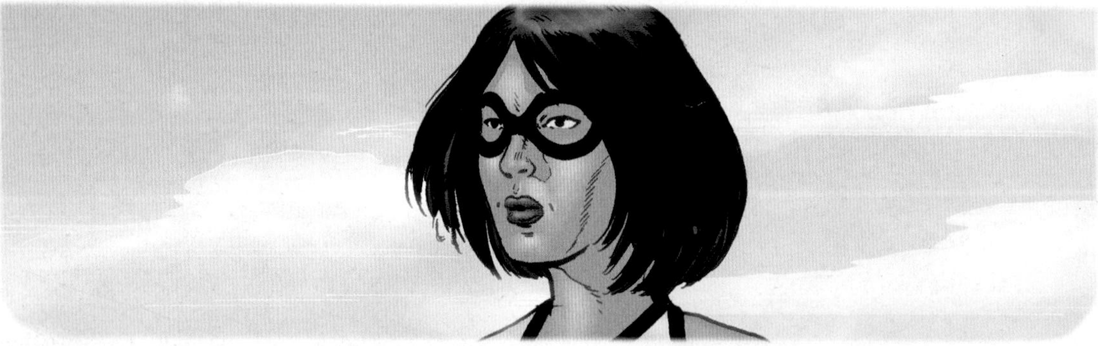
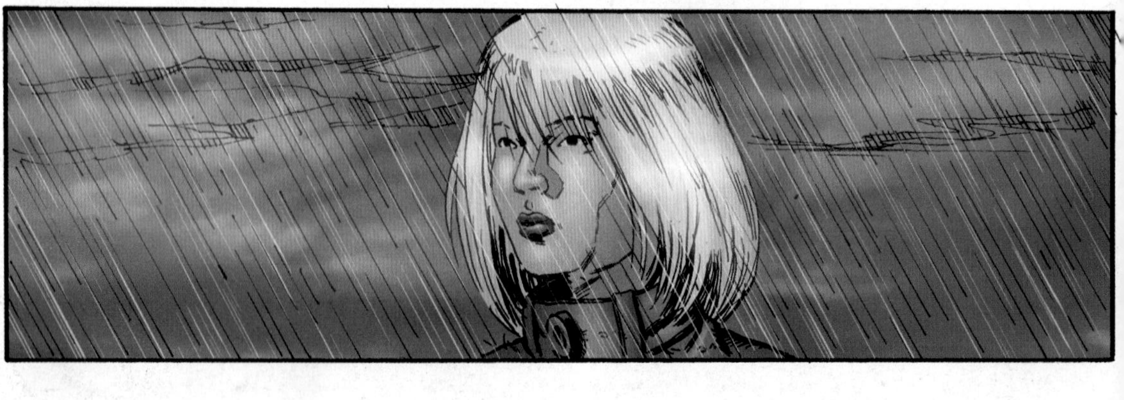

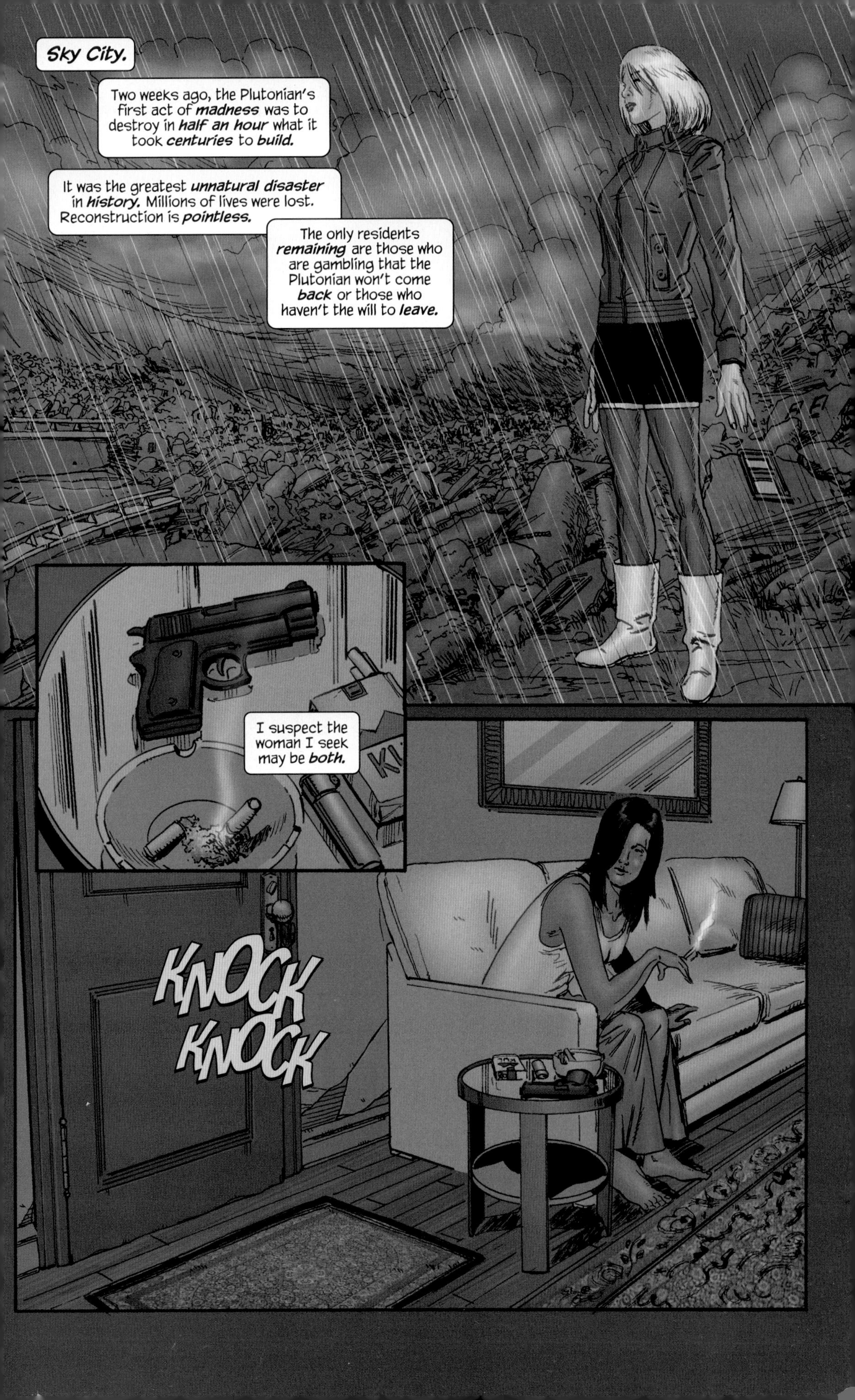
Sky City.
Two weeks ago, the Plutonian's first act of madness was to destroy in half an hour what it took centuries to build.
It was the greatest unnatural disaster in history. Millions of lives were lost. Reconstruction is pointless.
The only residents remaining are those who are gambling that the Plutonian won't come back or those who haven't the will to leave.
I suspect the woman I seek may be both.
KNOCK KNOCK

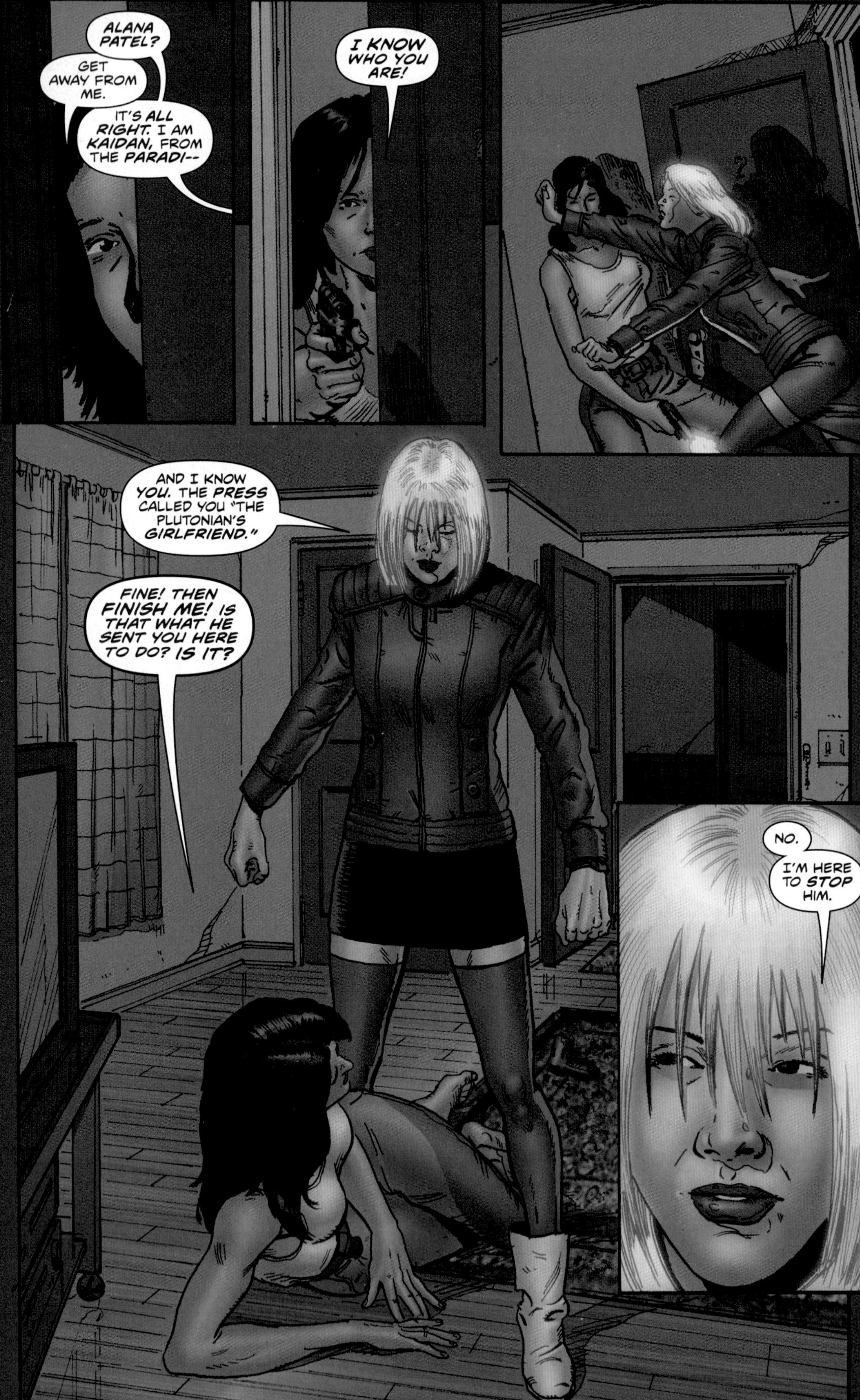
ALANA PATEL?
GET AWAY FROM ME.
IT'S ALL RIGHT. I AM KAIDAN, FROM THE PARADI--
I KNOW WHO YOU ARE!
AND I KNOW YOU. THE PRESS CALLED YOU "THE PLUTONIAN'S GIRLFRIEND."
FINE! THEN FINISH ME! IS THAT WHAT HE SENT YOU HERE TO DO? IS IT?
NO.
I'M HERE TO STOP HIM.

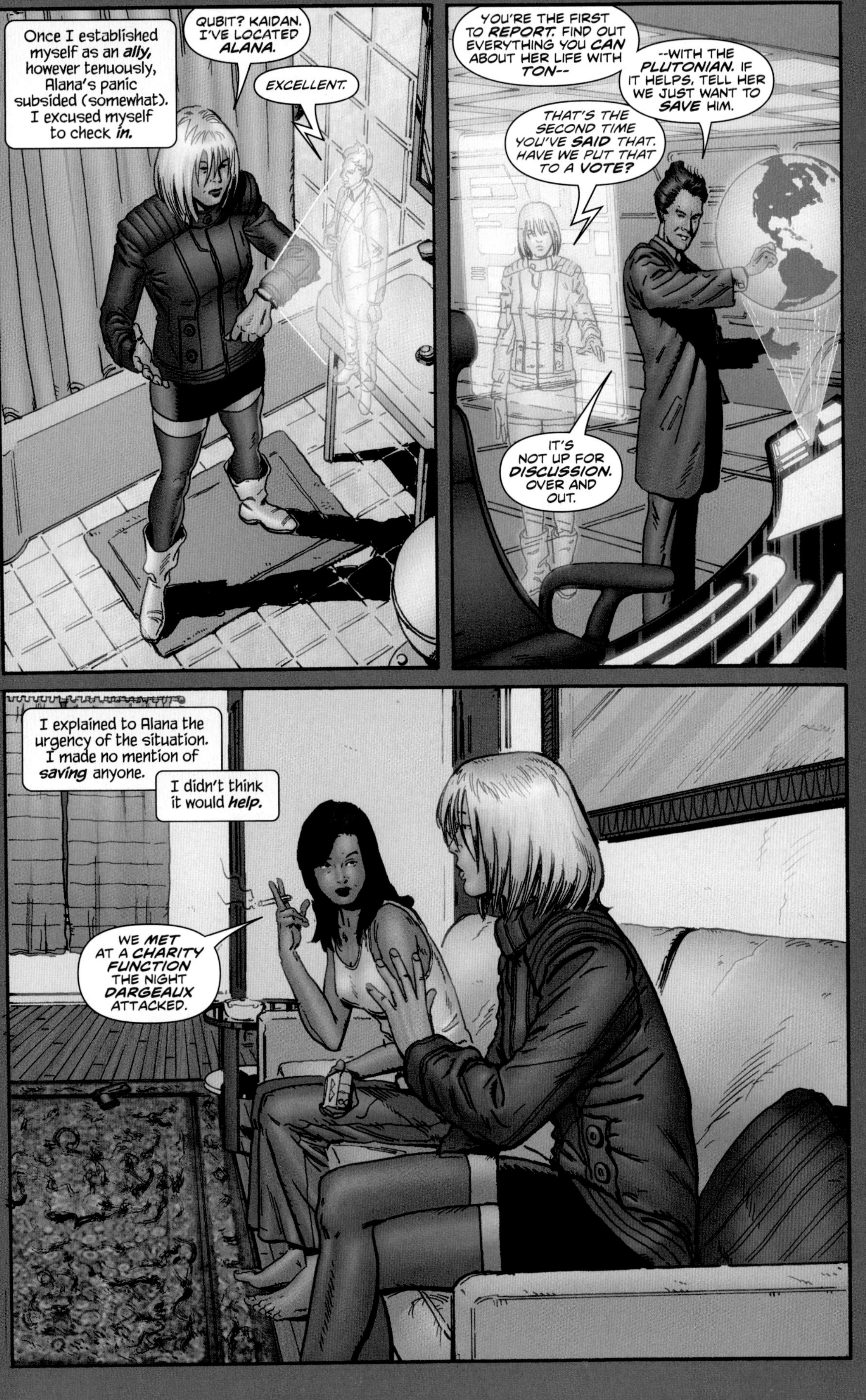
Once I established myself as an ally, however tenuously, Alana's panic subsided (somewhat). I excused myself to check in.
QUBIT? KAIDAN. I'VE LOCATED ALANA.
EXCELLENT.
YOU'RE THE FIRST TO REPORT. FIND OUT EVERYTHING YOU CAN ABOUT HER LIFE WITH TON--
--WITH THE PLUTONIAN. IF IT HELPS, TELL HER WE JUST WANT TO SAVE HIM.
THAT'S THE SECOND TIME YOU'VE SAID THAT. HAVE WE PUT THAT TO A VOTE?
IT'S NOT UP FOR DISCUSSION. OVER AND OUT.
I explained to Alana the urgency of the situation. I made no mention of saving anyone.
I didn't think it would help.
WE MET AT A CHARITY FUNCTION THE NIGHT DARGEAUX ATTACKED.

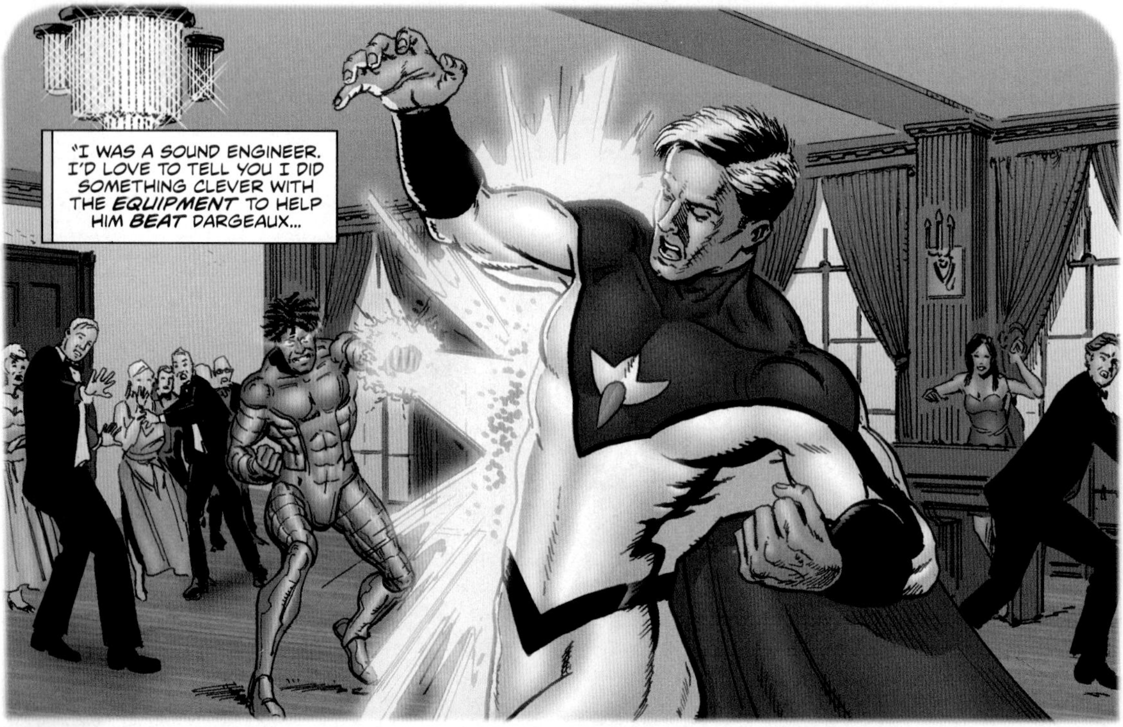
"I WAS A SOUND ENGINEER. I'D LOVE TO TELL YOU I DID SOMETHING CLEVER WITH THE *EQUIPMENT* TO HELP HIM *BEAT* DARGEAUX...

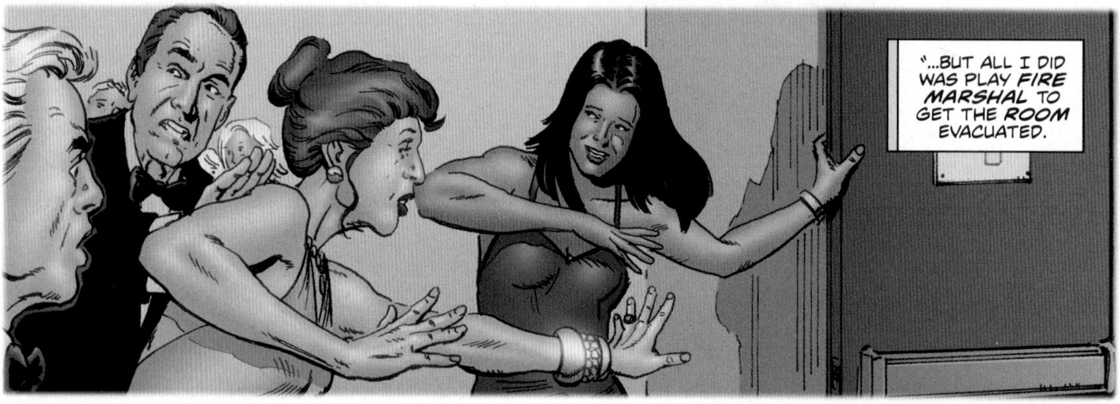
"...BUT ALL I DID WAS PLAY *FIRE MARSHAL* TO GET THE *ROOM* EVACUATED.

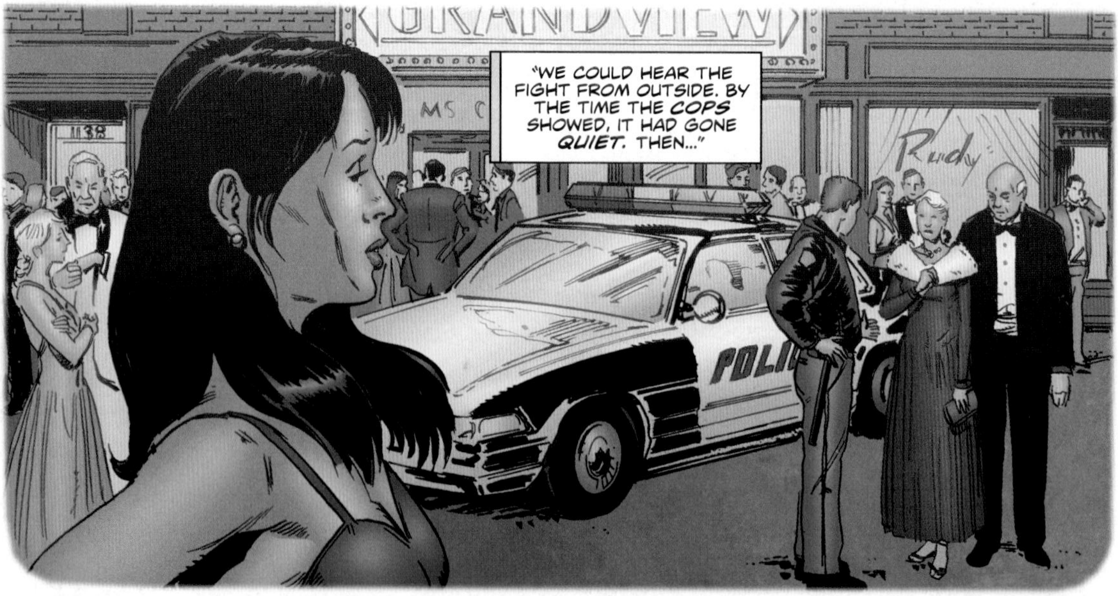
"WE COULD HEAR THE FIGHT FROM OUTSIDE. BY THE TIME THE *COPS* SHOWED, IT HAD GONE *QUIET*. THEN..."
Rudy
POLIC

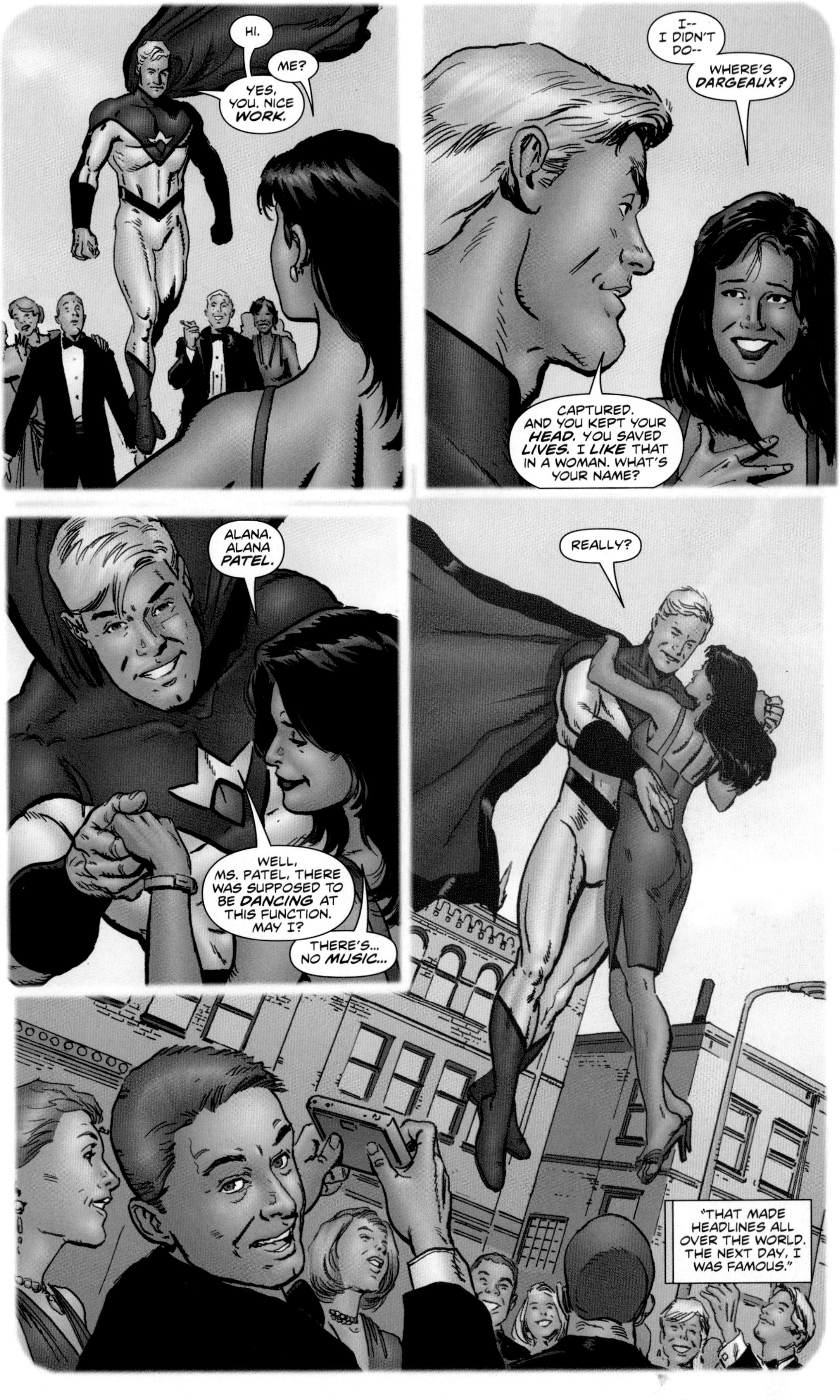
HI.
ME?
YES, YOU. NICE WORK.
I-- I DIDN'T DO--
WHERE'S DARGEAUX?
CAPTURED. AND YOU KEPT YOUR HEAD. YOU SAVED LIVES. I LIKE THAT IN A WOMAN. WHAT'S YOUR NAME?
ALANA. ALANA PATEL.
WELL, MS. PATEL, THERE WAS SUPPOSED TO BE DANCING AT THIS FUNCTION. MAY I?
THERE'S... NO MUSIC...
REALLY?
"THAT MADE HEADLINES ALL OVER THE WORLD. THE NEXT DAY, I WAS FAMOUS."

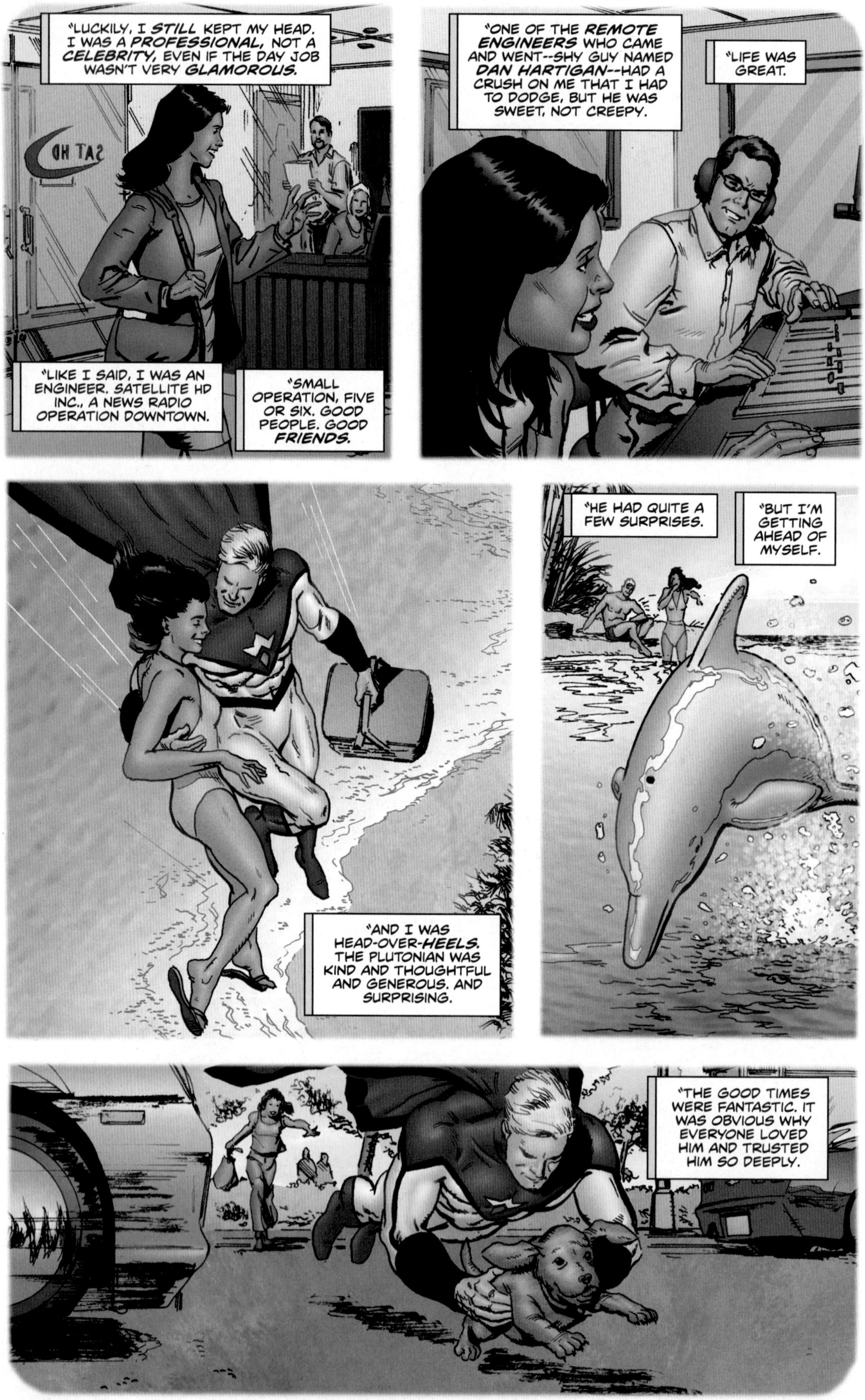
"LUCKILY, I STILL KEPT MY HEAD. I WAS A PROFESSIONAL, NOT A CELEBRITY, EVEN IF THE DAY JOB WASN'T VERY GLAMOROUS.
"LIKE I SAID, I WAS AN ENGINEER. SATELLITE HD INC., A NEWS RADIO OPERATION DOWNTOWN.
"SMALL OPERATION, FIVE OR SIX. GOOD PEOPLE. GOOD FRIENDS.
"ONE OF THE REMOTE ENGINEERS WHO CAME AND WENT--SHY GUY NAMED DAN HARTIGAN--HAD A CRUSH ON ME THAT I HAD TO DODGE, BUT HE WAS SWEET, NOT CREEPY.
"LIFE WAS GREAT.
"AND I WAS HEAD-OVER-HEELS. THE PLUTONIAN WAS KIND AND THOUGHTFUL AND GENEROUS. AND SURPRISING.
"HE HAD QUITE A FEW SURPRISES.
"BUT I'M GETTING AHEAD OF MYSELF.
"THE GOOD TIMES WERE FANTASTIC. IT WAS OBVIOUS WHY EVERYONE LOVED HIM AND TRUSTED HIM SO DEEPLY.

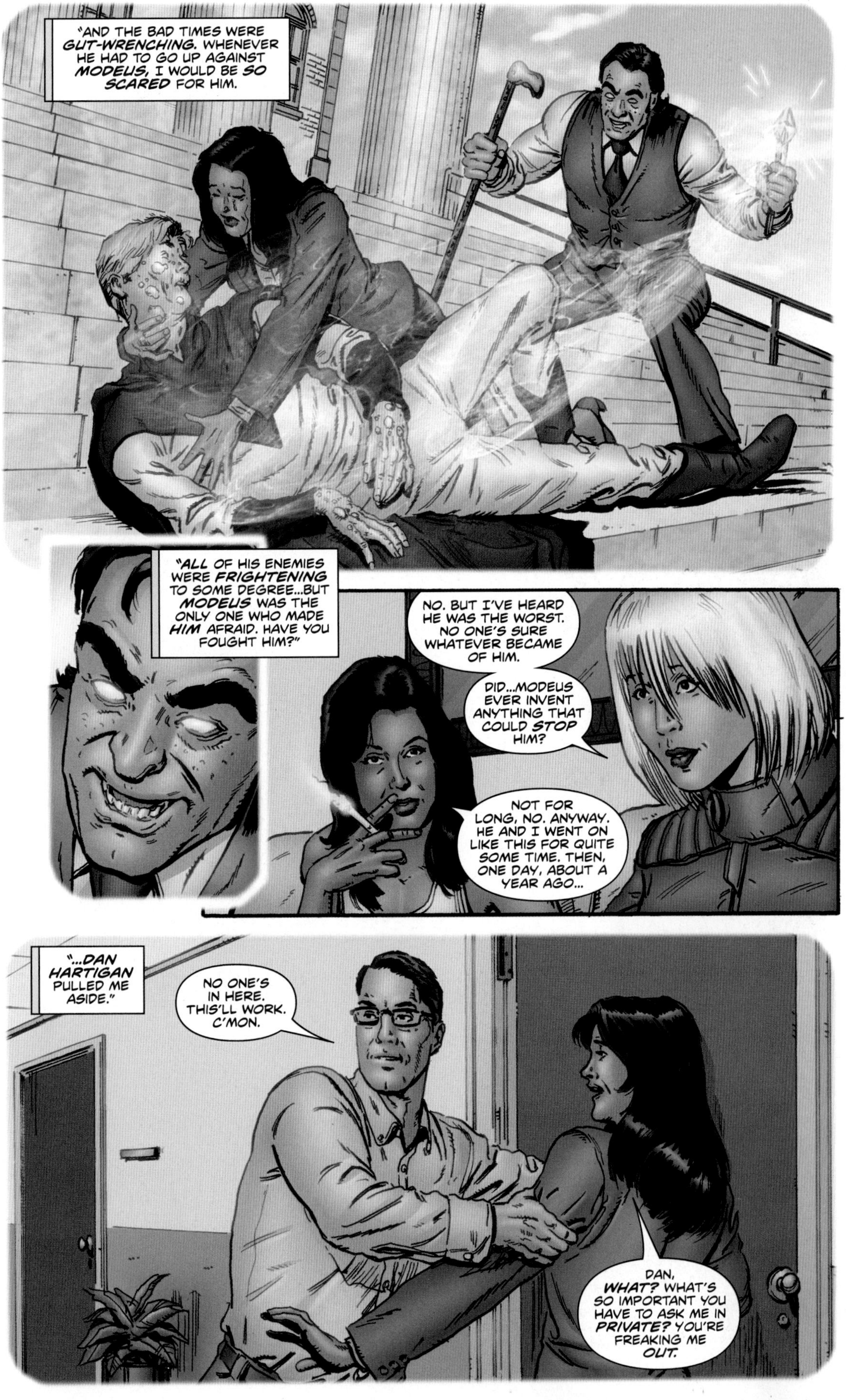
"AND THE BAD TIMES WERE GUT-WRENCHING. WHENEVER HE HAD TO GO UP AGAINST MODEUS, I WOULD BE SO SCARED FOR HIM.
"ALL OF HIS ENEMIES WERE FRIGHTENING TO SOME DEGREE...BUT MODEUS WAS THE ONLY ONE WHO MADE HIM AFRAID. HAVE YOU FOUGHT HIM?"
NO. BUT I'VE HEARD HE WAS THE WORST. NO ONE'S SURE WHATEVER BECAME OF HIM.
DID...MODEUS EVER INVENT ANYTHING THAT COULD STOP HIM?
NOT FOR LONG, NO. ANYWAY. HE AND I WENT ON LIKE THIS FOR QUITE SOME TIME. THEN, ONE DAY, ABOUT A YEAR AGO...
"...DAN HARTIGAN PULLED ME ASIDE."
NO ONE'S IN HERE. THIS'LL WORK. C'MON.
DAN, WHAT? WHAT'S SO IMPORTANT YOU HAVE TO ASK ME IN PRIVATE? YOU'RE FREAKING ME OUT.

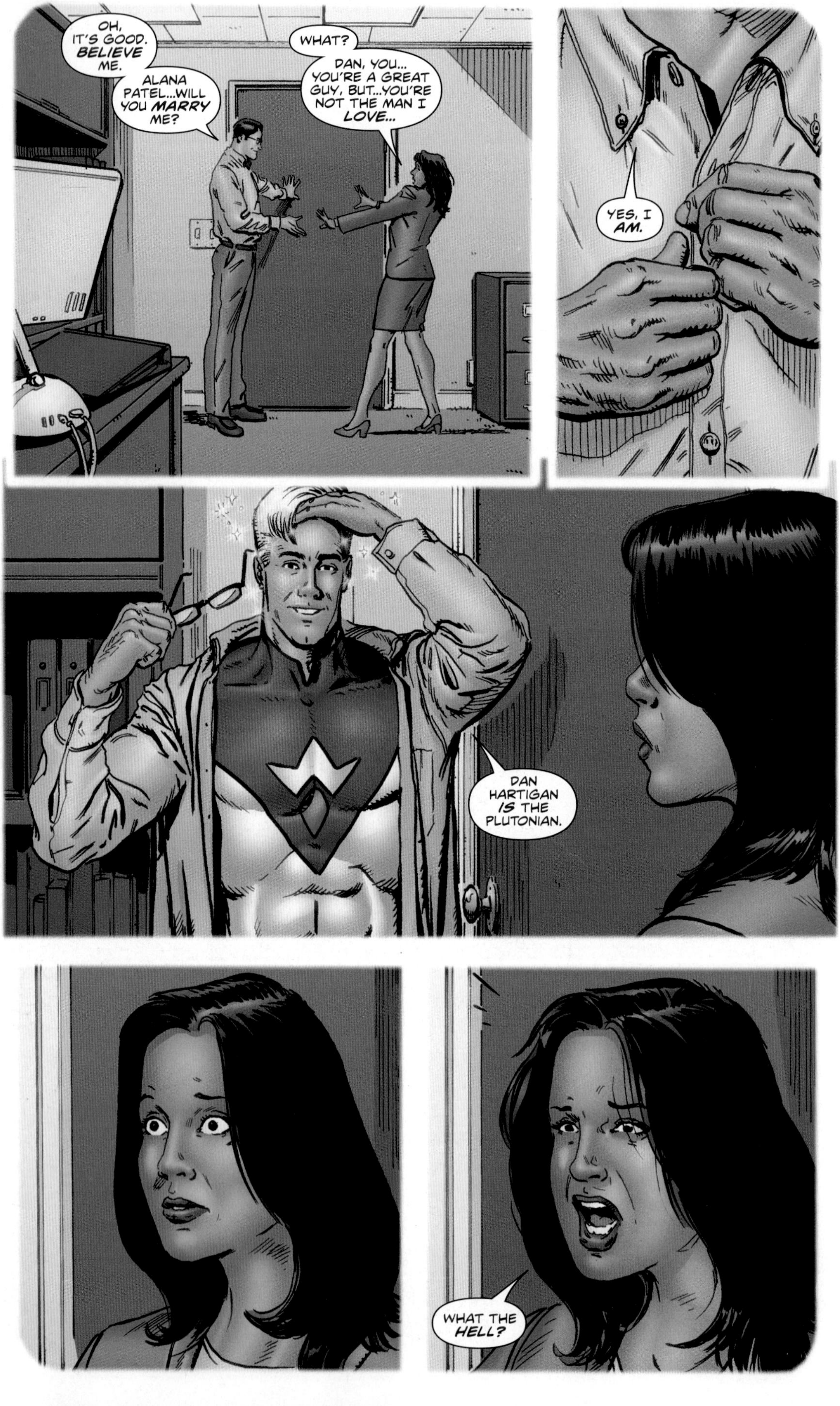
OH, IT'S GOOD. BELIEVE ME.
ALANA PATEL...WILL YOU MARRY ME?
WHAT?
DAN, YOU... YOU'RE A GREAT GUY, BUT...YOU'RE NOT THE MAN I LOVE...
YES, I AM.
DAN HARTIGAN IS THE PLUTONIAN.
WHAT THE HELL?

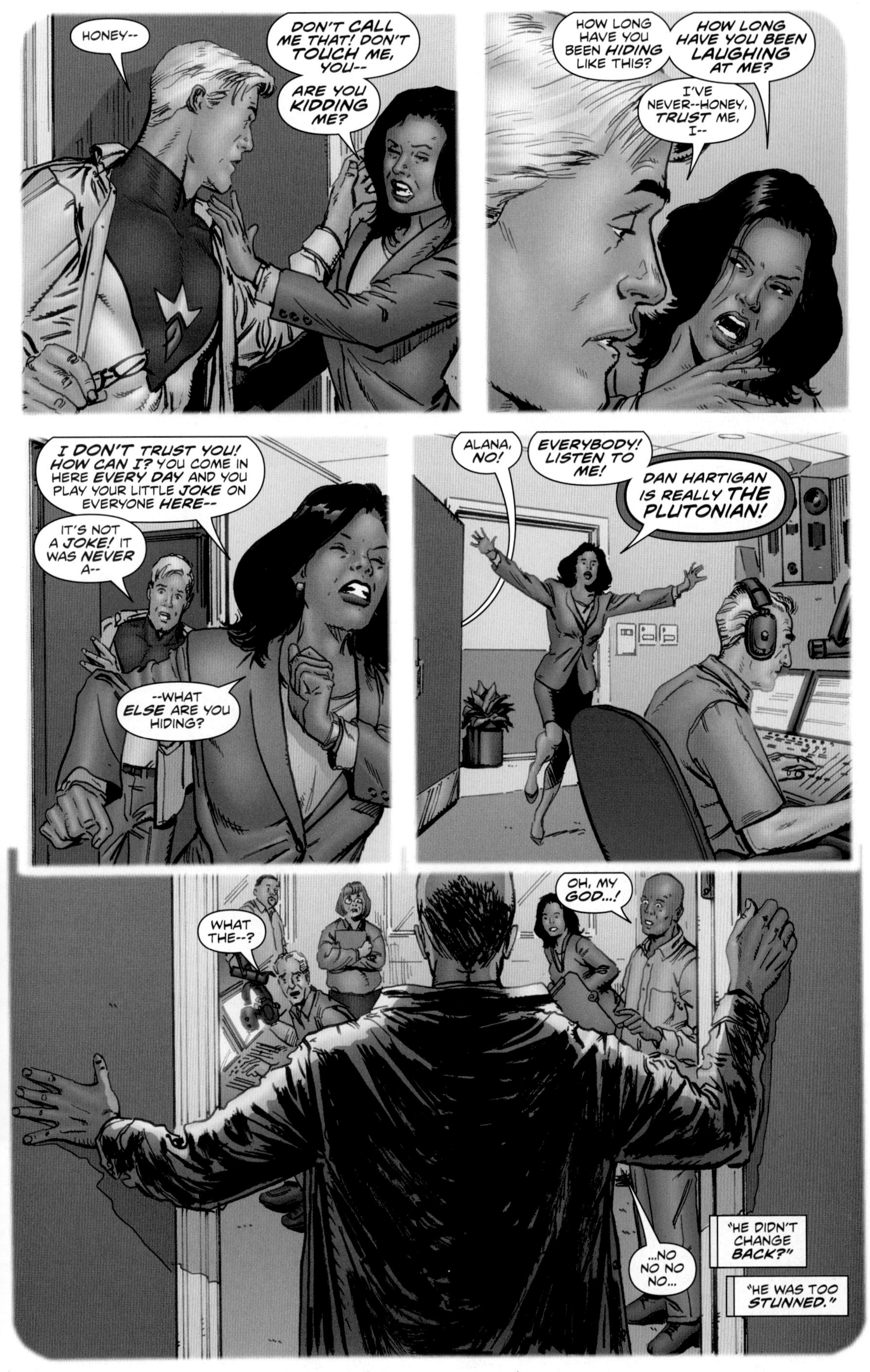
HONEY--
DON'T CALL ME THAT! DON'T TOUCH ME, YOU--
ARE YOU KIDDING ME?
HOW LONG HAVE YOU BEEN HIDING LIKE THIS?
HOW LONG HAVE YOU BEEN LAUGHING AT ME?
I'VE NEVER--HONEY, TRUST ME, I--
I DON'T TRUST YOU! HOW CAN I? YOU COME IN HERE EVERY DAY AND YOU PLAY YOUR LITTLE JOKE ON EVERYONE HERE--
IT'S NOT A JOKE! IT WAS NEVER A--
--WHAT ELSE ARE YOU HIDING?
ALANA, NO!
EVERYBODY! LISTEN TO ME!
DAN HARTIGAN IS REALLY THE PLUTONIAN!
WHAT THE--?
OH, MY GOD...!
...NO NO NO NO...
"HE DIDN'T CHANGE BACK?"
"HE WAS TOO STUNNED."

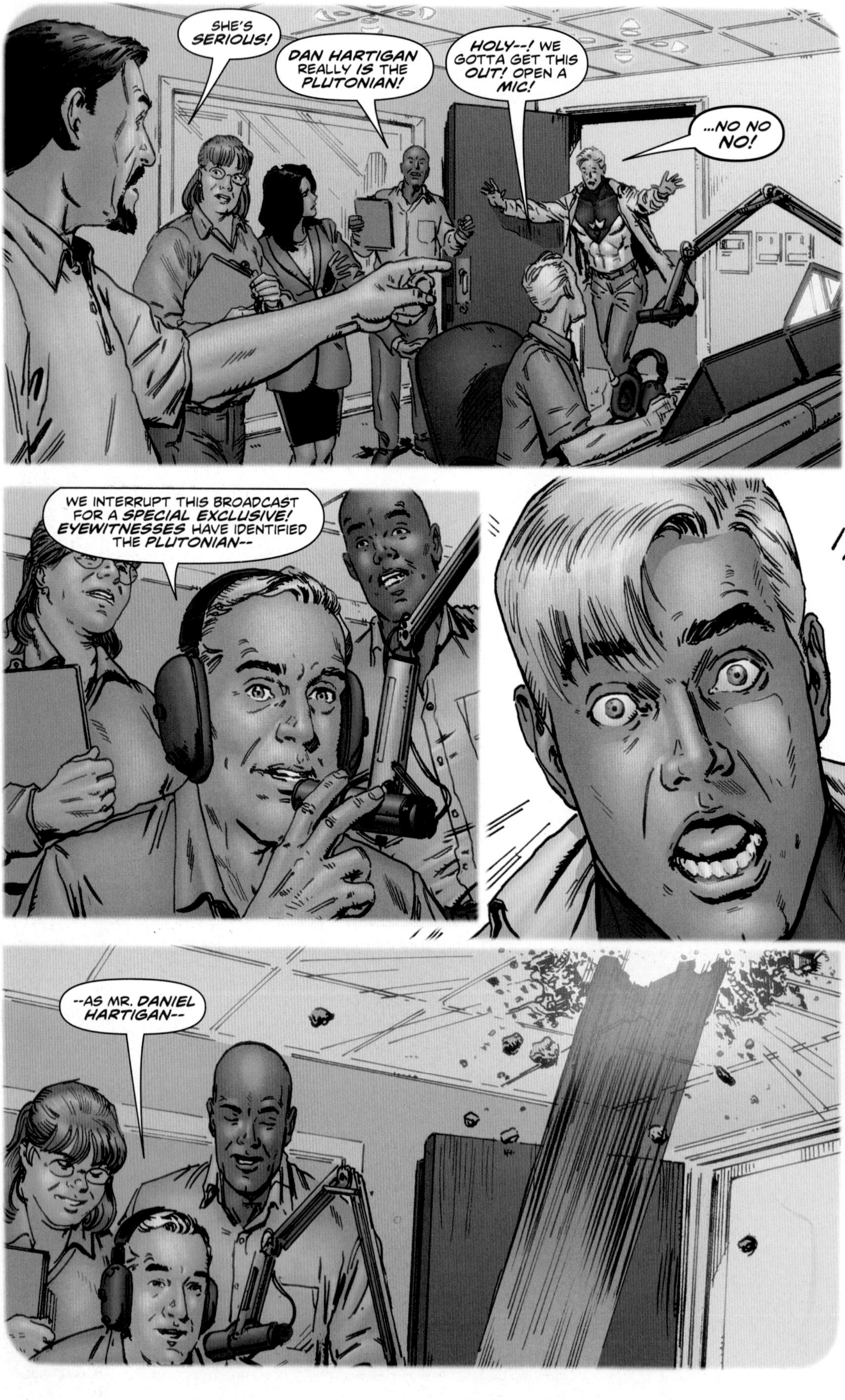
SHE'S SERIOUS!
DAN HARTIGAN REALLY IS THE PLUTONIAN!
HOLY--! WE GOTTA GET THIS OUT! OPEN A MIC!
...NO NO NO!
WE INTERRUPT THIS BROADCAST FOR A SPECIAL EXCLUSIVE! EYEWITNESSES HAVE IDENTIFIED THE PLUTONIAN--
--AS MR. DANIEL HARTIGAN--

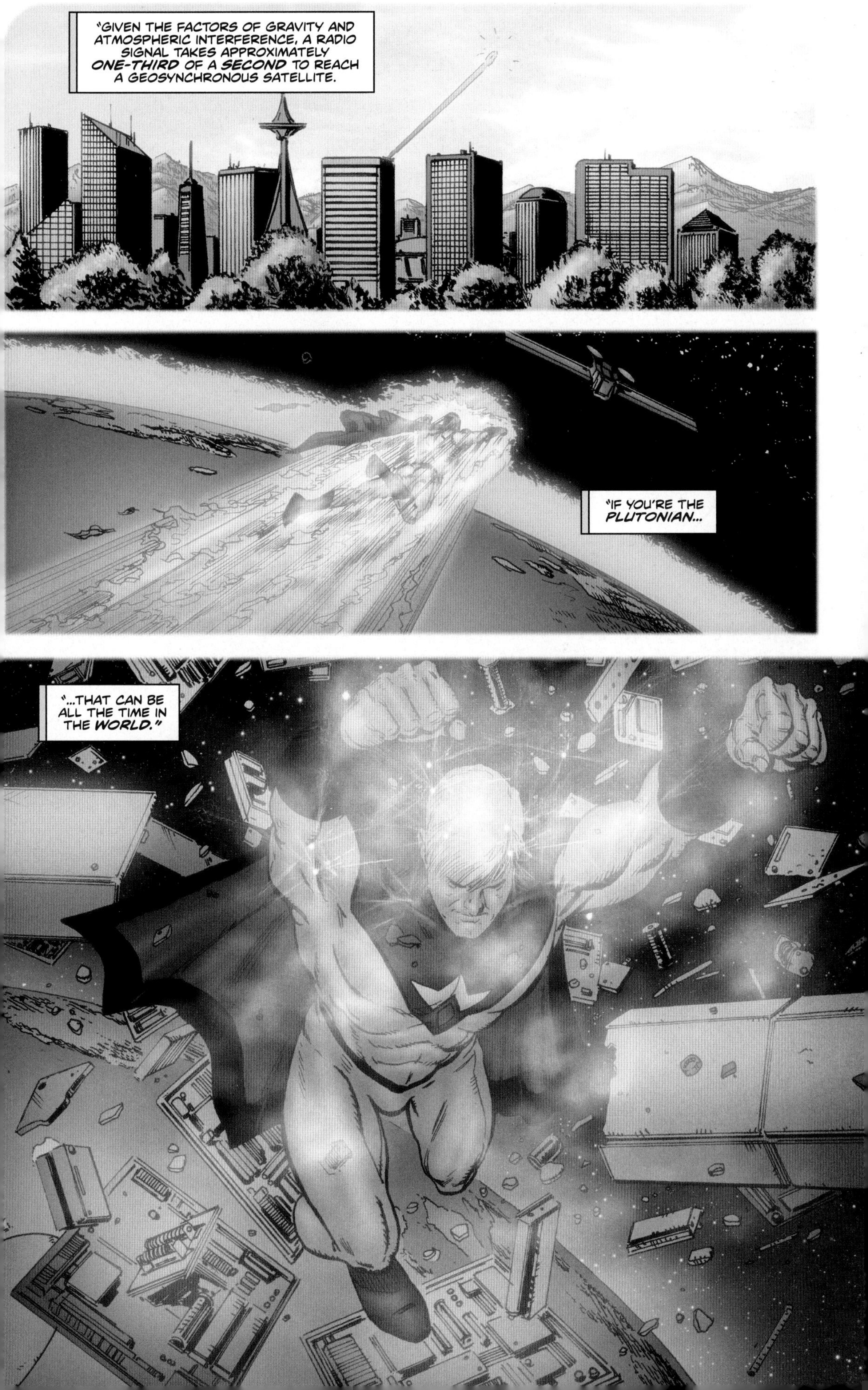
"GIVEN THE FACTORS OF GRAVITY AND ATMOSPHERIC INTERFERENCE, A RADIO SIGNAL TAKES APPROXIMATELY ONE-THIRD OF A SECOND TO REACH A GEOSYNCHRONOUS SATELLITE.
"IF YOU'RE THE PLUTONIAN...
"...THAT CAN BE ALL THE TIME IN THE WORLD."

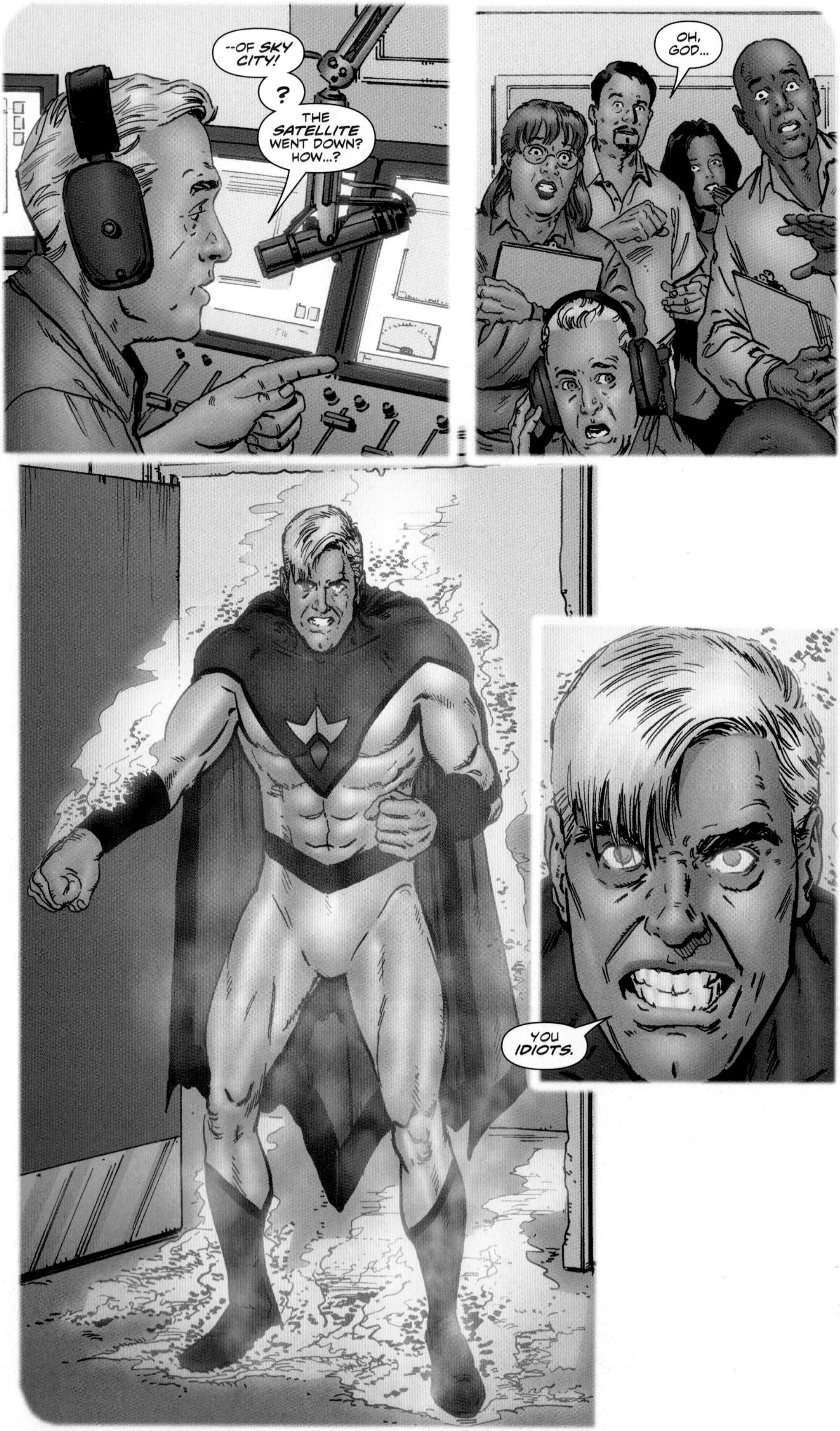
--OF SKY CITY!
?
THE SATELLITE WENT DOWN? HOW...?
OH, GOD...
YOU IDIOTS.

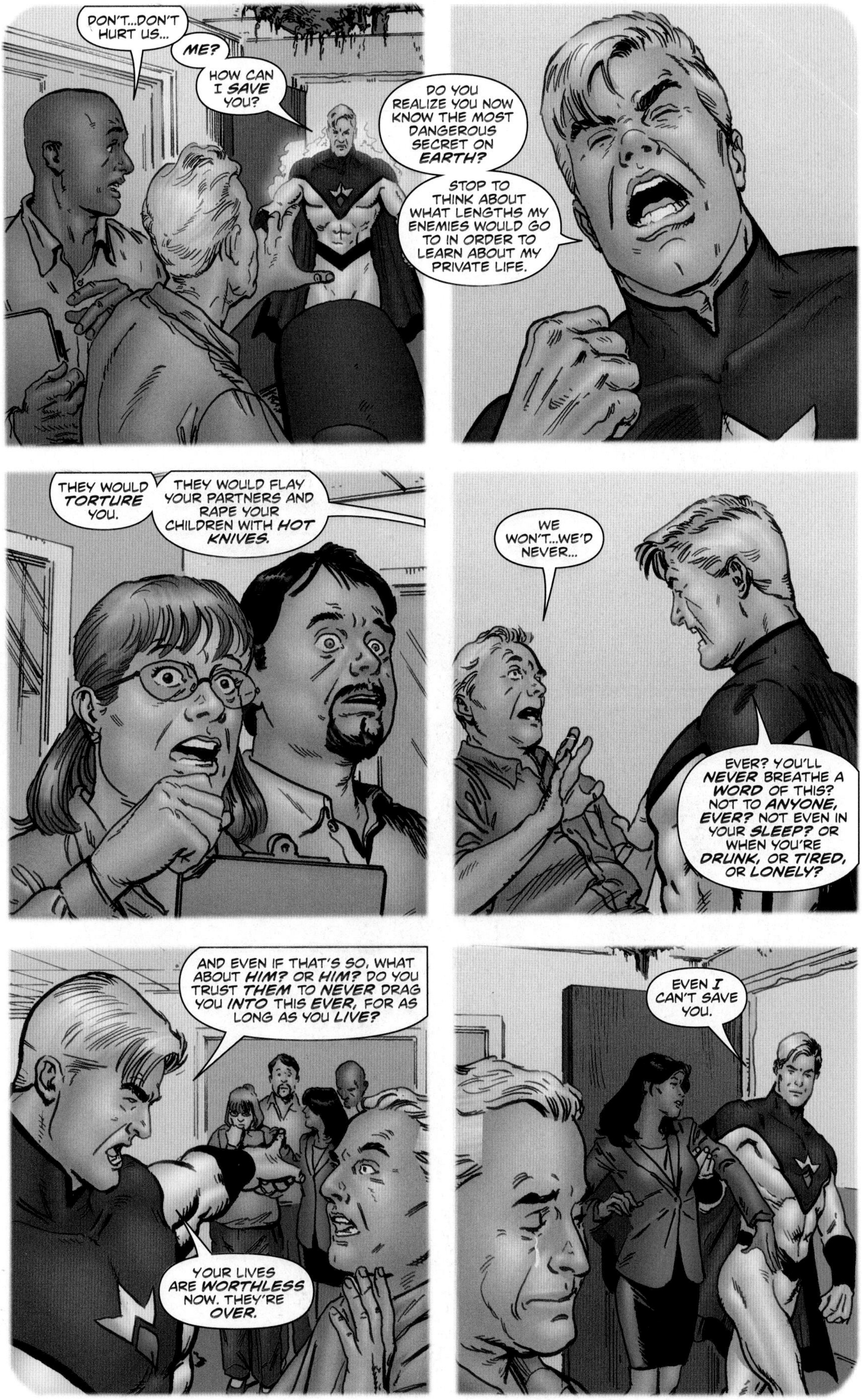
DON'T...DON'T HURT US...
ME?
HOW CAN I SAVE YOU?
DO YOU REALIZE YOU NOW KNOW THE MOST DANGEROUS SECRET ON EARTH?
STOP TO THINK ABOUT WHAT LENGTHS MY ENEMIES WOULD GO TO IN ORDER TO LEARN ABOUT MY PRIVATE LIFE.
THEY WOULD TORTURE YOU.
THEY WOULD FLAY YOUR PARTNERS AND RAPE YOUR CHILDREN WITH HOT KNIVES.
WE WON'T...WE'D NEVER...
EVER? YOU'LL NEVER BREATHE A WORD OF THIS? NOT TO ANYONE, EVER? NOT EVEN IN YOUR SLEEP? OR WHEN YOU'RE DRUNK, OR TIRED, OR LONELY?
AND EVEN IF THAT'S SO, WHAT ABOUT HIM? OR HIM? DO YOU TRUST THEM TO NEVER DRAG YOU INTO THIS EVER, FOR AS LONG AS YOU LIVE?
YOUR LIVES ARE WORTHLESS NOW. THEY'RE OVER.
EVEN I CAN'T SAVE YOU.

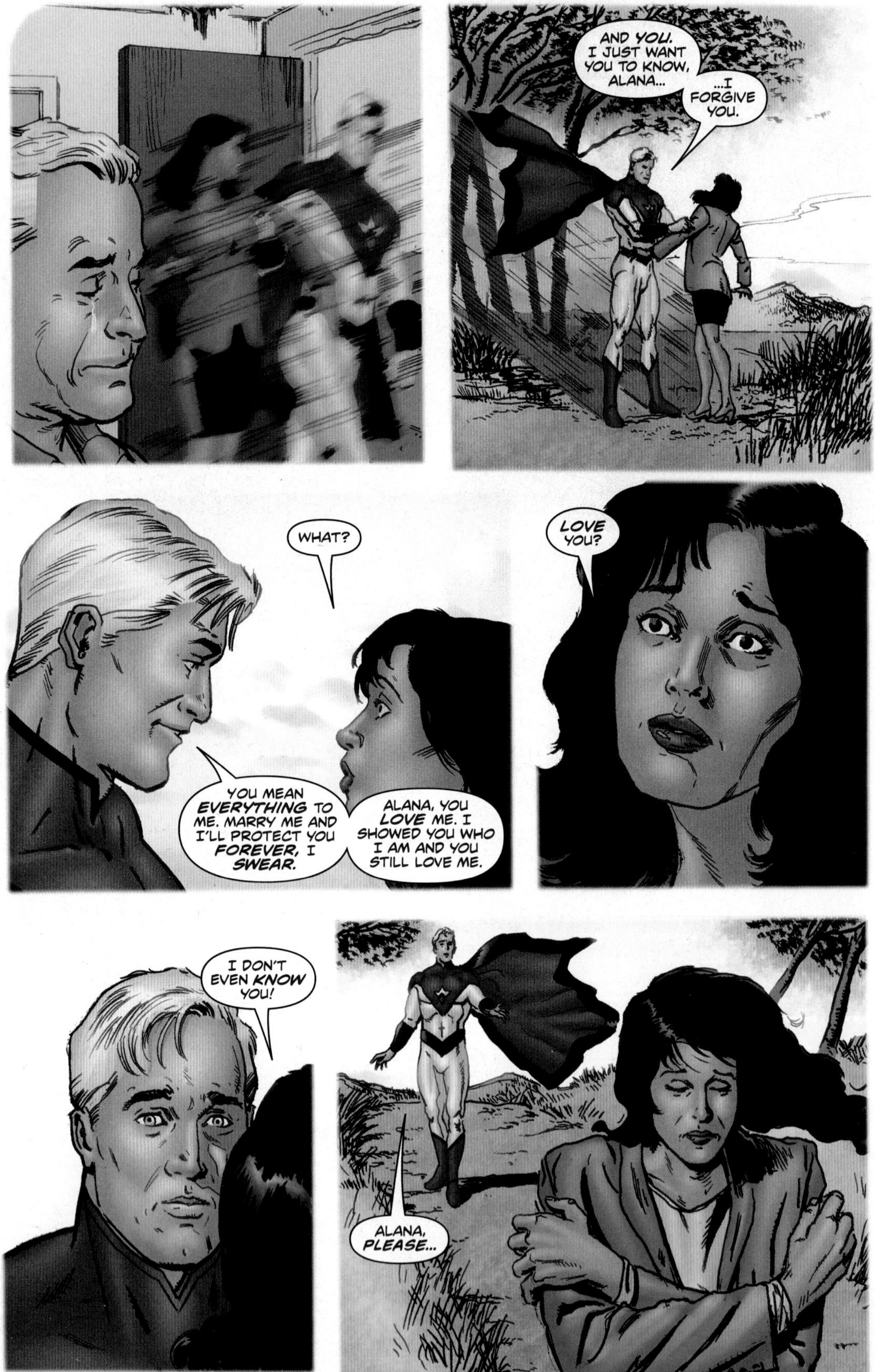
AND YOU. I JUST WANT YOU TO KNOW, ALANA...
...I FORGIVE YOU.
WHAT?
YOU MEAN EVERYTHING TO ME. MARRY ME AND I'LL PROTECT YOU FOREVER, I SWEAR.
ALANA, YOU LOVE ME. I SHOWED YOU WHO I AM AND YOU STILL LOVE ME.
LOVE YOU?
I DON'T EVEN KNOW YOU!
ALANA, PLEASE...

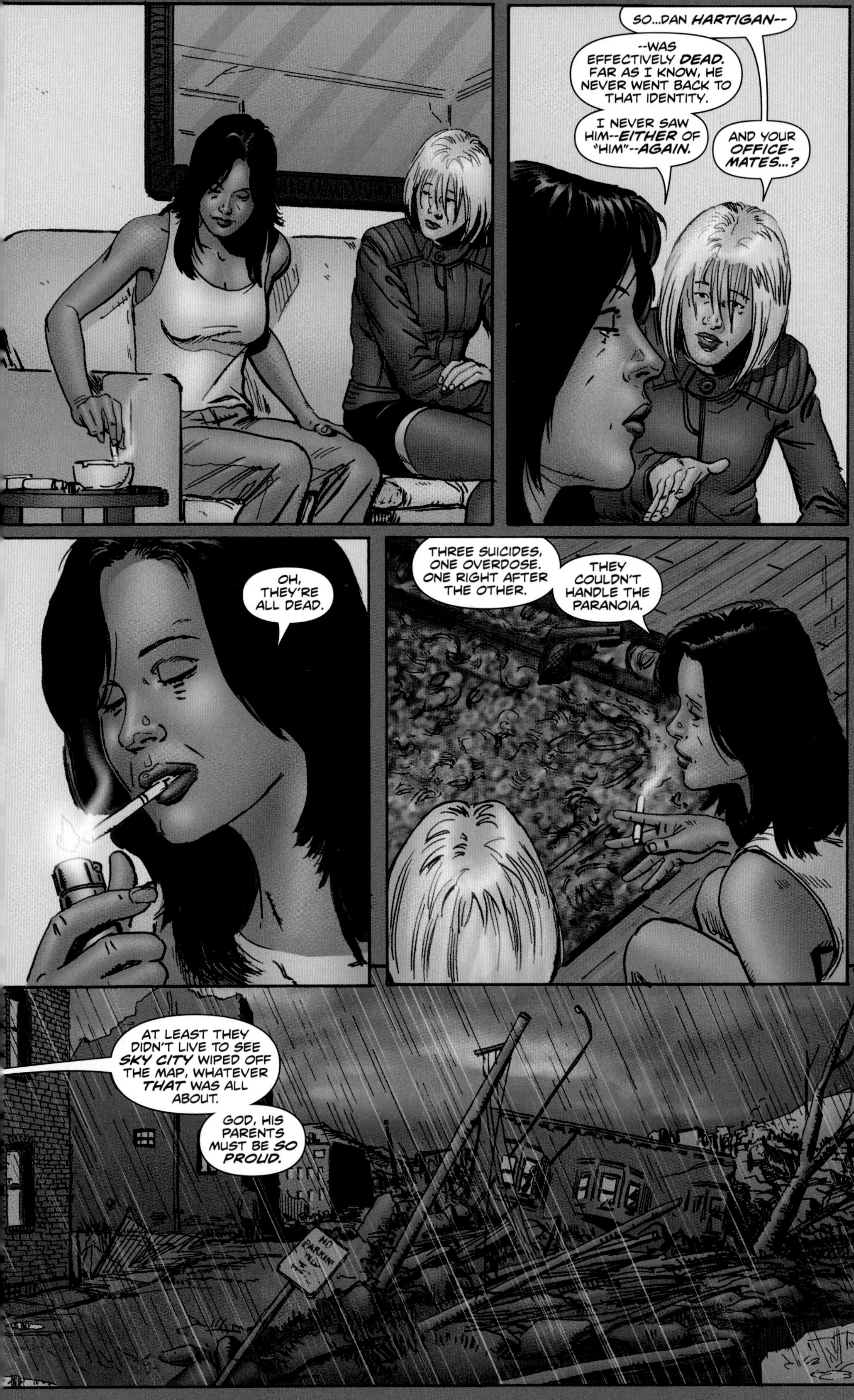
SO...DAN HARTIGAN--
--WAS EFFECTIVELY DEAD. FAR AS I KNOW, HE NEVER WENT BACK TO THAT IDENTITY.
I NEVER SAW HIM--EITHER OF "HIM"--AGAIN.
AND YOUR OFFICE-MATES...?
OH, THEY'RE ALL DEAD.
THREE SUICIDES, ONE OVERDOSE. ONE RIGHT AFTER THE OTHER.
THEY COULDN'T HANDLE THE PARANOIA.
AT LEAST THEY DIDN'T LIVE TO SEE SKY CITY WIPED OFF THE MAP, WHATEVER THAT WAS ALL ABOUT.
GOD, HIS PARENTS MUST BE SO PROUD.
NO PARKING

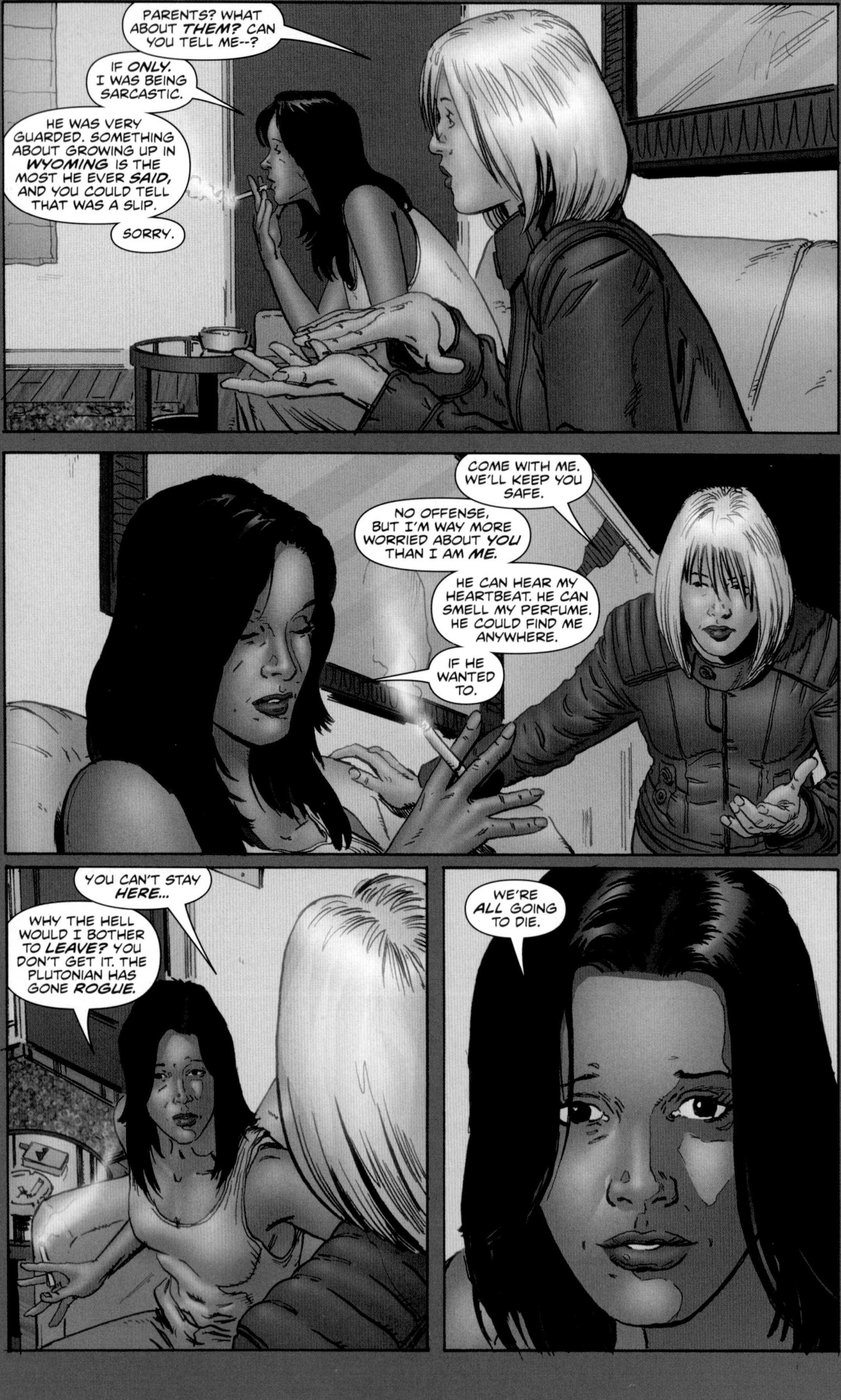
PARENTS? WHAT ABOUT THEM? CAN YOU TELL ME--?
IF ONLY. I WAS BEING SARCASTIC.
HE WAS VERY GUARDED. SOMETHING ABOUT GROWING UP IN WYOMING IS THE MOST HE EVER SAID, AND YOU COULD TELL THAT WAS A SLIP.
SORRY.
COME WITH ME. WE'LL KEEP YOU SAFE.
NO OFFENSE, BUT I'M WAY MORE WORRIED ABOUT YOU THAN I AM ME.
HE CAN HEAR MY HEARTBEAT. HE CAN SMELL MY PERFUME. HE COULD FIND ME ANYWHERE.
IF HE WANTED TO.
YOU CAN'T STAY HERE...
WHY THE HELL WOULD I BOTHER TO LEAVE? YOU DON'T GET IT. THE PLUTONIAN HAS GONE ROGUE.
WE'RE ALL GOING TO DIE.

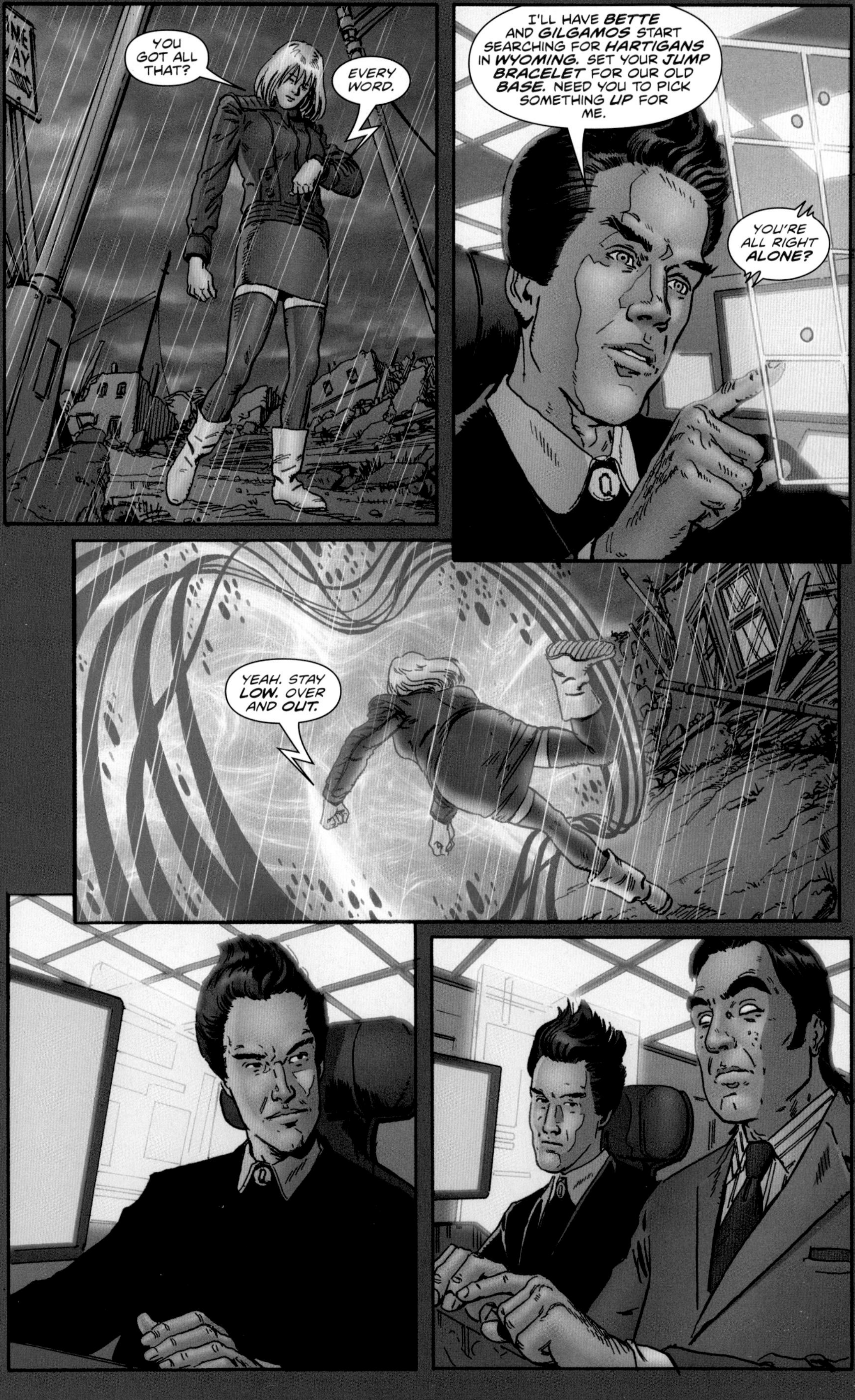

YOU GOT ALL THAT?
EVERY WORD.
I'LL HAVE BETTE AND GILGAMOS START SEARCHING FOR HARTIGANS IN WYOMING. SET YOUR JUMP BRACELET FOR OUR OLD BASE. NEED YOU TO PICK SOMETHING UP FOR ME.
YOU'RE ALL RIGHT ALONE?
YEAH. STAY LOW. OVER AND OUT.

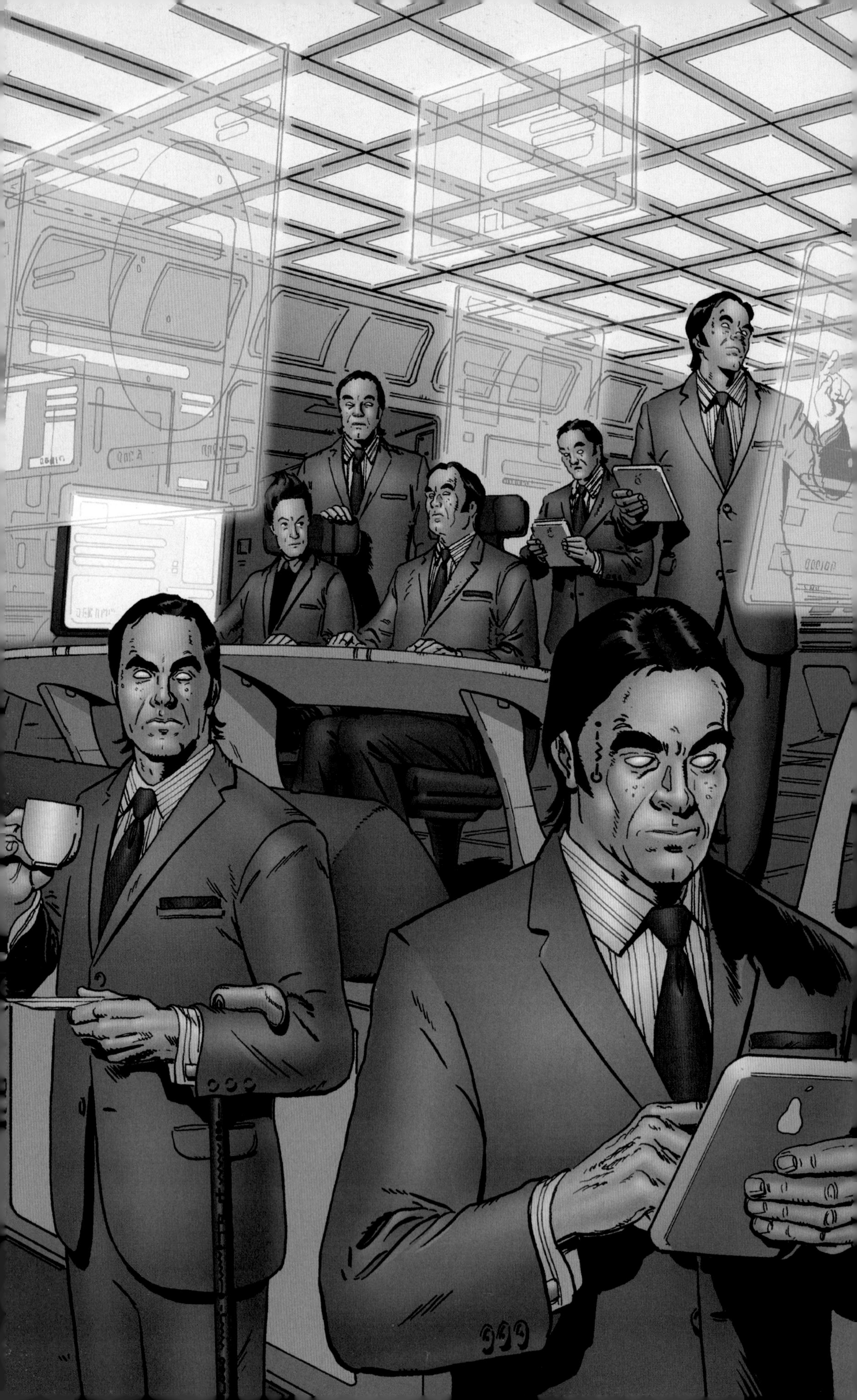

CHAPTER 3

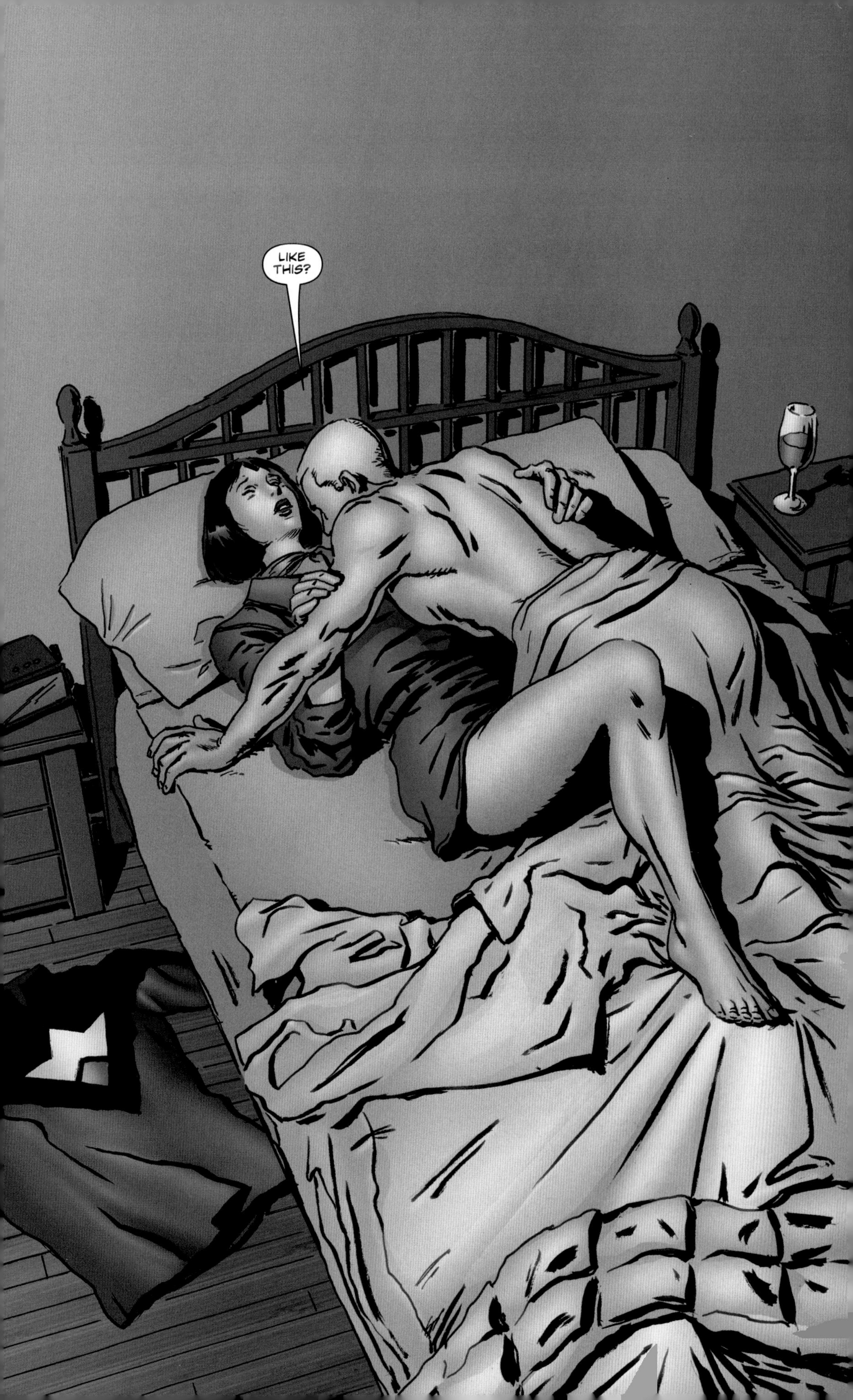
LIKE THIS?

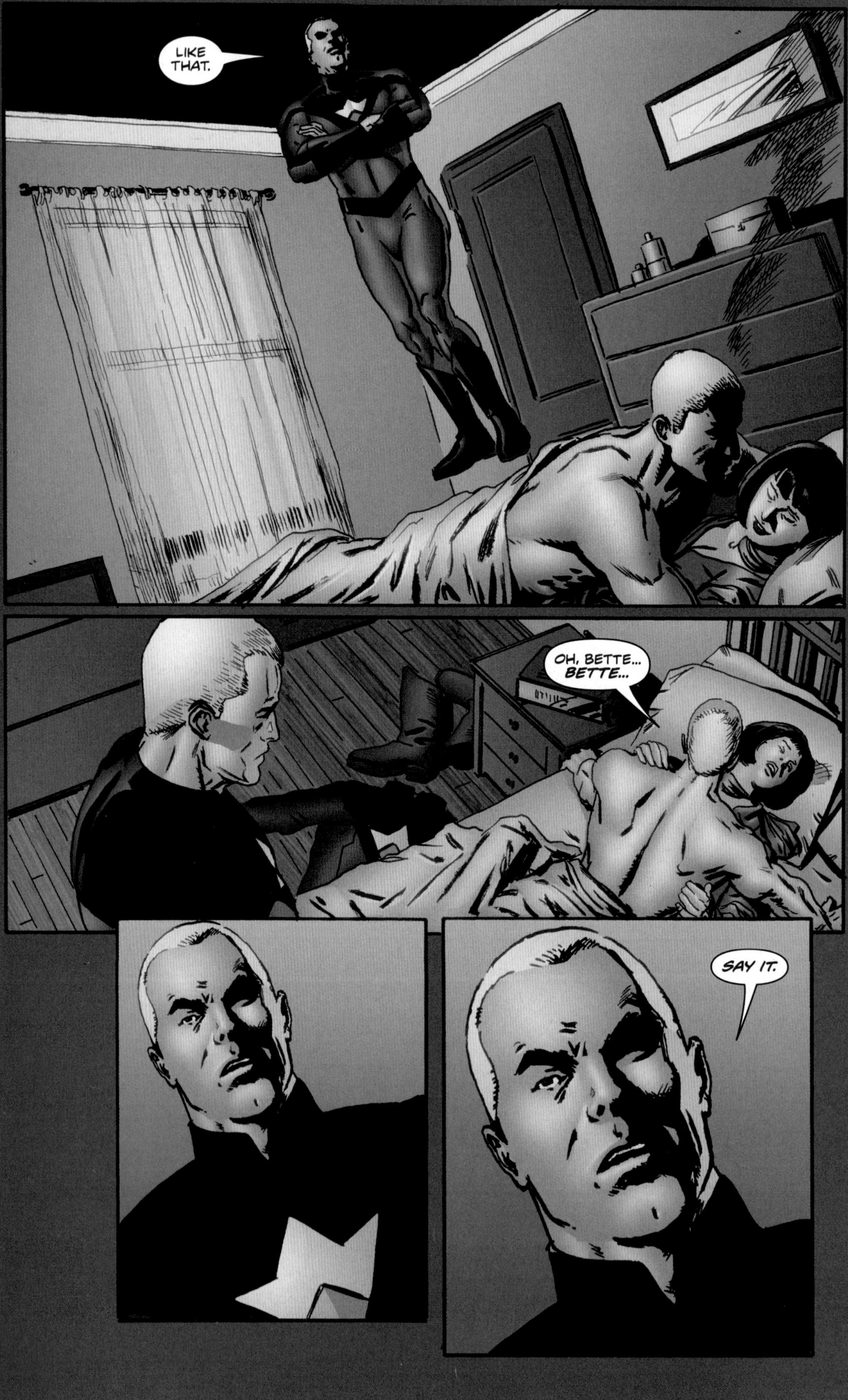
LIKE THAT.
OH, BETTE... BETTE...
SAY IT.

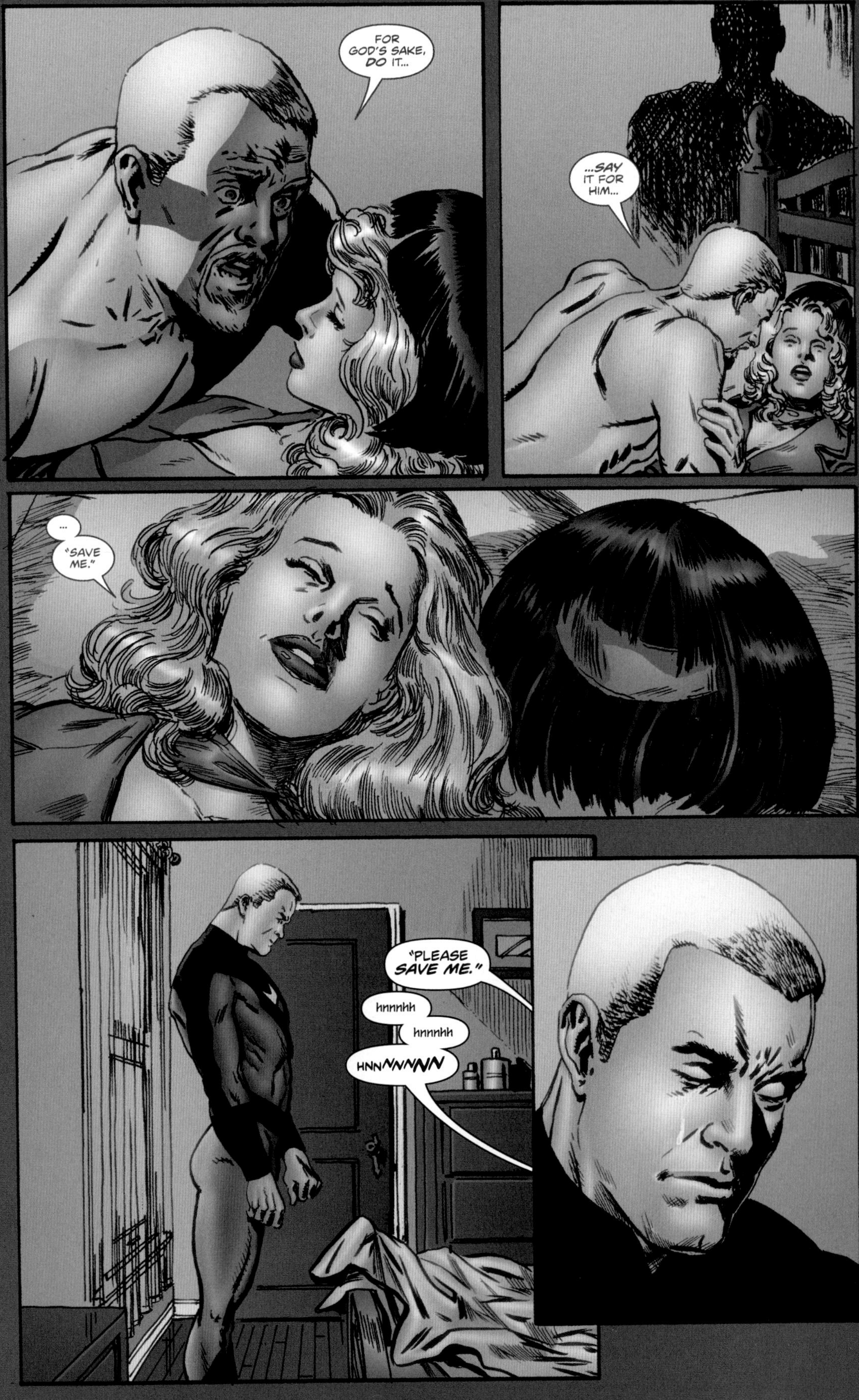
FOR GOD'S SAKE, DO IT...
...SAY IT FOR HIM...
... "SAVE ME."
"PLEASE SAVE ME."
hnnnhh
hnnnhh
HNNNNNNN

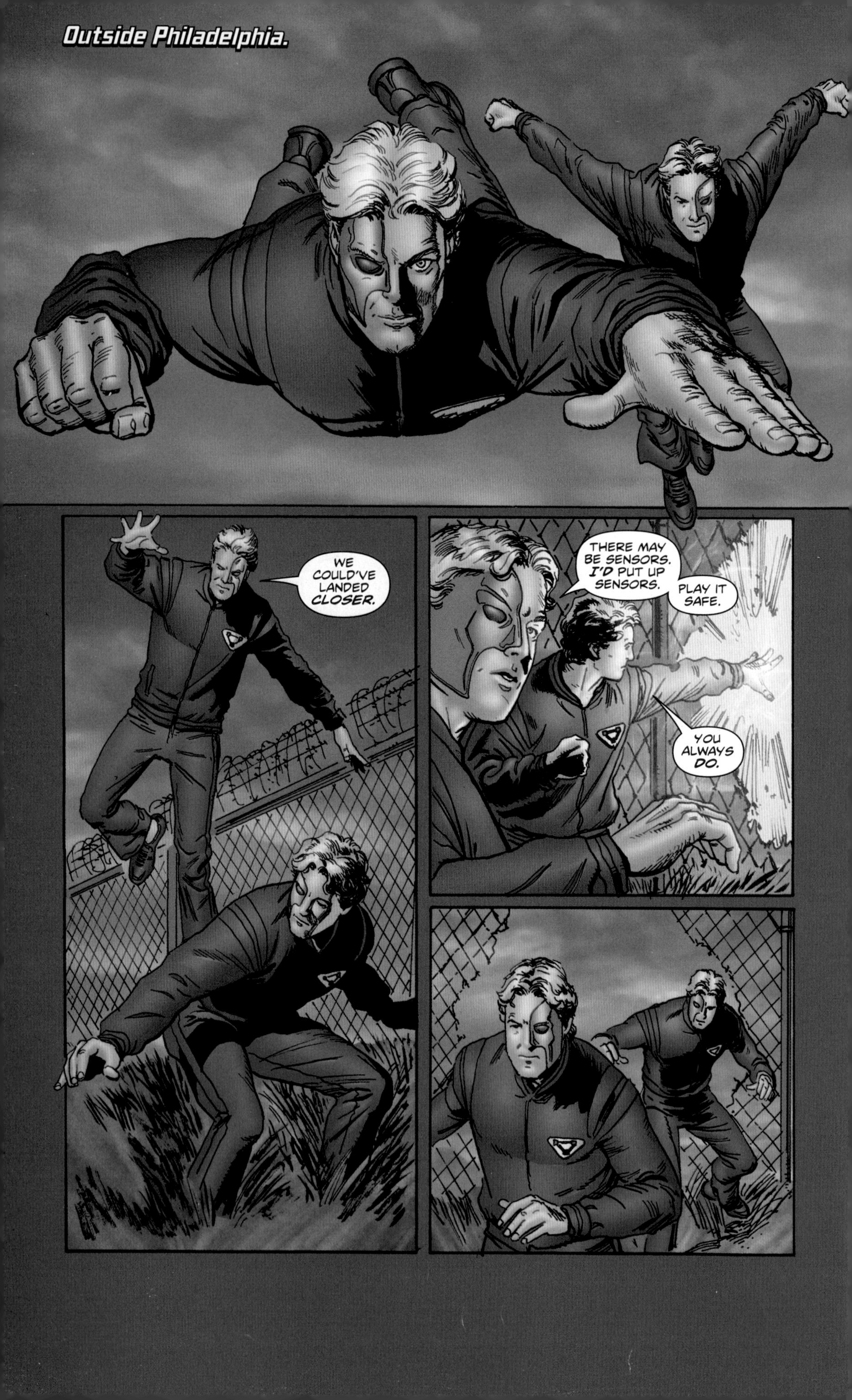
Outside Philadelphia.
WE COULD'VE LANDED CLOSER.
THERE MAY BE SENSORS. I'D PUT UP SENSORS.
PLAY IT SAFE.
YOU ALWAYS DO.

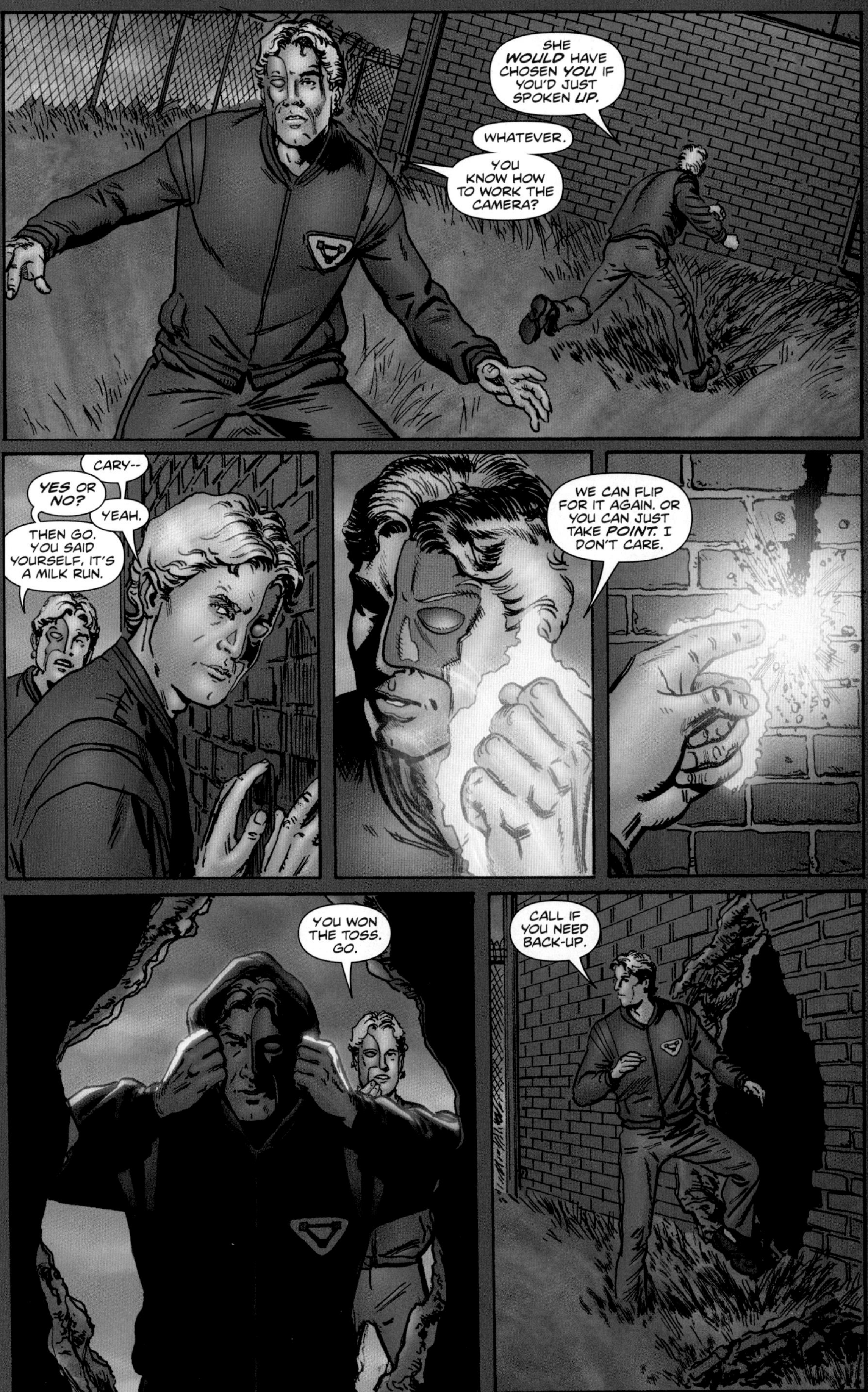
SHE WOULD HAVE CHOSEN YOU IF YOU'D JUST SPOKEN UP.
WHATEVER.
YOU KNOW HOW TO WORK THE CAMERA?
CARY--
YES OR NO?
YEAH.
THEN GO. YOU SAID YOURSELF, IT'S A MILK RUN.
WE CAN FLIP FOR IT AGAIN. OR YOU CAN JUST TAKE POINT. I DON'T CARE.
YOU WON THE TOSS. GO.
CALL IF YOU NEED BACK-UP.

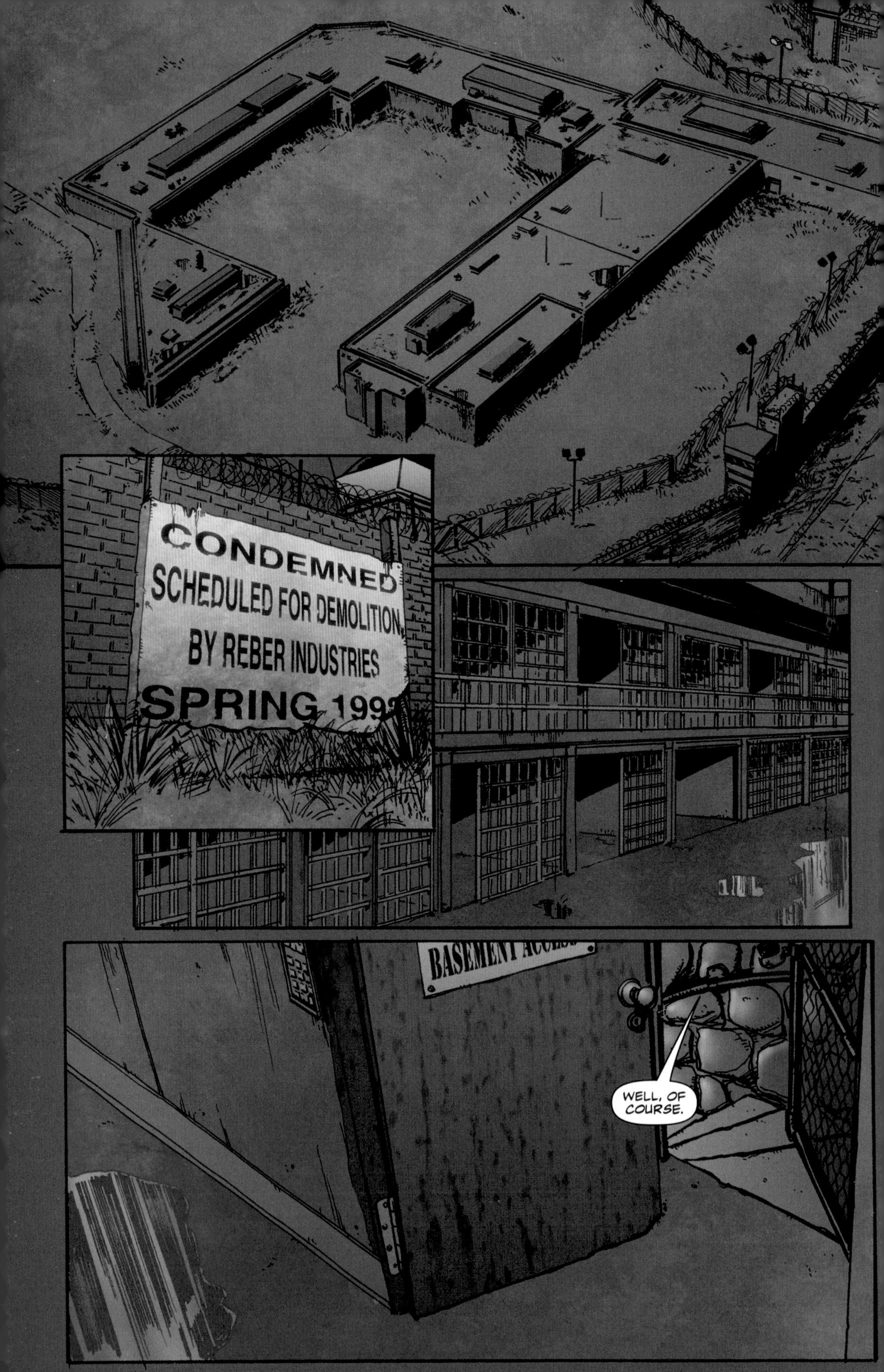
CONDEMNED
SCHEDULED FOR DEMOLITION
BY REBER INDUSTRIES
SPRING 199
BASEMENT
WELL, OF COURSE.

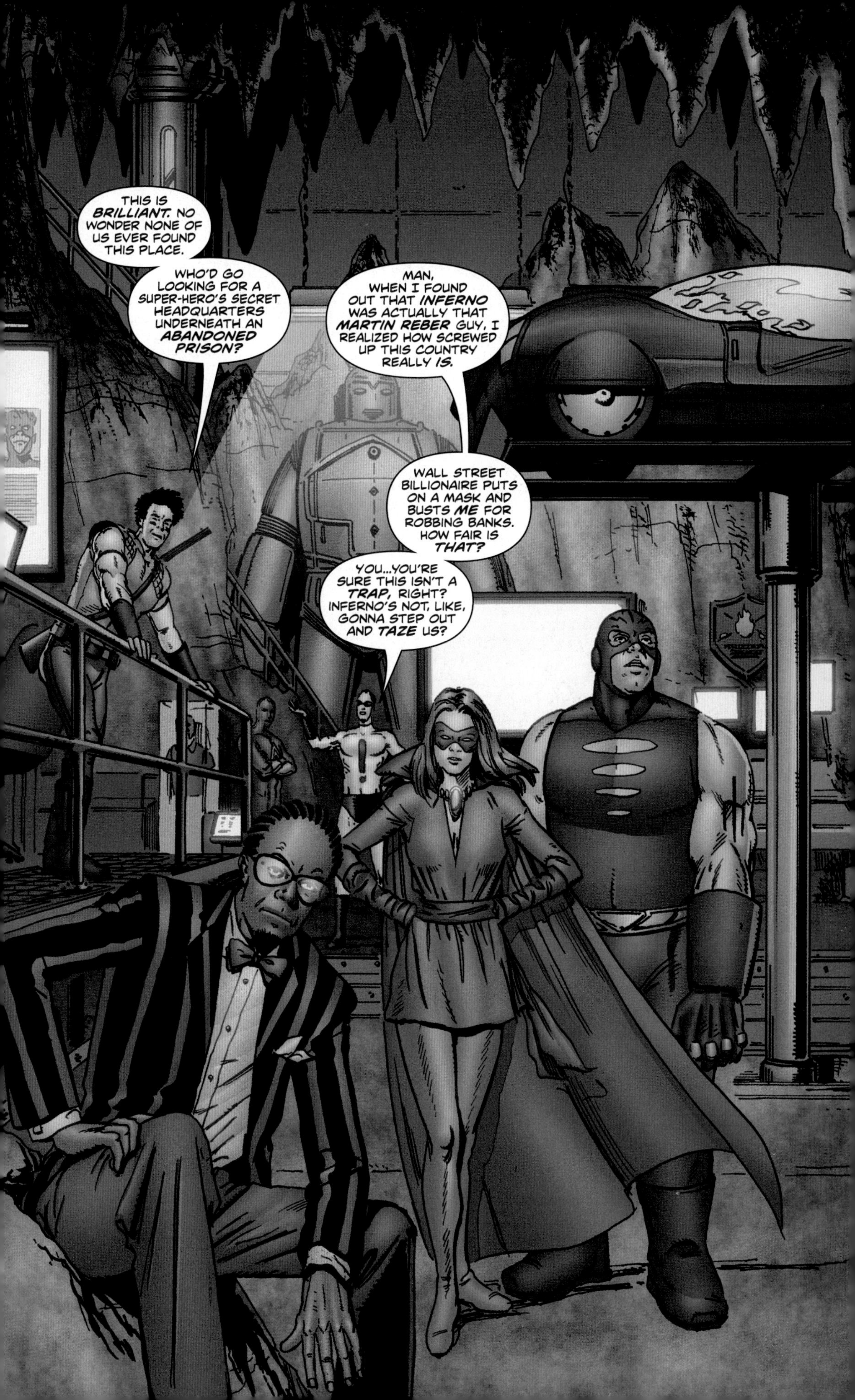
THIS IS BRILLIANT. NO WONDER NONE OF US EVER FOUND THIS PLACE.
WHO'D GO LOOKING FOR A SUPER-HERO'S SECRET HEADQUARTERS UNDERNEATH AN ABANDONED PRISON?
MAN, WHEN I FOUND OUT THAT INFERNO WAS ACTUALLY THAT MARTIN REBER GUY, I REALIZED HOW SCREWED UP THIS COUNTRY REALLY IS.
WALL STREET BILLIONAIRE PUTS ON A MASK AND BUSTS ME FOR ROBBING BANKS. HOW FAIR IS THAT?
YOU...YOU'RE SURE THIS ISN'T A TRAP, RIGHT? INFERNO'S NOT, LIKE, GONNA STEP OUT AND TAZE US?

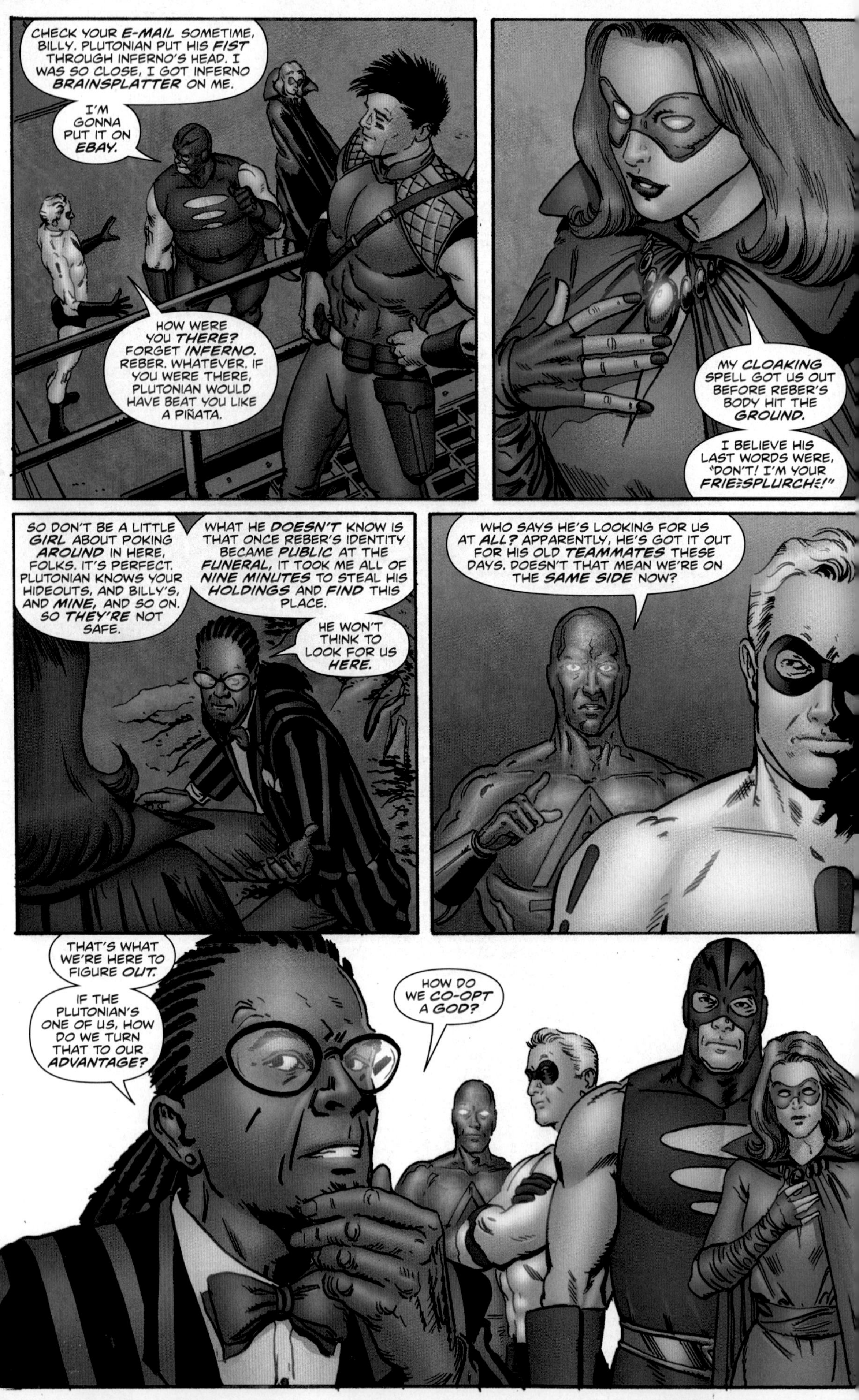
CHECK YOUR E-MAIL SOMETIME, BILLY. PLUTONIAN PUT HIS FIST THROUGH INFERNO'S HEAD. I WAS SO CLOSE, I GOT INFERNO BRAINSPLATTER ON ME.
I'M GONNA PUT IT ON EBAY.
HOW WERE YOU THERE? FORGET INFERNO. REBER. WHATEVER. IF YOU WERE THERE, PLUTONIAN WOULD HAVE BEAT YOU LIKE A PIÑATA.
MY CLOAKING SPELL GOT US OUT BEFORE REBER'S BODY HIT THE GROUND.
I BELIEVE HIS LAST WORDS WERE, "DON'T! I'M YOUR FRIE=SPLURCH=!"
SO DON'T BE A LITTLE GIRL ABOUT POKING AROUND IN HERE, FOLKS. IT'S PERFECT. PLUTONIAN KNOWS YOUR HIDEOUTS, AND BILLY'S, AND MINE, AND SO ON. SO THEY'RE NOT SAFE.
WHAT HE DOESN'T KNOW IS THAT ONCE REBER'S IDENTITY BECAME PUBLIC AT THE FUNERAL, IT TOOK ME ALL OF NINE MINUTES TO STEAL HIS HOLDINGS AND FIND THIS PLACE.
HE WON'T THINK TO LOOK FOR US HERE.
WHO SAYS HE'S LOOKING FOR US AT ALL? APPARENTLY, HE'S GOT IT OUT FOR HIS OLD TEAMMATES THESE DAYS. DOESN'T THAT MEAN WE'RE ON THE SAME SIDE NOW?
THAT'S WHAT WE'RE HERE TO FIGURE OUT.
IF THE PLUTONIAN'S ONE OF US, HOW DO WE TURN THAT TO OUR ADVANTAGE?
HOW DO WE CO-OPT A GOD?

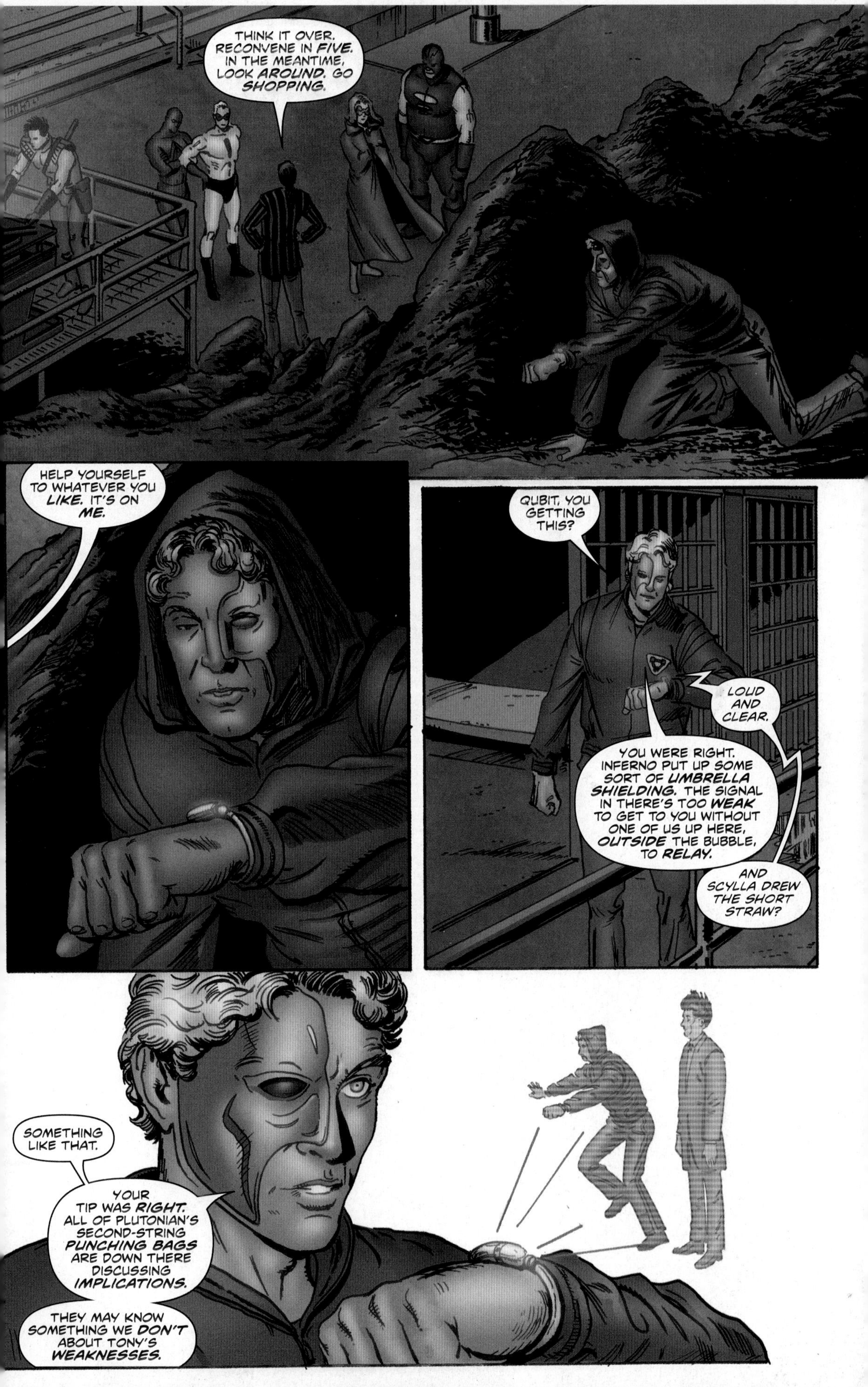
THINK IT OVER. RECONVENE IN FIVE. IN THE MEANTIME, LOOK AROUND. GO SHOPPING.
HELP YOURSELF TO WHATEVER YOU LIKE. IT'S ON ME.
QUBIT, YOU GETTING THIS?
LOUD AND CLEAR.
YOU WERE RIGHT. INFERNO PUT UP SOME SORT OF UMBRELLA SHIELDING. THE SIGNAL IN THERE'S TOO WEAK TO GET TO YOU WITHOUT ONE OF US UP HERE, OUTSIDE THE BUBBLE, TO RELAY.
AND SCYLLA DREW THE SHORT STRAW?
SOMETHING LIKE THAT.
YOUR TIP WAS RIGHT. ALL OF PLUTONIAN'S SECOND-STRING PUNCHING BAGS ARE DOWN THERE DISCUSSING IMPLICATIONS.
THEY MAY KNOW SOMETHING WE DON'T ABOUT TONY'S WEAKNESSES.

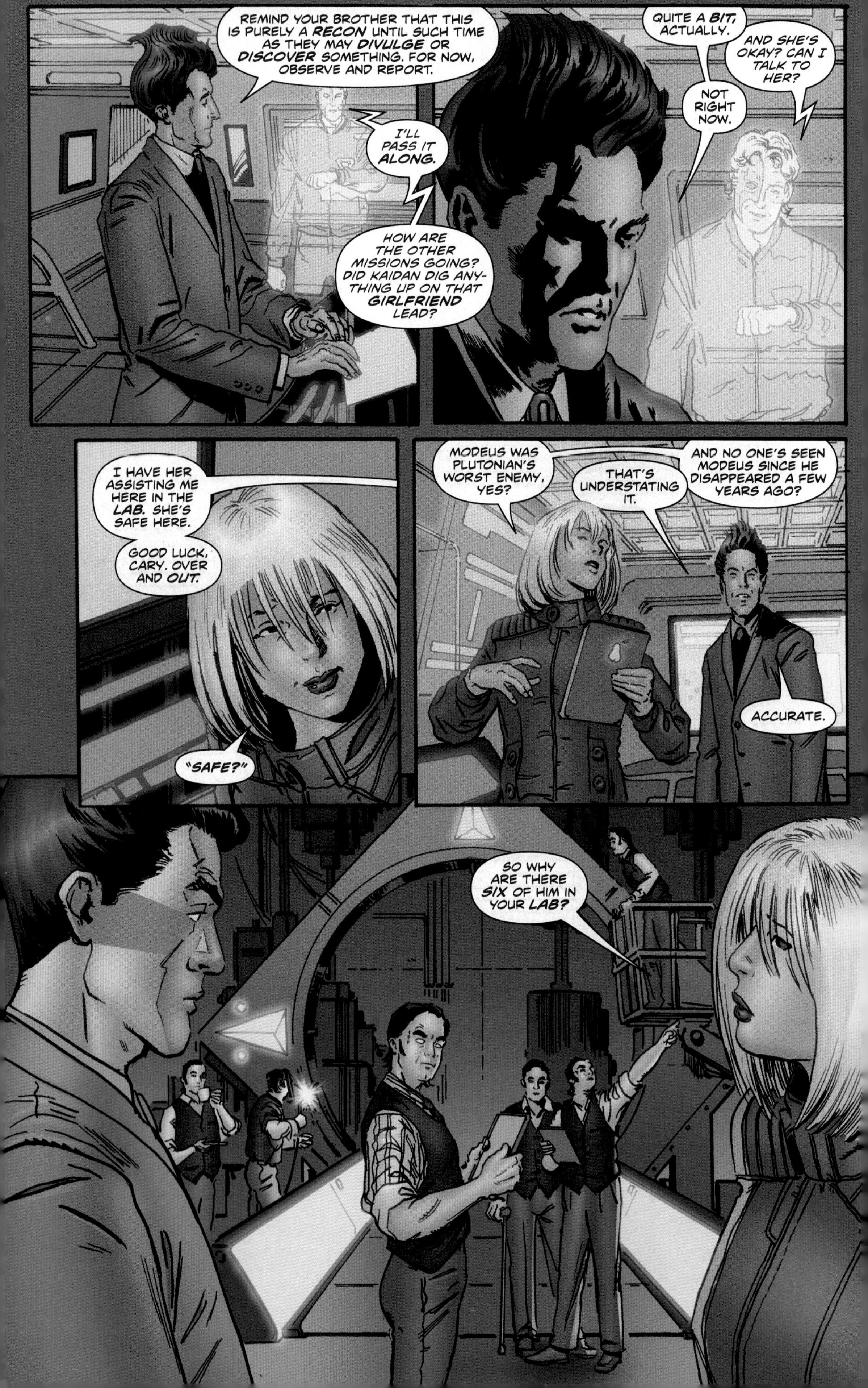
REMIND YOUR BROTHER THAT THIS IS PURELY A RECON UNTIL SUCH TIME AS THEY MAY DIVULGE OR DISCOVER SOMETHING. FOR NOW, OBSERVE AND REPORT.
I'LL PASS IT ALONG.
HOW ARE THE OTHER MISSIONS GOING? DID KAIDAN DIG ANYTHING UP ON THAT GIRLFRIEND LEAD?
QUITE A BIT, ACTUALLY.
AND SHE'S OKAY? CAN I TALK TO HER?
NOT RIGHT NOW.
I HAVE HER ASSISTING ME HERE IN THE LAB. SHE'S SAFE HERE.
GOOD LUCK, CARY. OVER AND OUT.
"SAFE?"
MODEUS WAS PLUTONIAN'S WORST ENEMY, YES?
THAT'S UNDERSTATING IT.
AND NO ONE'S SEEN MODEUS SINCE HE DISAPPEARED A FEW YEARS AGO?
ACCURATE.
SO WHY ARE THERE SIX OF HIM IN YOUR LAB?

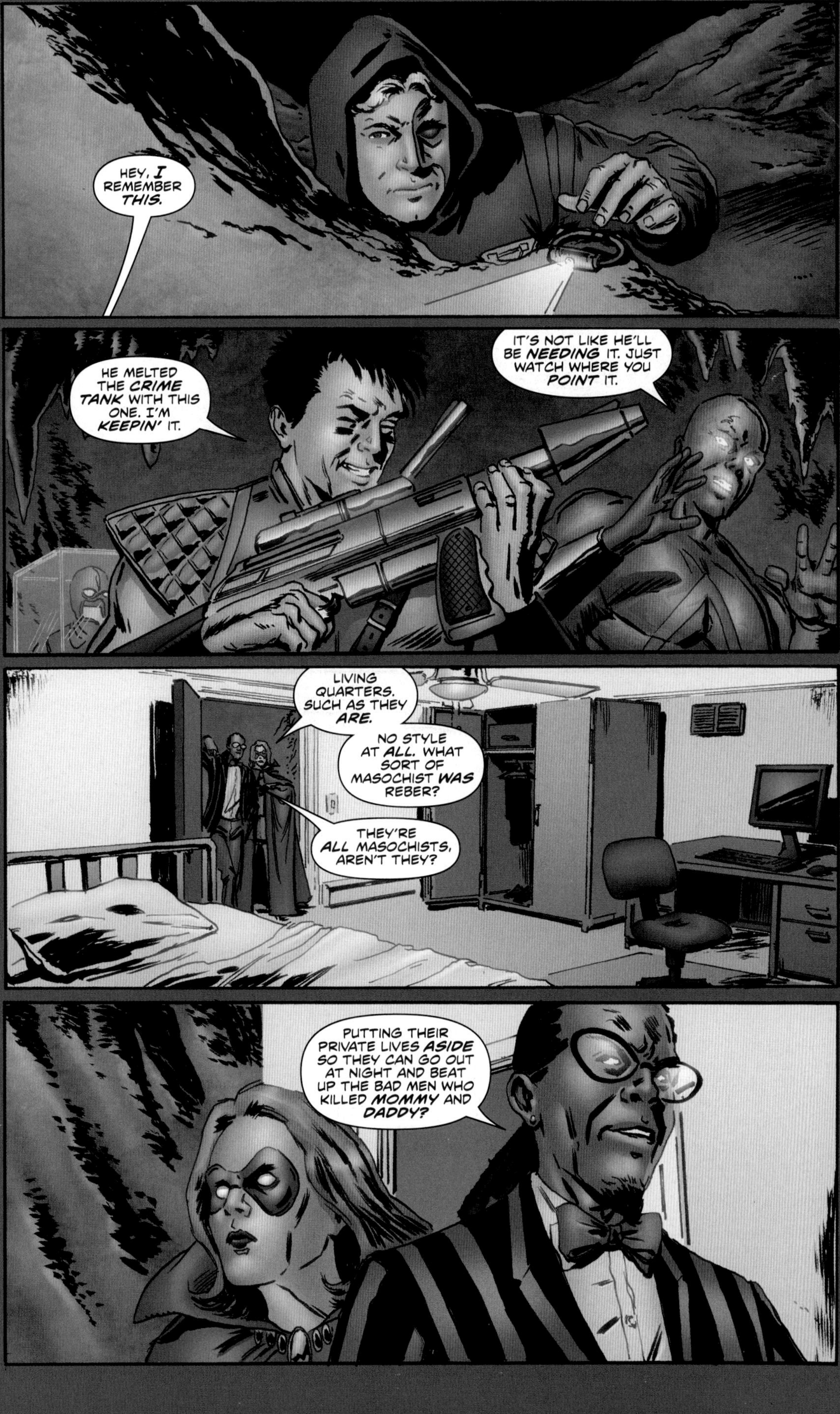
HEY, *I* REMEMBER *THIS.*
HE MELTED THE *CRIME TANK* WITH THIS ONE. I'M *KEEPIN'* IT.
IT'S NOT LIKE HE'LL BE *NEEDING* IT. JUST WATCH WHERE YOU *POINT* IT.
LIVING QUARTERS. SUCH AS THEY *ARE.*
NO STYLE AT *ALL.* WHAT SORT OF MASOCHIST *WAS* REBER?
THEY'RE *ALL* MASOCHISTS, AREN'T THEY?
PUTTING THEIR PRIVATE LIVES *ASIDE* SO THEY CAN GO OUT AT NIGHT AND BEAT UP THE BAD MEN WHO KILLED *MOMMY* AND *DADDY?*

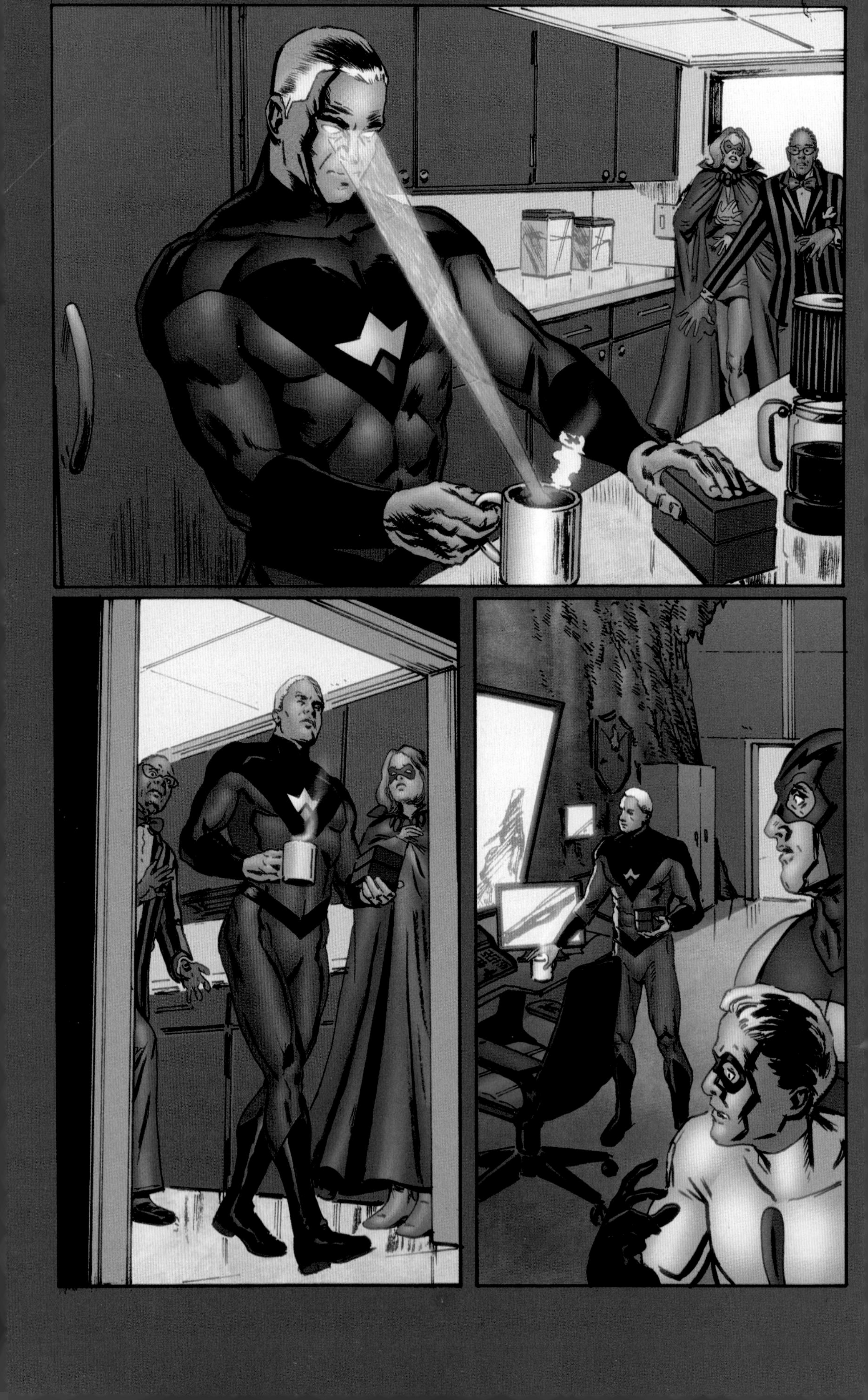

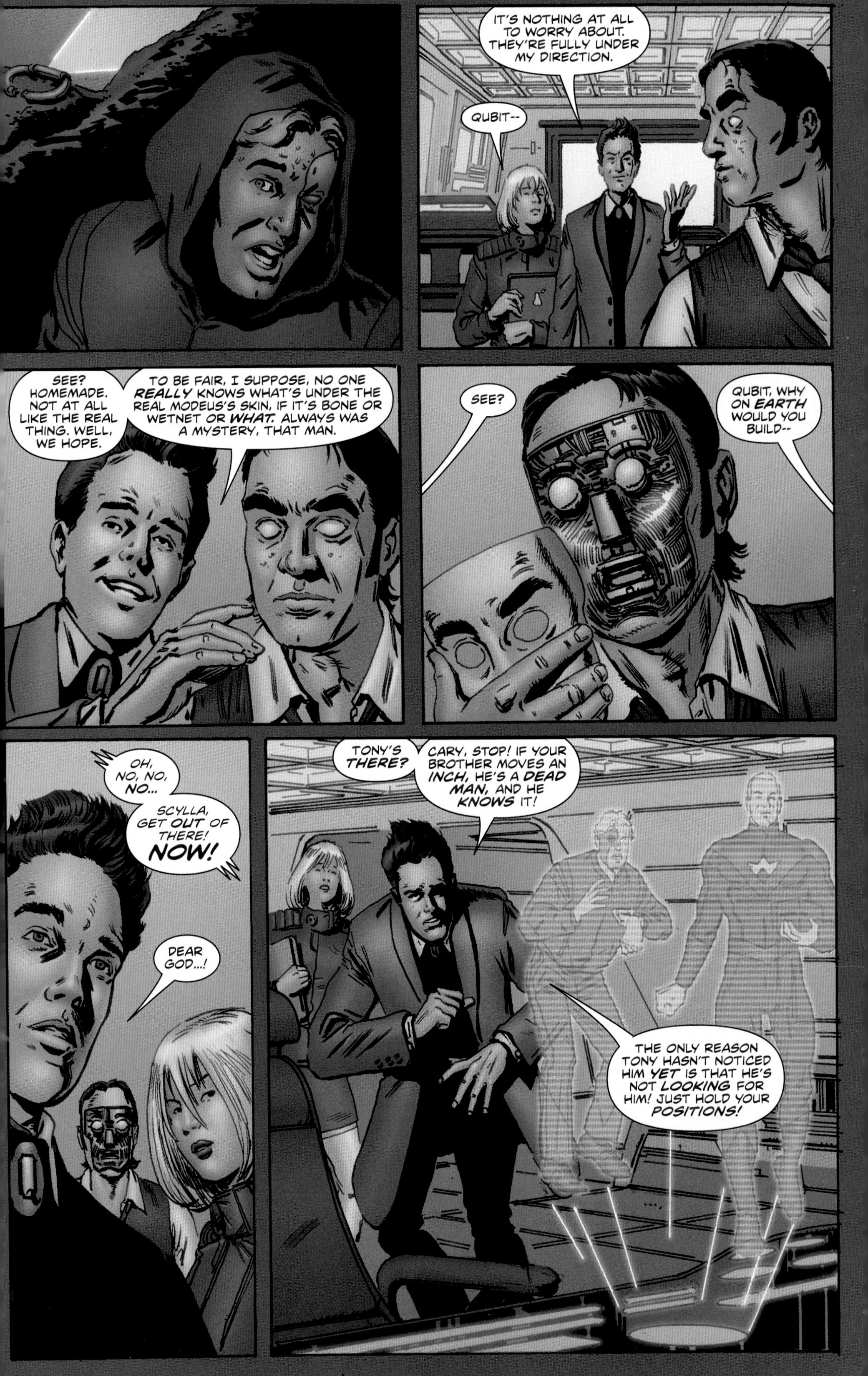
IT'S NOTHING AT ALL TO WORRY ABOUT. THEY'RE FULLY UNDER MY DIRECTION.
QUBIT--
SEE? HOMEMADE. NOT AT ALL LIKE THE REAL THING. WELL, WE HOPE.
TO BE FAIR, I SUPPOSE, NO ONE REALLY KNOWS WHAT'S UNDER THE REAL MODEUS'S SKIN, IF IT'S BONE OR WETNET OR WHAT. ALWAYS WAS A MYSTERY, THAT MAN.
SEE?
QUBIT, WHY ON EARTH WOULD YOU BUILD--
OH, NO, NO, NO...
SCYLLA, GET OUT OF THERE! NOW!
DEAR GOD...!
TONY'S THERE?
CARY, STOP! IF YOUR BROTHER MOVES AN INCH, HE'S A DEAD MAN, AND HE KNOWS IT!
THE ONLY REASON TONY HASN'T NOTICED HIM YET IS THAT HE'S NOT LOOKING FOR HIM! JUST HOLD YOUR POSITIONS!

HE'S GOT HIS *JUMP-BRACELET!* WE CAN 'PORT--

HE'LL *HEAR* IT! STAY *CALM* AND LET ME *THINK!*

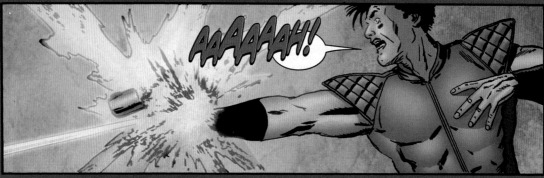

AaAAAAH!

ANYONE ELSE? NO? BECAUSE I IMAGINE YOU'RE ALL *DYING* TO SCRATCH THAT SAME *ITCH.*

DON'T LOOK SURPRISED THAT I'M HERE. WHAT, JUST BECAUSE I CAN RAM THROUGH A MOUNTAIN WITH MY *HEAD,* IT MEANS I'M NOT *SMART?*

I KNEW IT WAS JUST A MATTER OF TIME BEFORE YOU ALL PULLED TOGETHER. SAFETY IN *NUMBERS...*

...RIGHT?

AAAAA AAAAA AAAAAA

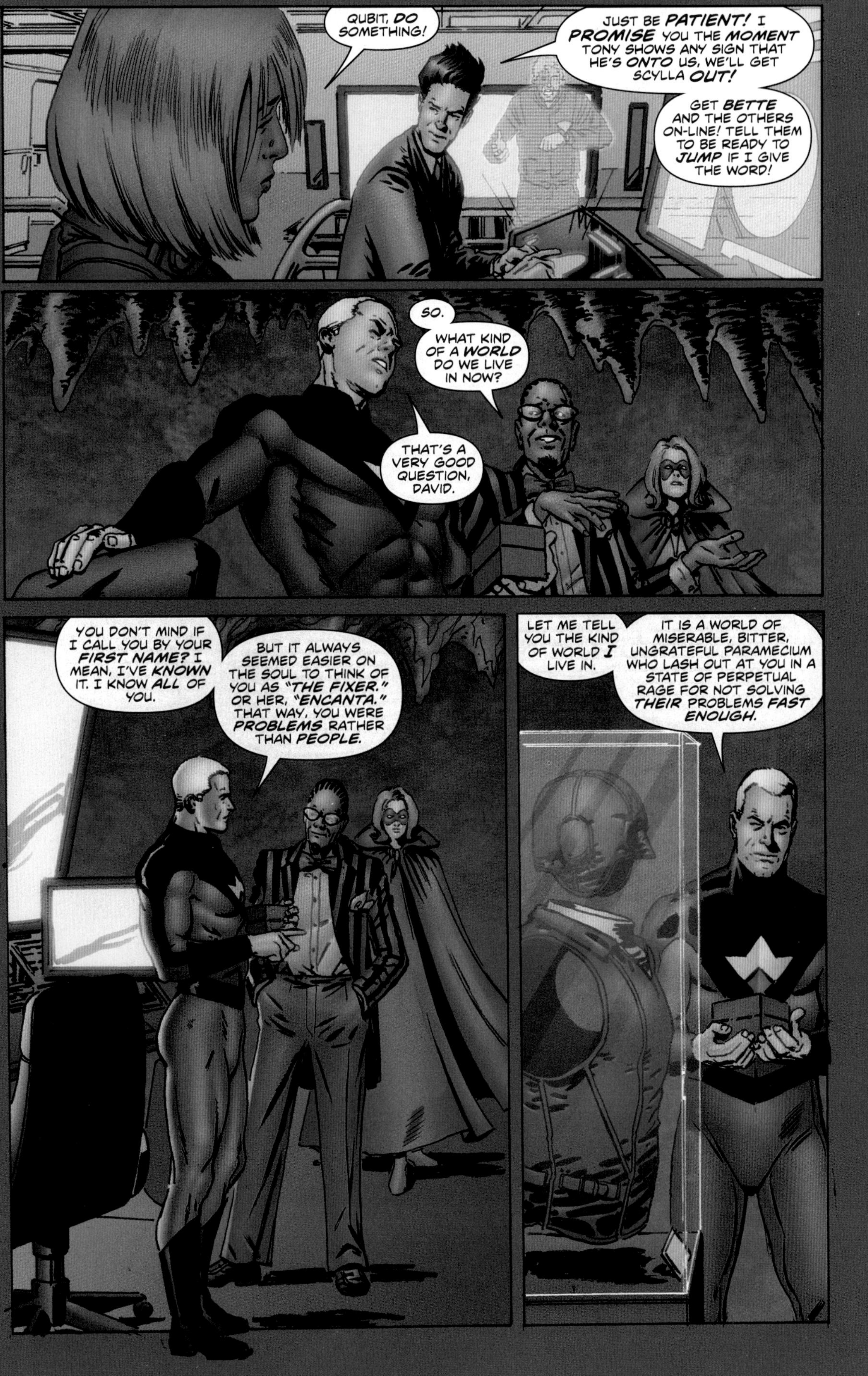
QUBIT, DO SOMETHING!
JUST BE PATIENT! I PROMISE YOU THE MOMENT TONY SHOWS ANY SIGN THAT HE'S ONTO US, WE'LL GET SCYLLA OUT!
GET BETTE AND THE OTHERS ON-LINE! TELL THEM TO BE READY TO JUMP IF I GIVE THE WORD!
SO.
WHAT KIND OF A WORLD DO WE LIVE IN NOW?
THAT'S A VERY GOOD QUESTION, DAVID.
YOU DON'T MIND IF I CALL YOU BY YOUR FIRST NAME? I MEAN, I'VE KNOWN IT. I KNOW ALL OF YOU.
BUT IT ALWAYS SEEMED EASIER ON THE SOUL TO THINK OF YOU AS "THE FIXER." OR HER, "ENCANTA." THAT WAY, YOU WERE PROBLEMS RATHER THAN PEOPLE.
LET ME TELL YOU THE KIND OF WORLD I LIVE IN.
IT IS A WORLD OF MISERABLE, BITTER, UNGRATEFUL PARAMECIUM WHO LASH OUT AT YOU IN A STATE OF PERPETUAL RAGE FOR NOT SOLVING THEIR PROBLEMS FAST ENOUGH.

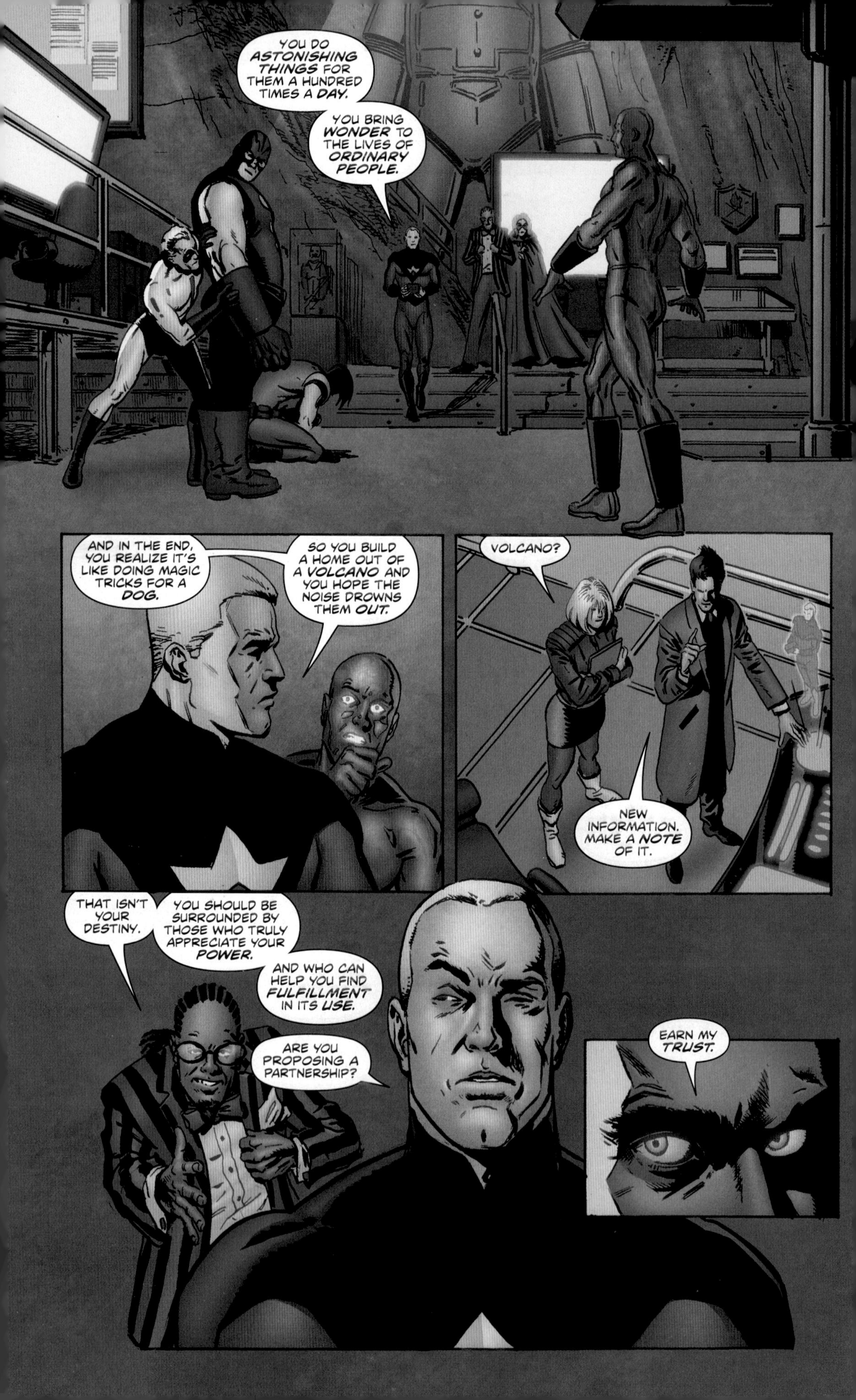
YOU DO ASTONISHING THINGS FOR THEM A HUNDRED TIMES A DAY.
YOU BRING WONDER TO THE LIVES OF ORDINARY PEOPLE.
AND IN THE END, YOU REALIZE IT'S LIKE DOING MAGIC TRICKS FOR A DOG.
SO YOU BUILD A HOME OUT OF A VOLCANO AND YOU HOPE THE NOISE DROWNS THEM OUT.
VOLCANO?
NEW INFORMATION. MAKE A NOTE OF IT.
THAT ISN'T YOUR DESTINY.
YOU SHOULD BE SURROUNDED BY THOSE WHO TRULY APPRECIATE YOUR POWER.
AND WHO CAN HELP YOU FIND FULFILLMENT IN ITS USE.
ARE YOU PROPOSING A PARTNERSHIP?
EARN MY TRUST.

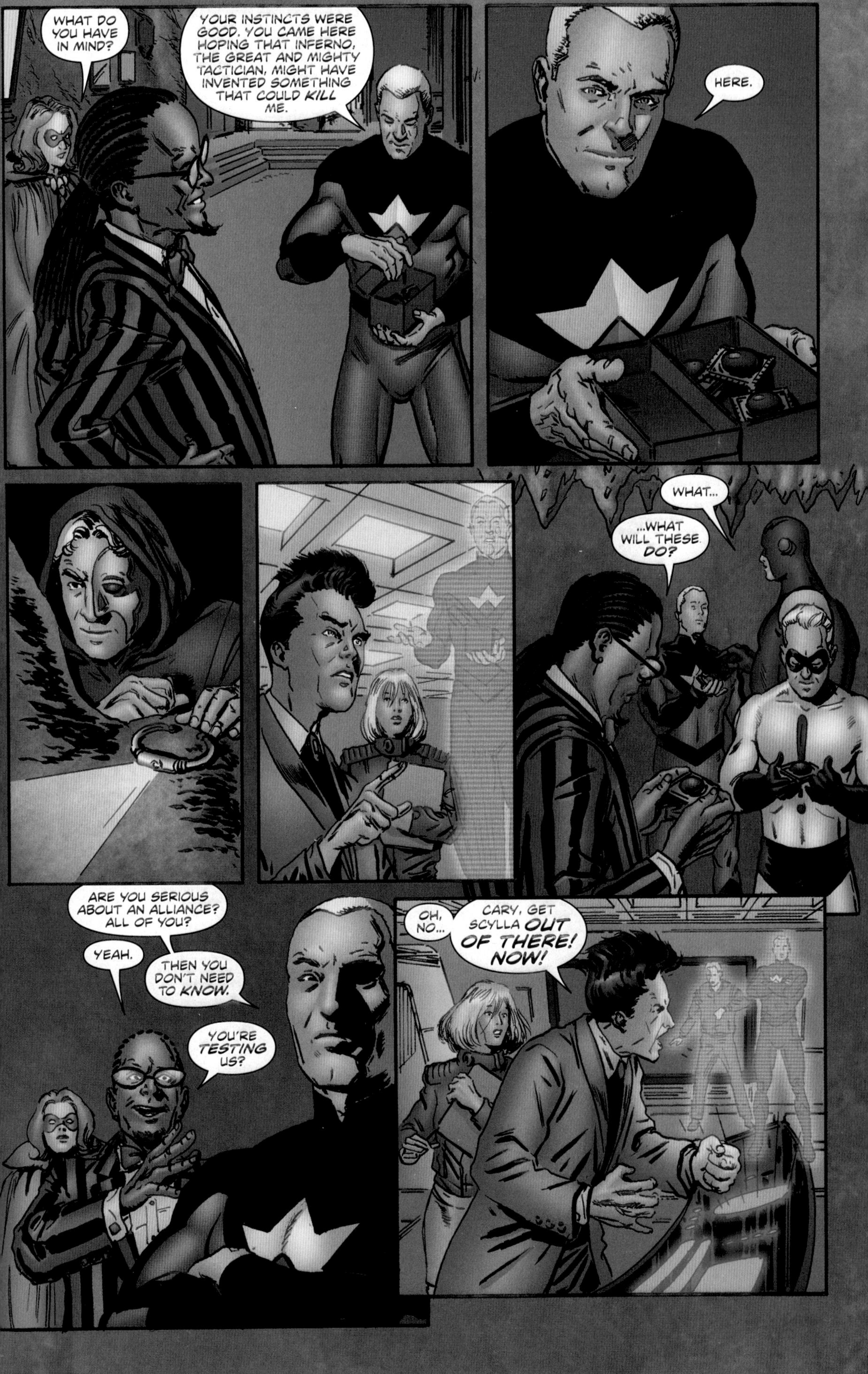
WHAT DO YOU HAVE IN MIND?
YOUR INSTINCTS WERE GOOD. YOU CAME HERE HOPING THAT INFERNO, THE GREAT AND MIGHTY TACTICIAN, MIGHT HAVE INVENTED SOMETHING THAT COULD KILL ME.
HERE.
WHAT...
...WHAT WILL THESE DO?
ARE YOU SERIOUS ABOUT AN ALLIANCE? ALL OF YOU?
YEAH.
THEN YOU DON'T NEED TO KNOW.
YOU'RE TESTING US?
OH, NO...
CARY, GET SCYLLA OUT OF THERE! NOW!

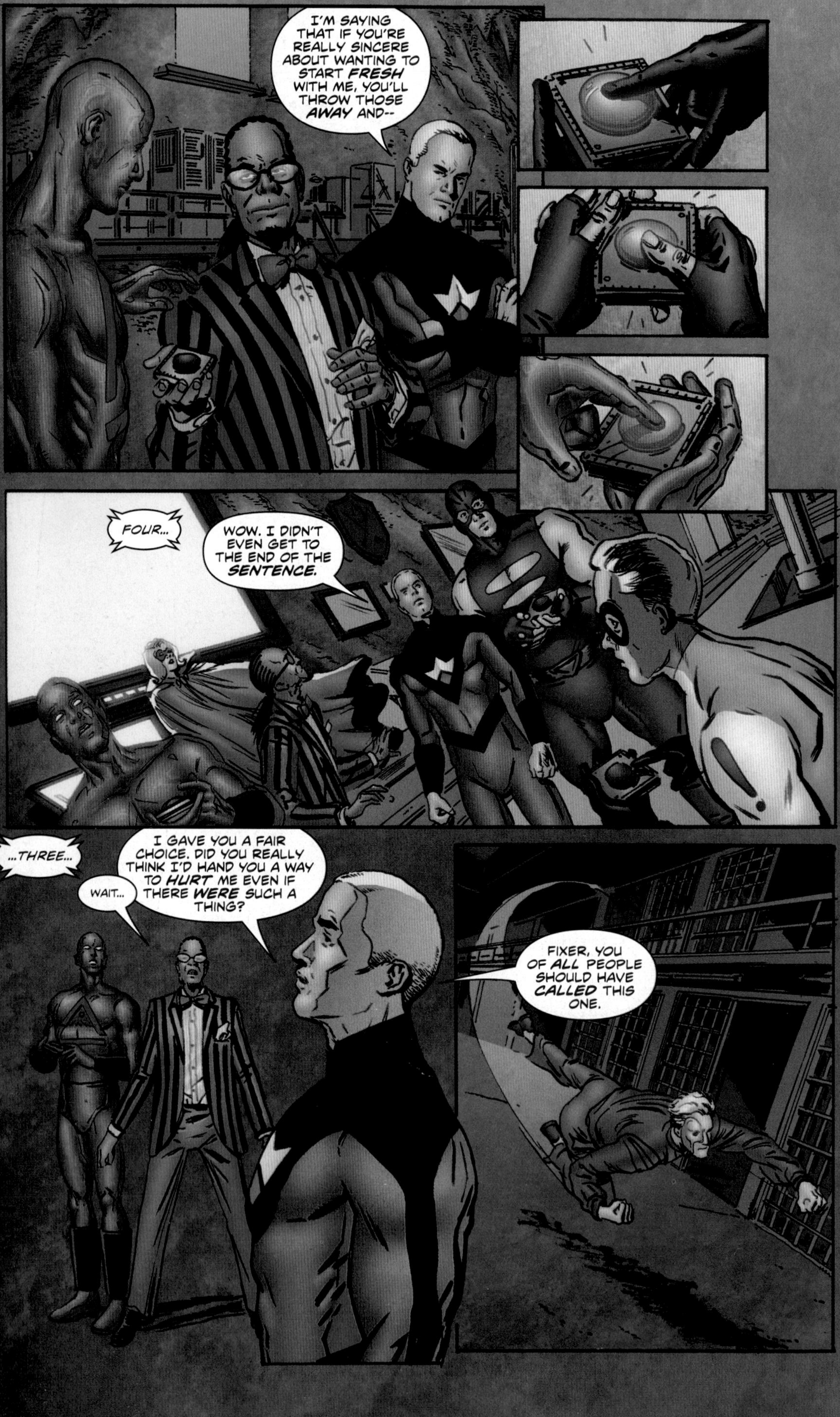
I'M SAYING THAT IF YOU'RE REALLY SINCERE ABOUT WANTING TO START FRESH WITH ME, YOU'LL THROW THOSE AWAY AND--
FOUR...
WOW. I DIDN'T EVEN GET TO THE END OF THE SENTENCE.
...THREE...
WAIT...
I GAVE YOU A FAIR CHOICE. DID YOU REALLY THINK I'D HAND YOU A WAY TO HURT ME EVEN IF THERE WERE SUCH A THING?
FIXER, YOU OF ALL PEOPLE SHOULD HAVE CALLED THIS ONE.

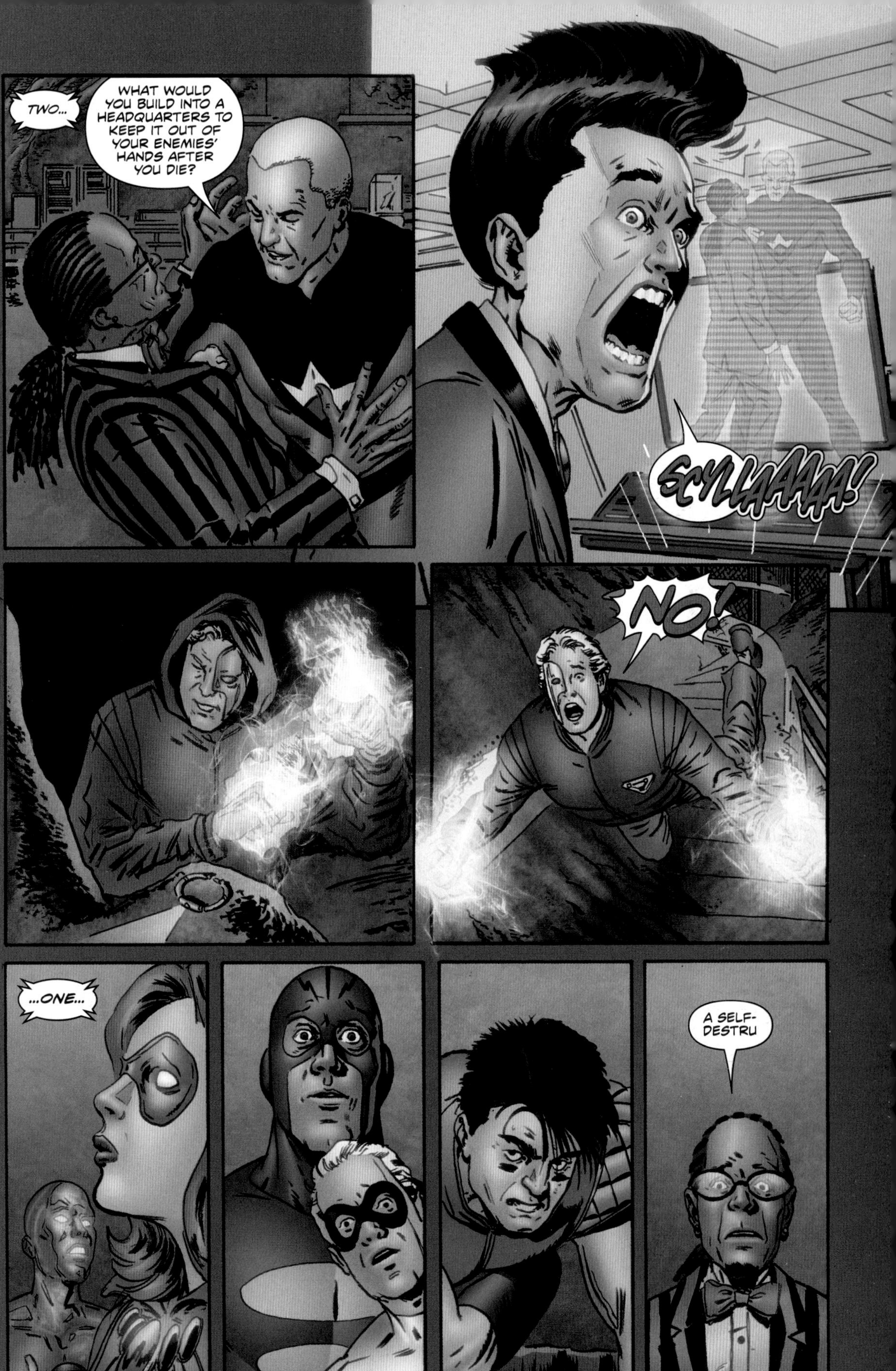
TWO...
WHAT WOULD YOU BUILD INTO A HEADQUARTERS TO KEEP IT OUT OF YOUR ENEMIES' HANDS AFTER YOU DIE?
SCYLLAAAAA!
NO!
...ONE...
A SELF-DESTRU

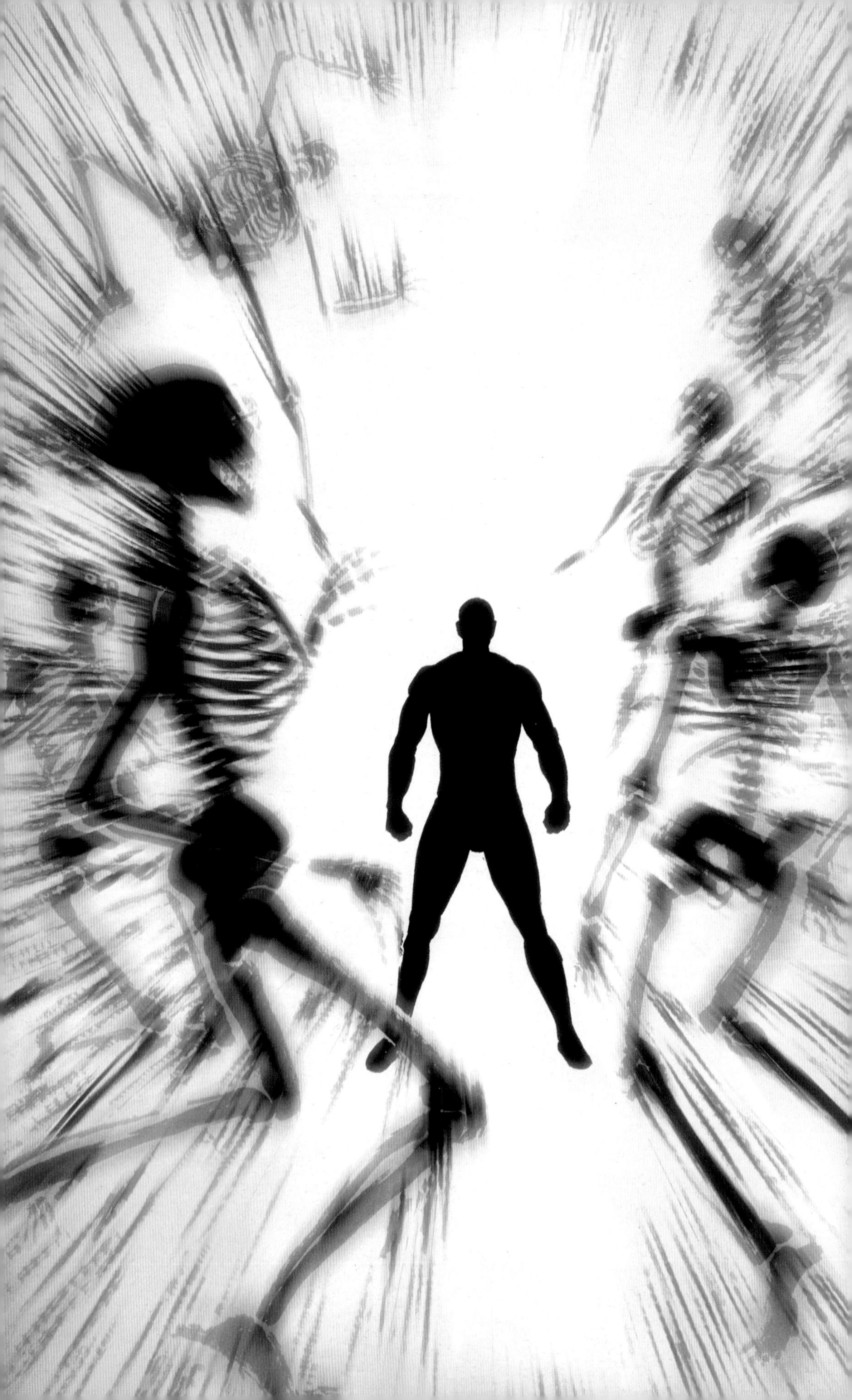

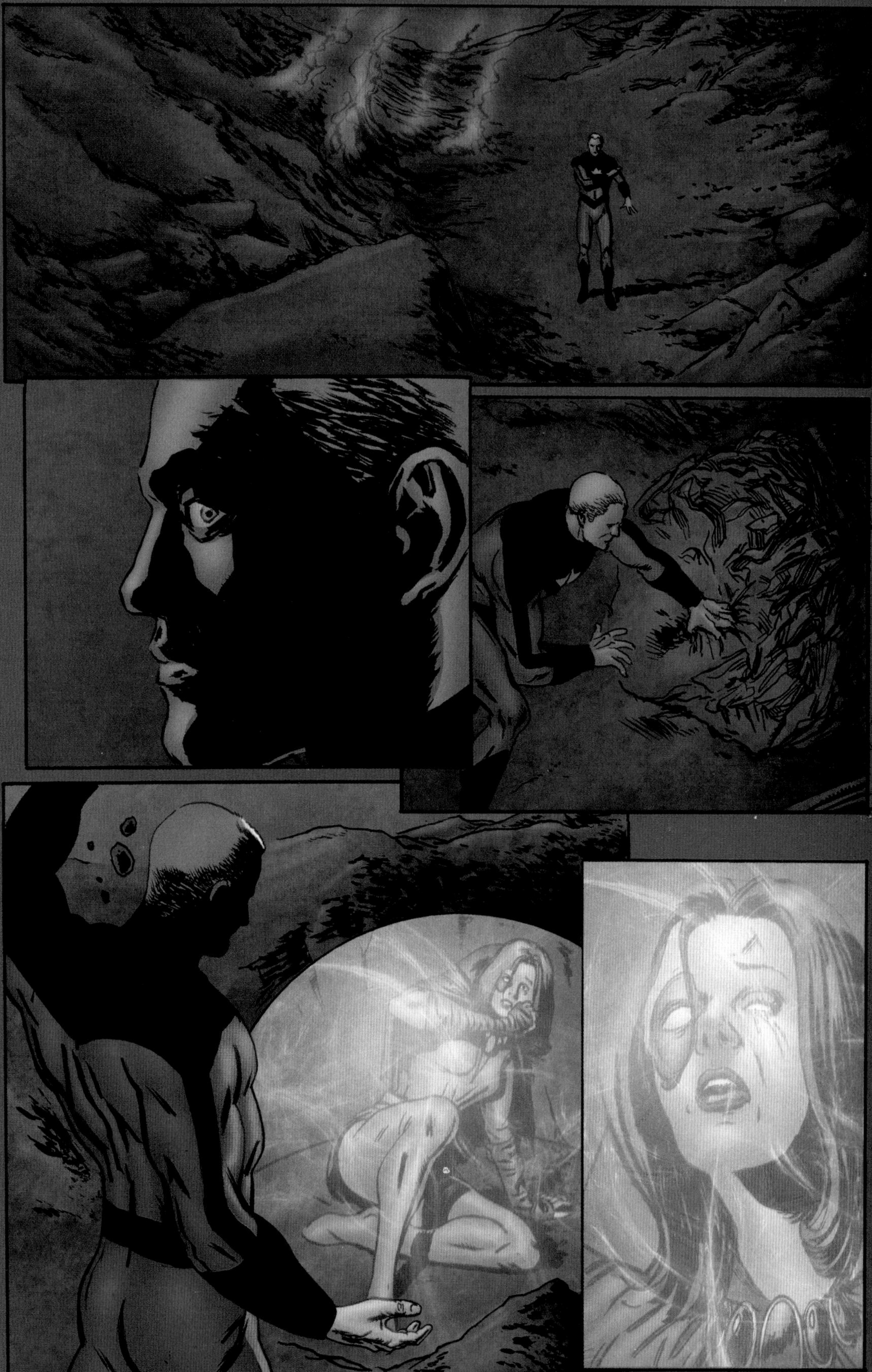

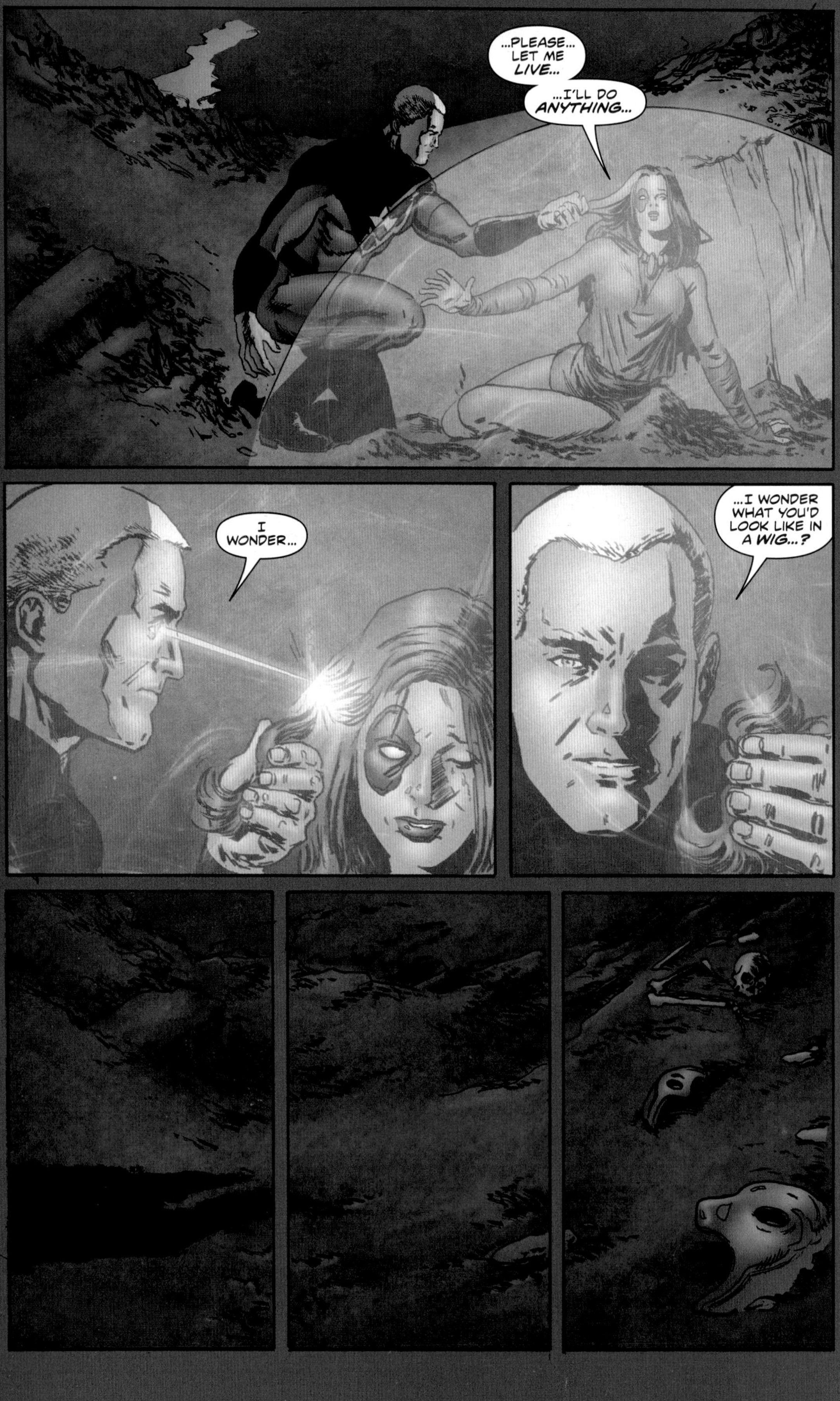
...PLEASE... LET ME LIVE...
...I'LL DO ANYTHING...
I WONDER...
...I WONDER WHAT YOU'D LOOK LIKE IN A WIG...?

CHAPTER 4

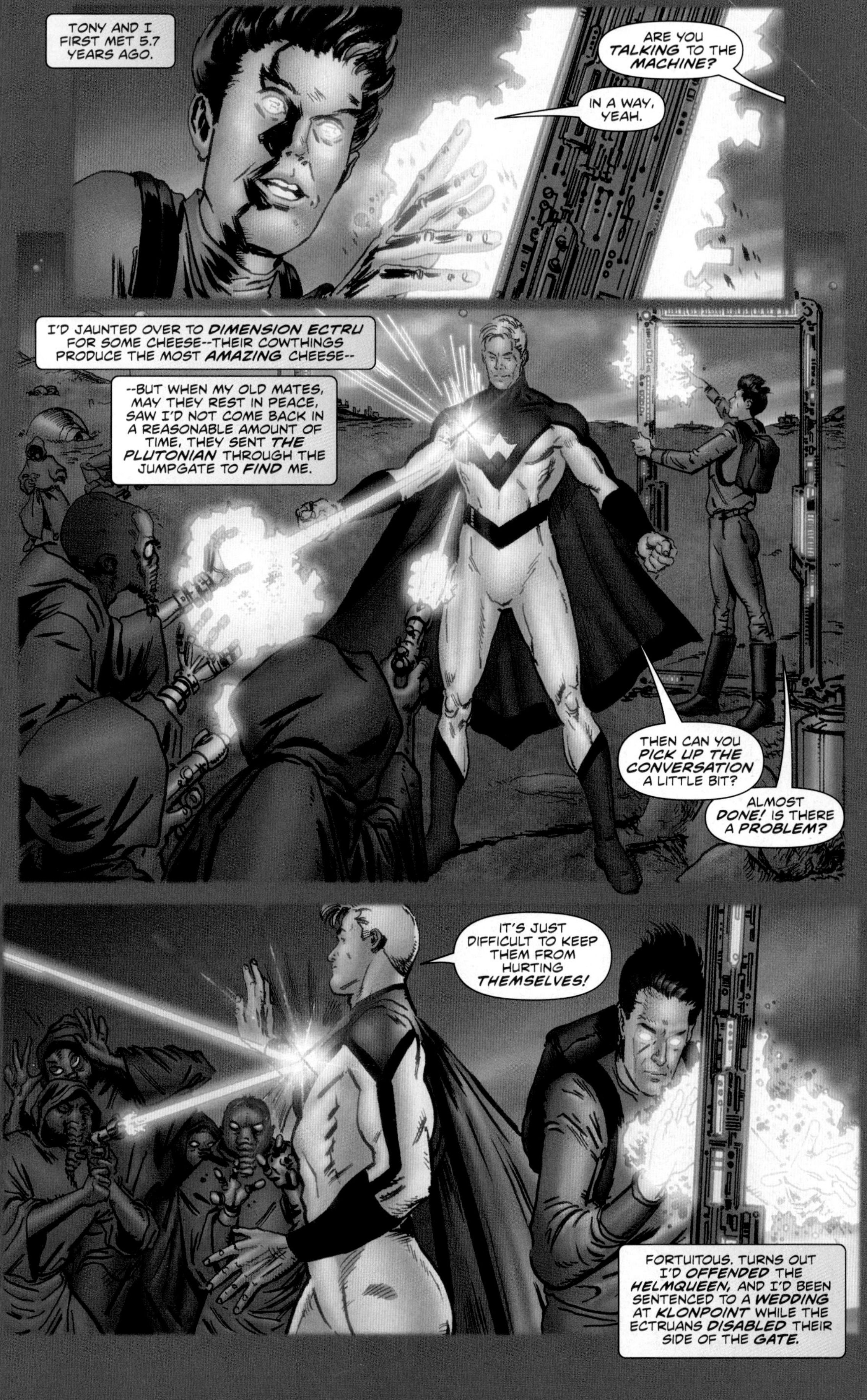
TONY AND I FIRST MET 5.7 YEARS AGO.
ARE YOU TALKING TO THE MACHINE?
IN A WAY, YEAH.
I'D JAUNTED OVER TO DIMENSION ECTRU FOR SOME CHEESE--THEIR COWTHINGS PRODUCE THE MOST AMAZING CHEESE--
--BUT WHEN MY OLD MATES, MAY THEY REST IN PEACE, SAW I'D NOT COME BACK IN A REASONABLE AMOUNT OF TIME, THEY SENT THE PLUTONIAN THROUGH THE JUMPGATE TO FIND ME.
THEN CAN YOU PICK UP THE CONVERSATION A LITTLE BIT?
ALMOST DONE! IS THERE A PROBLEM?
IT'S JUST DIFFICULT TO KEEP THEM FROM HURTING THEMSELVES!
FORTUITOUS. TURNS OUT I'D OFFENDED THE HELMQUEEN, AND I'D BEEN SENTENCED TO A WEDDING AT KLONPOINT WHILE THE ECTRUANS DISABLED THEIR SIDE OF THE GATE.

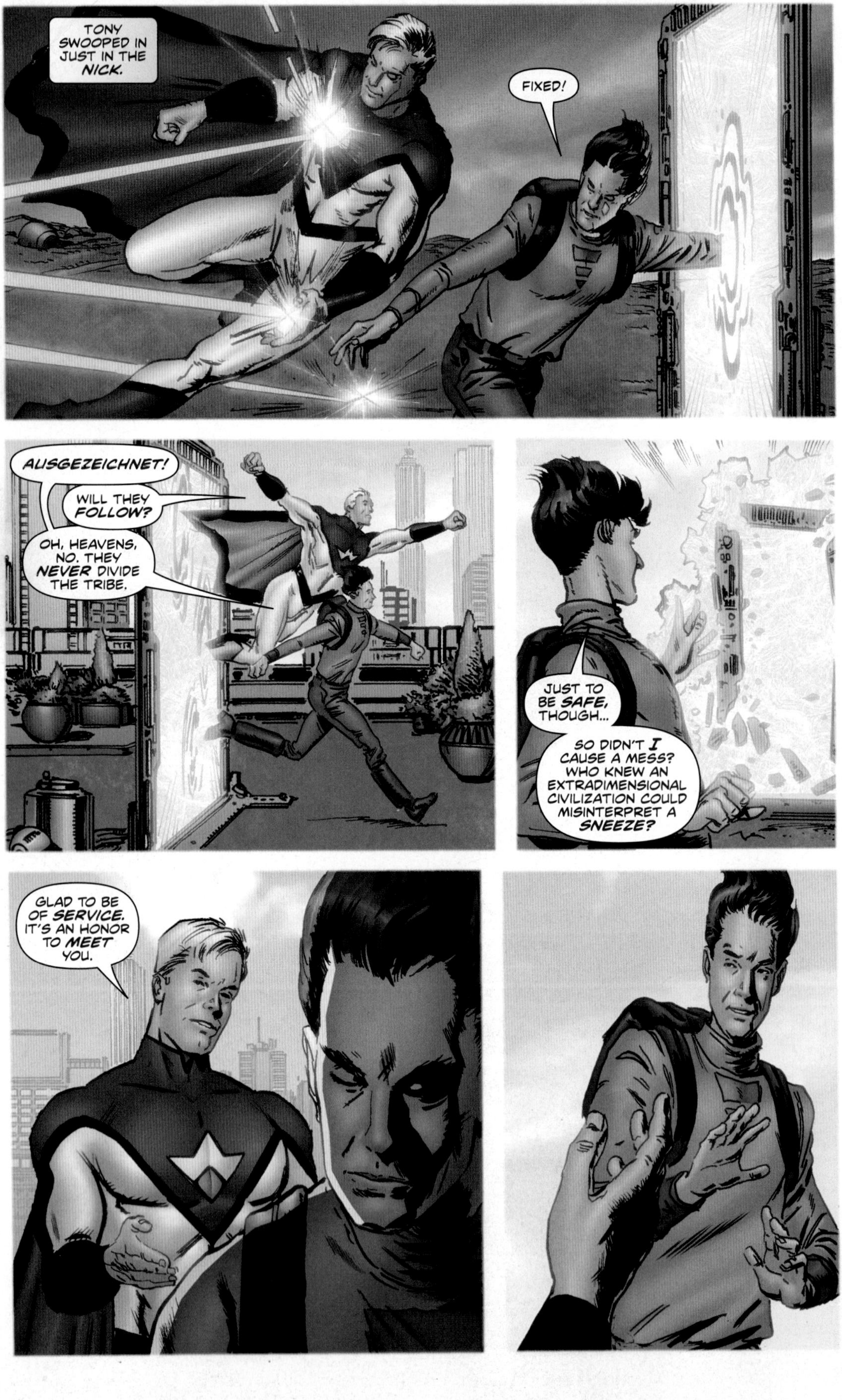

TONY SWOOPED IN JUST IN THE NICK.
FIXED!
AUSGEZEICHNET!
WILL THEY FOLLOW?
OH, HEAVENS, NO. THEY NEVER DIVIDE THE TRIBE.
JUST TO BE SAFE, THOUGH...
SO DIDN'T I CAUSE A MESS? WHO KNEW AN EXTRADIMENSIONAL CIVILIZATION COULD MISINTERPRET A SNEEZE?
GLAD TO BE OF SERVICE. IT'S AN HONOR TO MEET YOU.

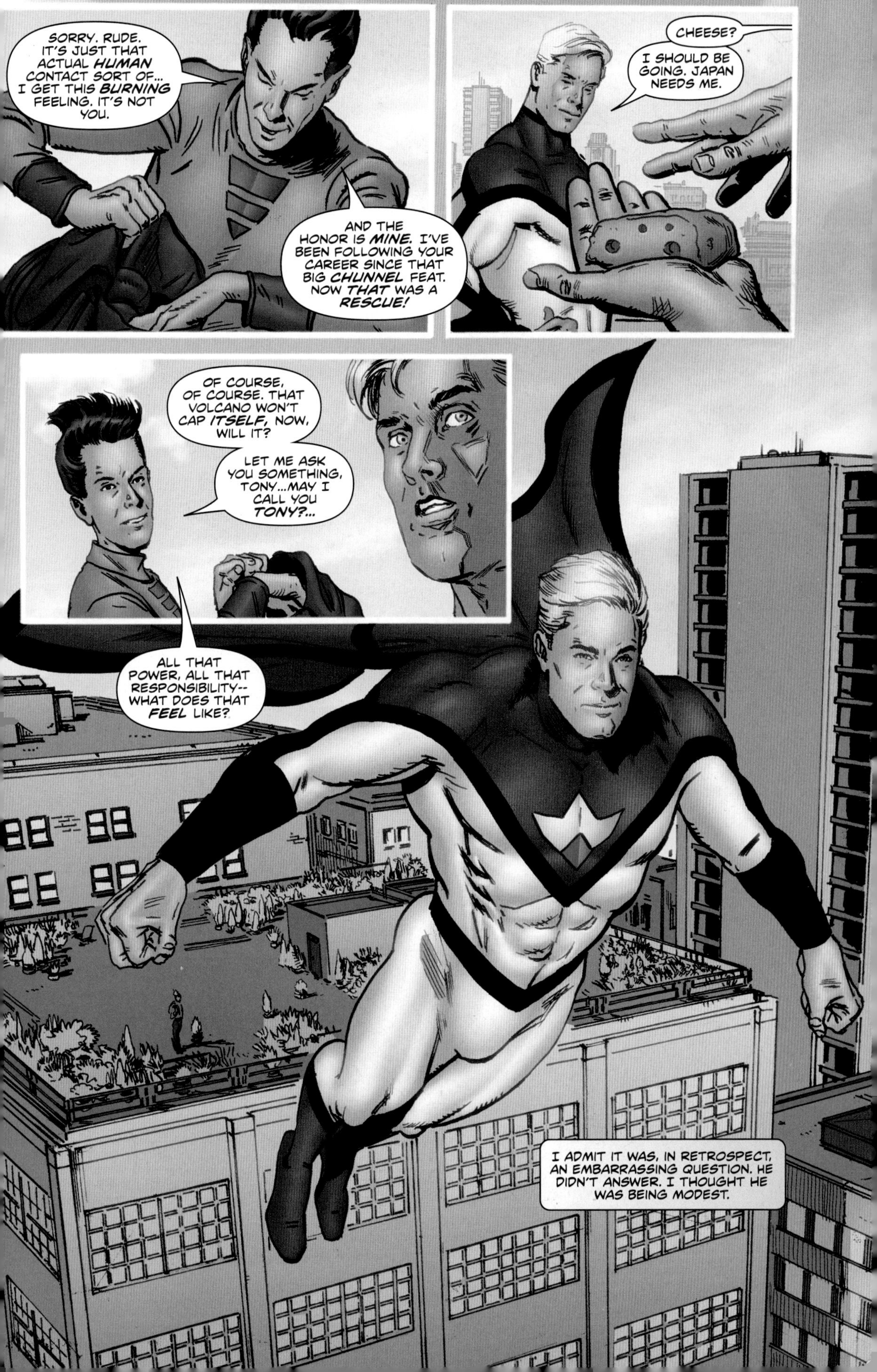
SORRY. RUDE. IT'S JUST THAT ACTUAL HUMAN CONTACT SORT OF... I GET THIS BURNING FEELING. IT'S NOT YOU.
AND THE HONOR IS MINE. I'VE BEEN FOLLOWING YOUR CAREER SINCE THAT BIG CHUNNEL FEAT. NOW THAT WAS A RESCUE!
CHEESE?
I SHOULD BE GOING. JAPAN NEEDS ME.
OF COURSE, OF COURSE. THAT VOLCANO WON'T CAP ITSELF, NOW, WILL IT?
LET ME ASK YOU SOMETHING, TONY...MAY I CALL YOU TONY?...
ALL THAT POWER, ALL THAT RESPONSIBILITY-- WHAT DOES THAT FEEL LIKE?
I ADMIT IT WAS, IN RETROSPECT, AN EMBARRASSING QUESTION. HE DIDN'T ANSWER. I THOUGHT HE WAS BEING MODEST.

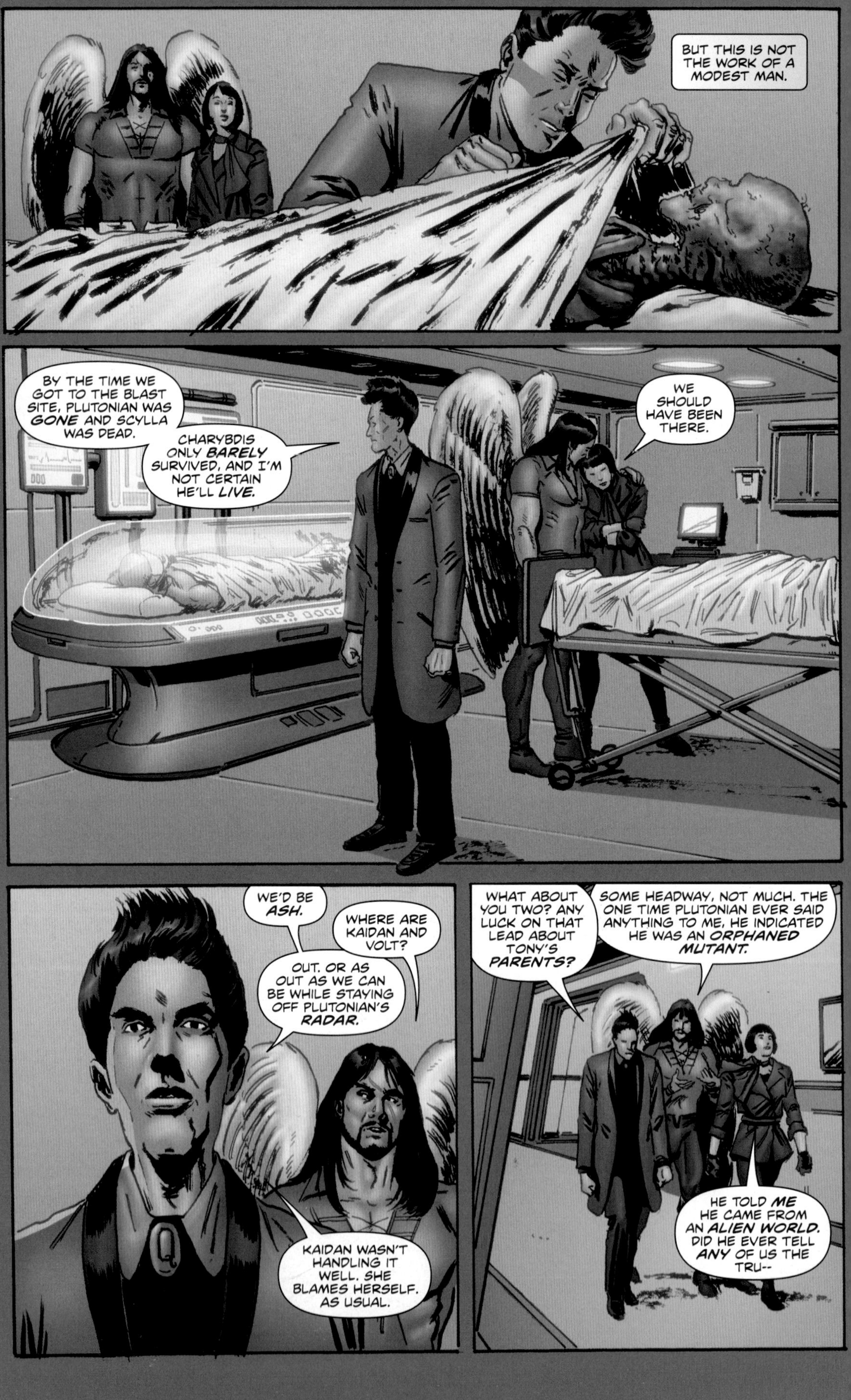
BUT THIS IS NOT THE WORK OF A MODEST MAN.
BY THE TIME WE GOT TO THE BLAST SITE, PLUTONIAN WAS GONE AND SCYLLA WAS DEAD.
CHARYBDIS ONLY BARELY SURVIVED, AND I'M NOT CERTAIN HE'LL LIVE.
WE SHOULD HAVE BEEN THERE.
WE'D BE ASH.
WHERE ARE KAIDAN AND VOLT?
OUT. OR AS OUT AS WE CAN BE WHILE STAYING OFF PLUTONIAN'S RADAR.
KAIDAN WASN'T HANDLING IT WELL. SHE BLAMES HERSELF. AS USUAL.
WHAT ABOUT YOU TWO? ANY LUCK ON THAT LEAD ABOUT TONY'S PARENTS?
SOME HEADWAY, NOT MUCH. THE ONE TIME PLUTONIAN EVER SAID ANYTHING TO ME, HE INDICATED HE WAS AN ORPHANED MUTANT.
HE TOLD ME HE CAME FROM AN ALIEN WORLD. DID HE EVER TELL ANY OF US THE TRU--

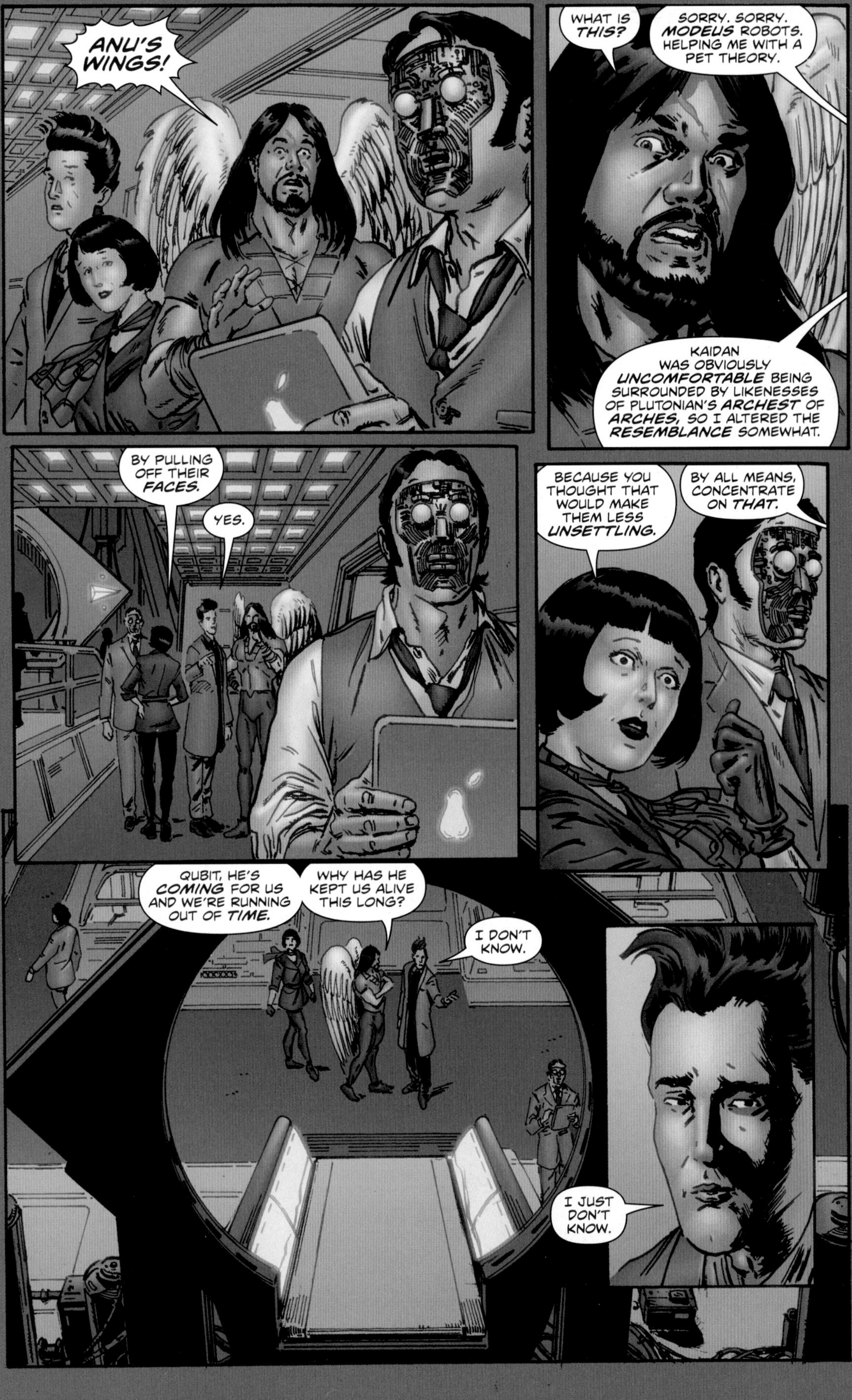
ANU'S WINGS!
WHAT IS THIS?
SORRY. SORRY. MODEUS ROBOTS. HELPING ME WITH A PET THEORY.
KAIDAN WAS OBVIOUSLY UNCOMFORTABLE BEING SURROUNDED BY LIKENESSES OF PLUTONIAN'S ARCHEST OF ARCHES, SO I ALTERED THE RESEMBLANCE SOMEWHAT.
BY PULLING OFF THEIR FACES.
YES.
BECAUSE YOU THOUGHT THAT WOULD MAKE THEM LESS UNSETTLING.
BY ALL MEANS, CONCENTRATE ON THAT.
QUBIT, HE'S COMING FOR US AND WE'RE RUNNING OUT OF TIME.
WHY HAS HE KEPT US ALIVE THIS LONG?
I DON'T KNOW.
I JUST DON'T KNOW.

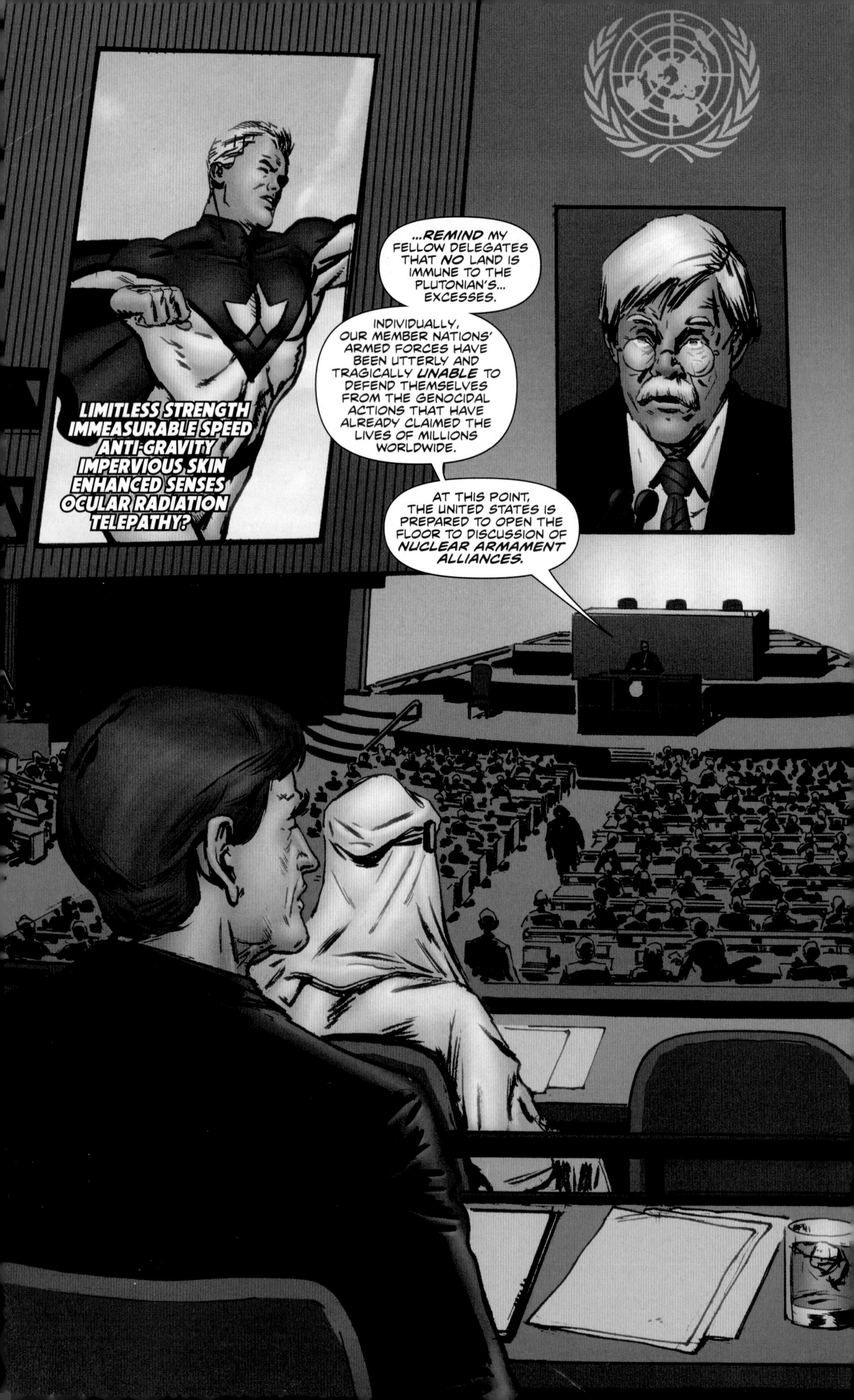

LIMITLESS STRENGTH
IMMEASURABLE SPEED
ANTI-GRAVITY
IMPERVIOUS SKIN
ENHANCED SENSES
OCULAR RADIATION
TELEPATHY?
...REMIND MY FELLOW DELEGATES THAT NO LAND IS IMMUNE TO THE PLUTONIAN'S... EXCESSES.
INDIVIDUALLY, OUR MEMBER NATIONS' ARMED FORCES HAVE BEEN UTTERLY AND TRAGICALLY UNABLE TO DEFEND THEMSELVES FROM THE GENOCIDAL ACTIONS THAT HAVE ALREADY CLAIMED THE LIVES OF MILLIONS WORLDWIDE.
AT THIS POINT, THE UNITED STATES IS PREPARED TO OPEN THE FLOOR TO DISCUSSION OF NUCLEAR ARMAMENT ALLIANCES.

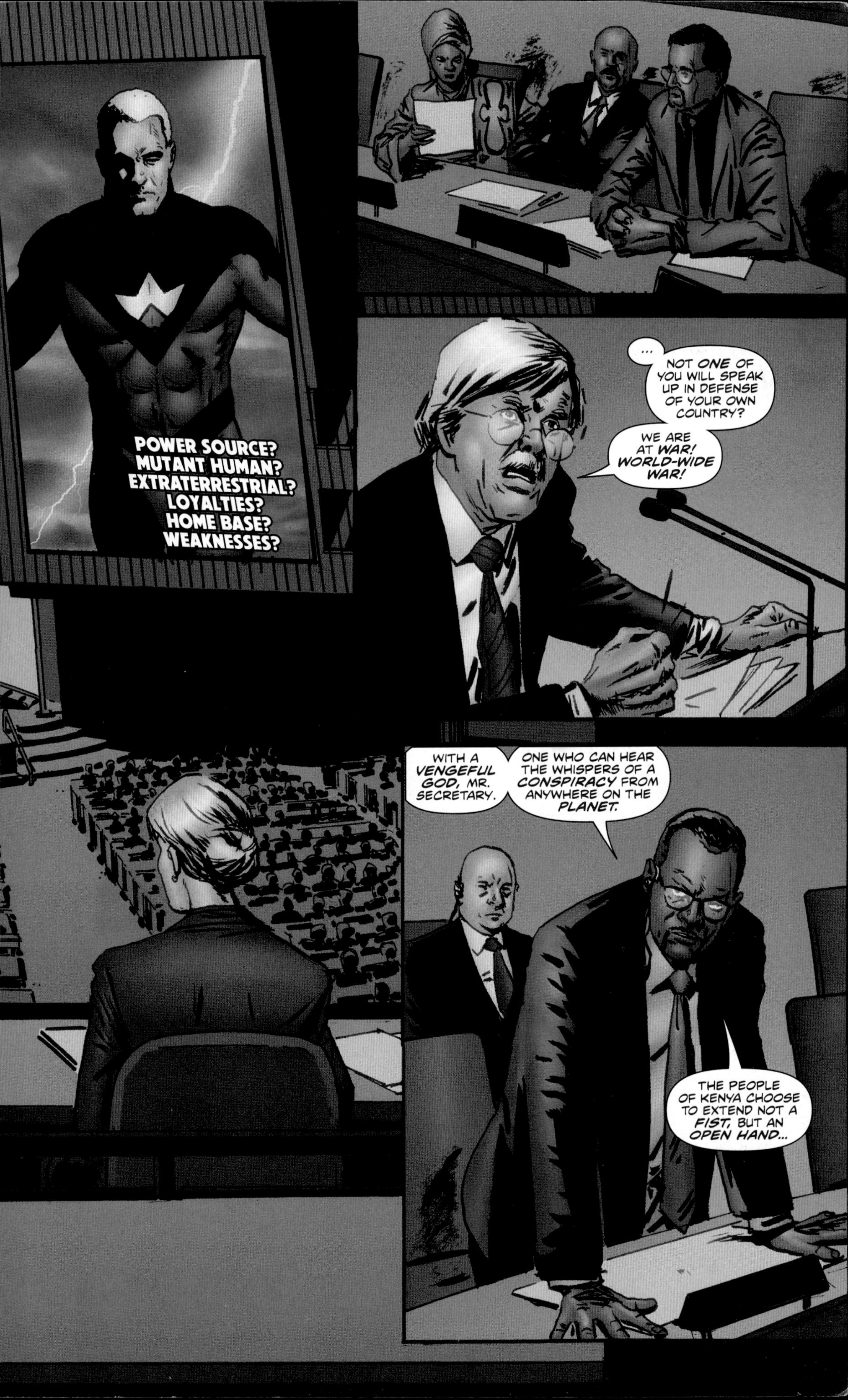
POWER SOURCE?
MUTANT HUMAN?
EXTRATERRESTRIAL?
LOYALTIES?
HOME BASE?
WEAKNESSES?
...
NOT ONE OF YOU WILL SPEAK UP IN DEFENSE OF YOUR OWN COUNTRY?
WE ARE AT WAR! WORLD-WIDE WAR!
WITH A VENGEFUL GOD, MR. SECRETARY.
ONE WHO CAN HEAR THE WHISPERS OF A CONSPIRACY FROM ANYWHERE ON THE PLANET.
THE PEOPLE OF KENYA CHOOSE TO EXTEND NOT A FIST, BUT AN OPEN HAND...

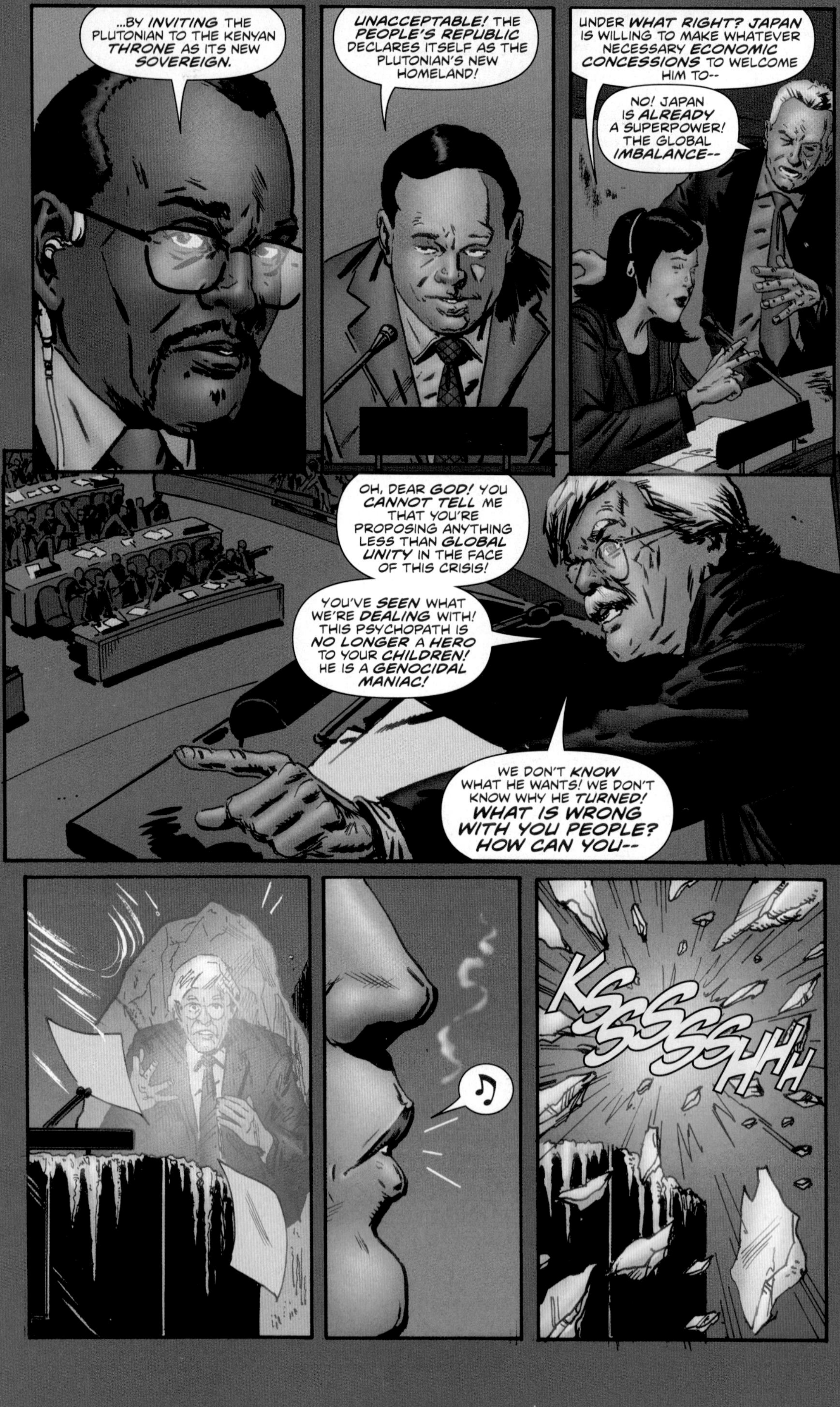
...BY INVITING THE PLUTONIAN TO THE KENYAN THRONE AS ITS NEW SOVEREIGN.
UNACCEPTABLE! THE PEOPLE'S REPUBLIC DECLARES ITSELF AS THE PLUTONIAN'S NEW HOMELAND!
UNDER WHAT RIGHT? JAPAN IS WILLING TO MAKE WHATEVER NECESSARY ECONOMIC CONCESSIONS TO WELCOME HIM TO--
NO! JAPAN IS ALREADY A SUPERPOWER! THE GLOBAL IMBALANCE--
OH, DEAR GOD! YOU CANNOT TELL ME THAT YOU'RE PROPOSING ANYTHING LESS THAN GLOBAL UNITY IN THE FACE OF THIS CRISIS!
YOU'VE SEEN WHAT WE'RE DEALING WITH! THIS PSYCHOPATH IS NO LONGER A HERO TO YOUR CHILDREN! HE IS A GENOCIDAL MANIAC!
WE DON'T KNOW WHAT HE WANTS! WE DON'T KNOW WHY HE TURNED! WHAT IS WRONG WITH YOU PEOPLE? HOW CAN YOU--
♪
KSSSSSHHHH

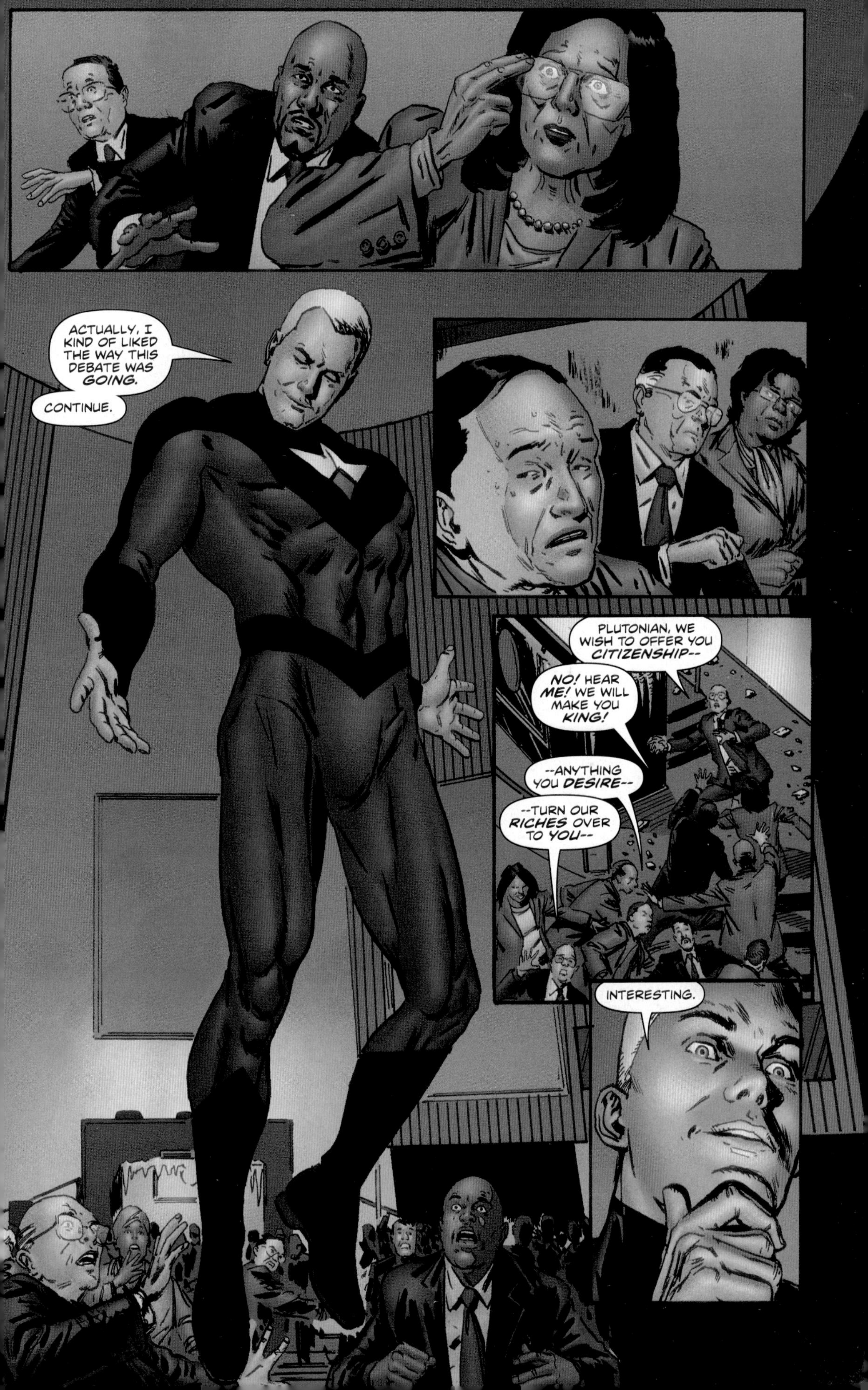
ACTUALLY, I KIND OF LIKED THE WAY THIS DEBATE WAS GOING.
CONTINUE.
PLUTONIAN, WE WISH TO OFFER YOU CITIZENSHIP--
NO! HEAR ME! WE WILL MAKE YOU KING!
--ANYTHING YOU DESIRE--
--TURN OUR RICHES OVER TO YOU--
INTERESTING.

YOU. YOU'RE FROM...

SINGAPORE.

SINGAPORE. TELL ME, SINGAPORE, YOU WANT TO BE MY HOME BECAUSE...

BECAUSE WE SEEK YOUR STRENGTH AND YOUR GUIDANCE IN A HOSTILE WORLD.

DO YOU UNDERSTAND THE EXPRESSION, "A TIGER BY THE TAIL"? DO YOU?

I'M LISTENING...

WE DO. BUT WE ALSO RECOGNIZE YOUR LONG HISTORY OF SERVICE TO OUR NATION.

WE EMBRACE YOU BECAUSE...

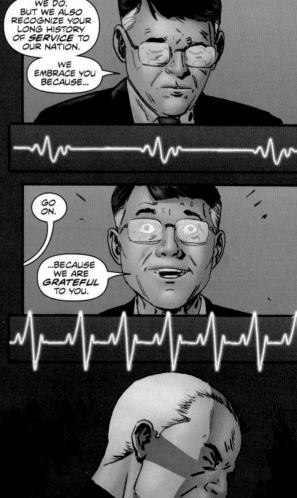

GO ON.

...BECAUSE WE ARE GRATEFUL TO YOU.

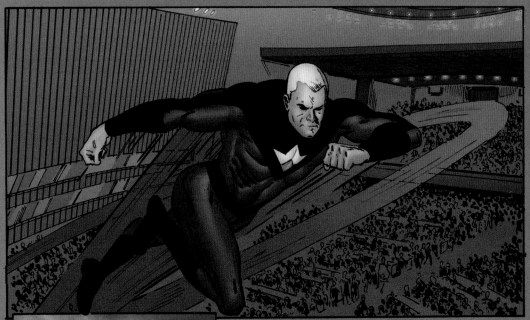

Singapore

WHAT ARE THOSE? AIRPLANES?

I CAN'T TELL. THEY'RE SHINY--

--LIKE DIAMONDS.

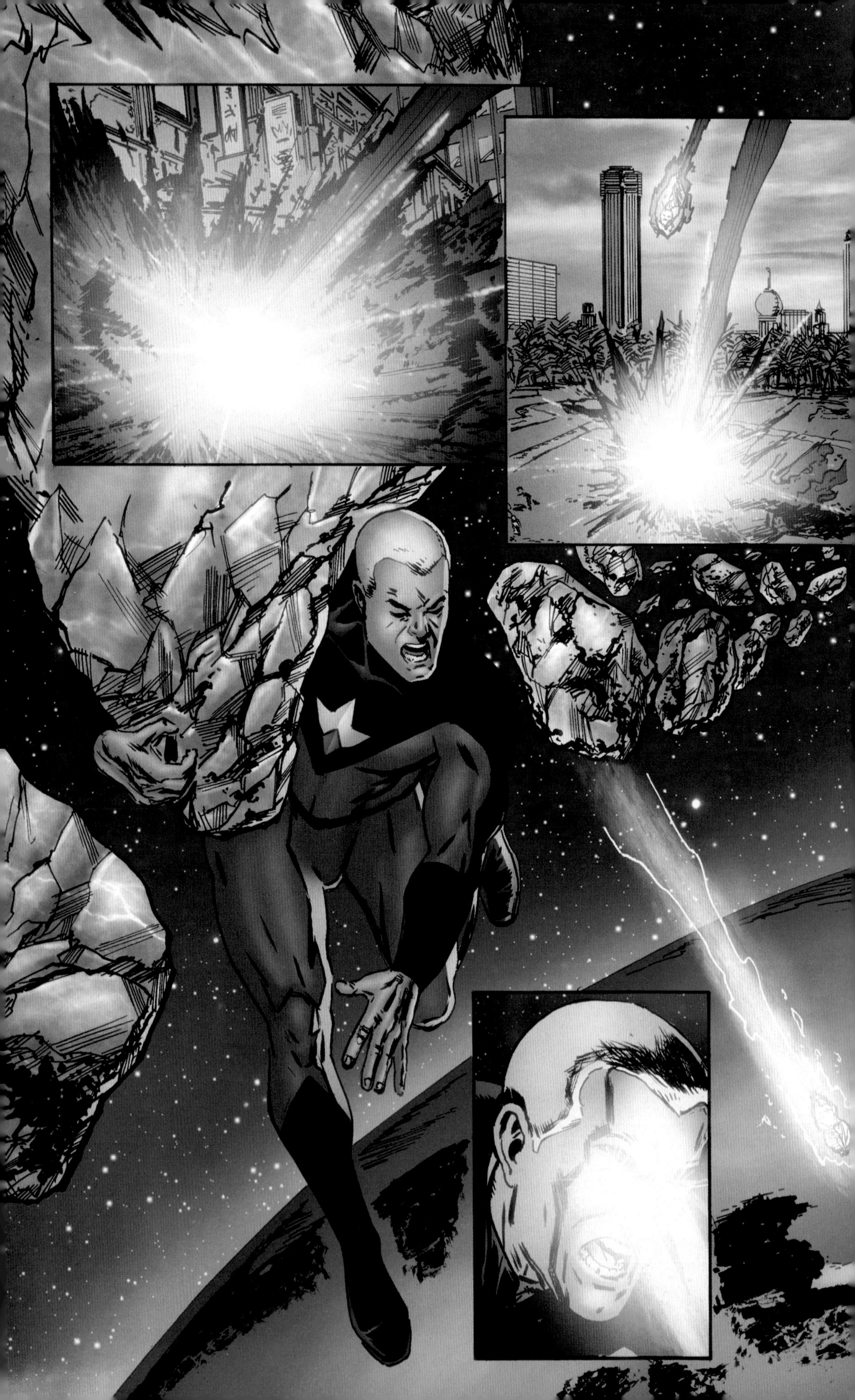

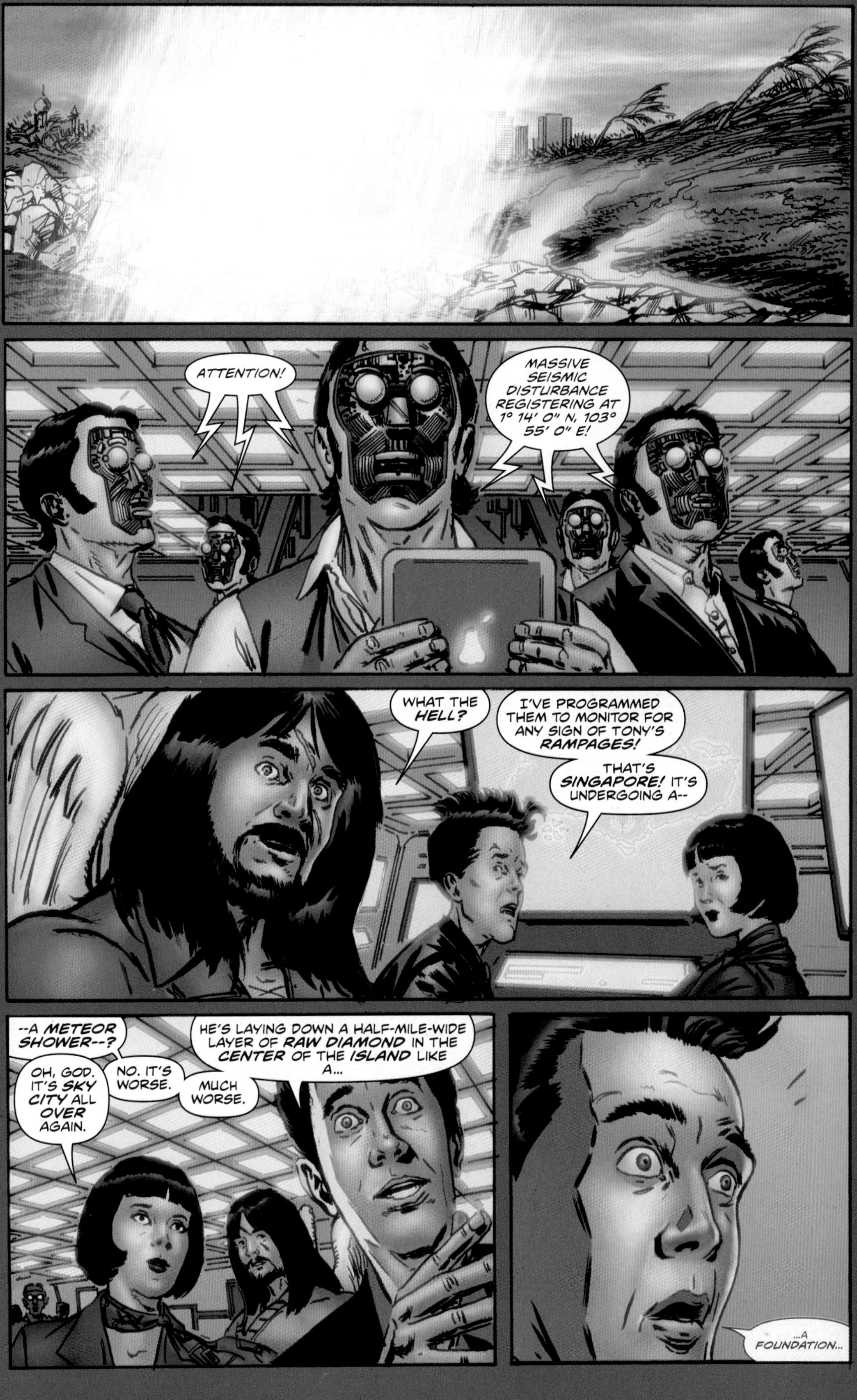

ATTENTION!
MASSIVE SEISMIC DISTURBANCE REGISTERING AT 1° 14' 0" N, 103° 55' 0" E!
WHAT THE HELL?
I'VE PROGRAMMED THEM TO MONITOR FOR ANY SIGN OF TONY'S RAMPAGES!
THAT'S SINGAPORE! IT'S UNDERGOING A--
--A METEOR SHOWER--?
OH, GOD. IT'S SKY CITY ALL OVER AGAIN.
NO. IT'S WORSE.
MUCH WORSE.
HE'S LAYING DOWN A HALF-MILE-WIDE LAYER OF RAW DIAMOND IN THE CENTER OF THE ISLAND LIKE A...
...A FOUNDATION...

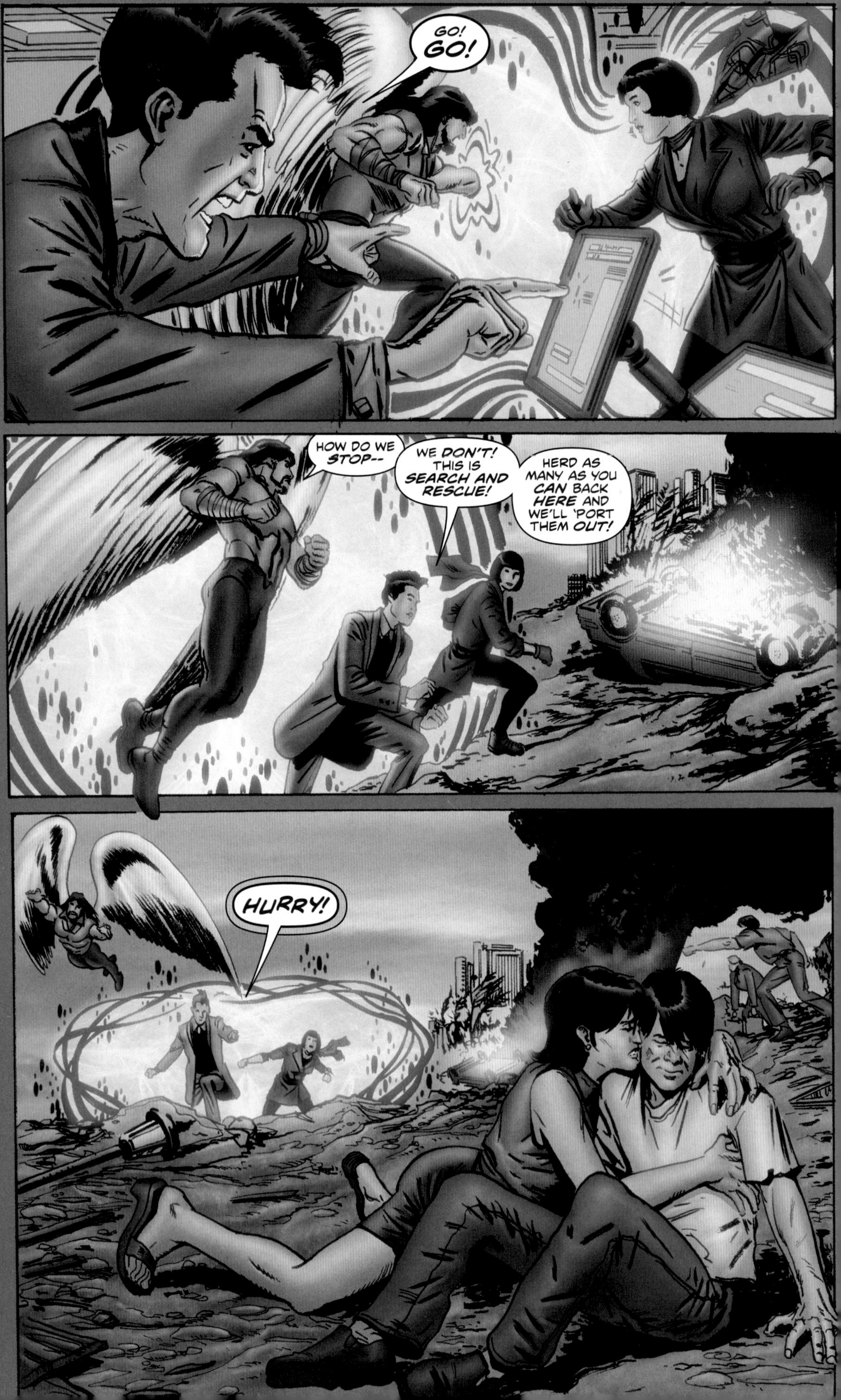
GO! GO!
HOW DO WE STOP--
WE DON'T! THIS IS SEARCH AND RESCUE!
HERD AS MANY AS YOU CAN BACK HERE AND WE'LL 'PORT THEM OUT!
HURRY!

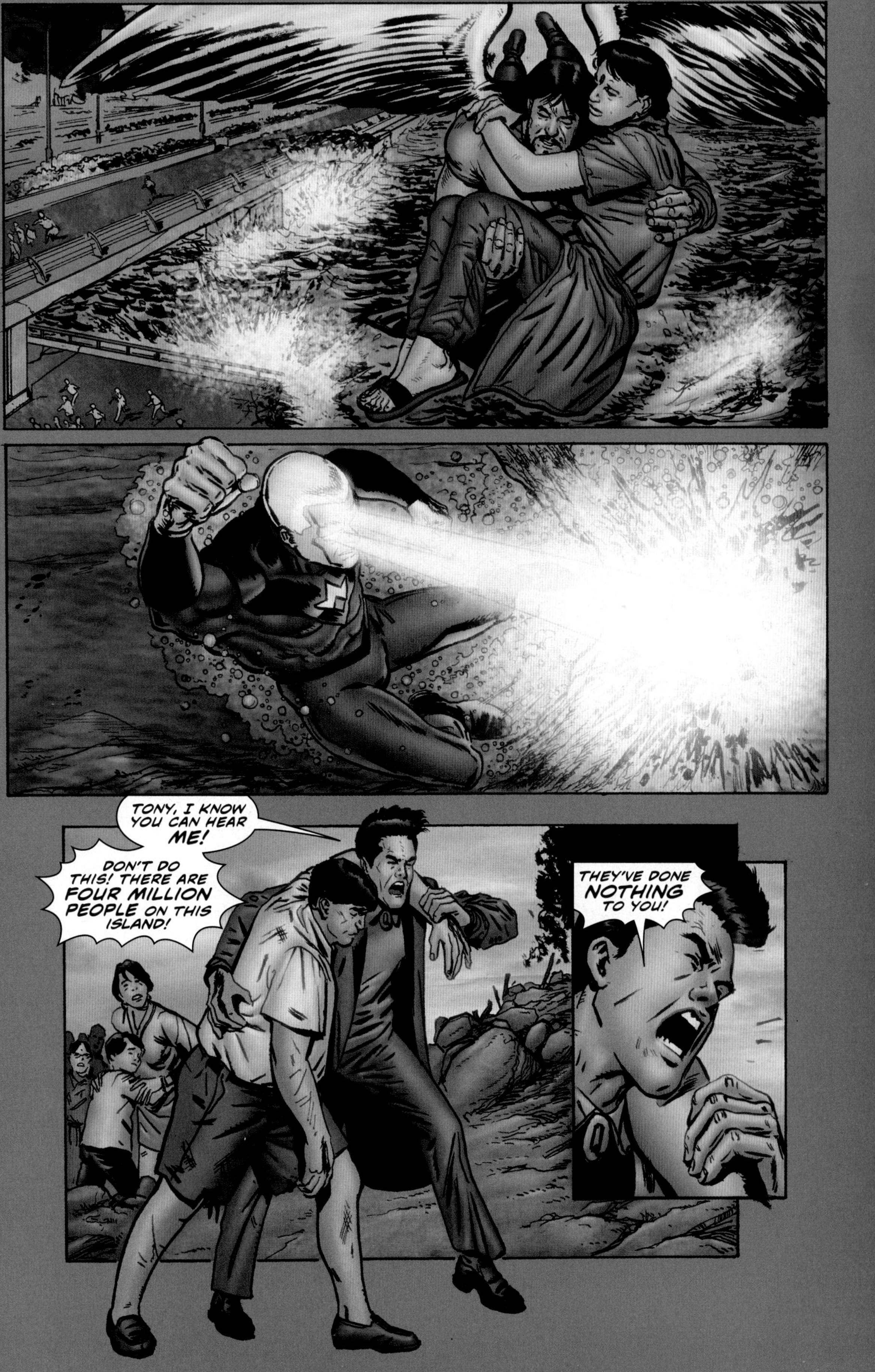
TONY, I KNOW YOU CAN HEAR ME!
DON'T DO THIS! THERE ARE FOUR MILLION PEOPLE ON THIS ISLAND!
THEY'VE DONE NOTHING TO YOU!

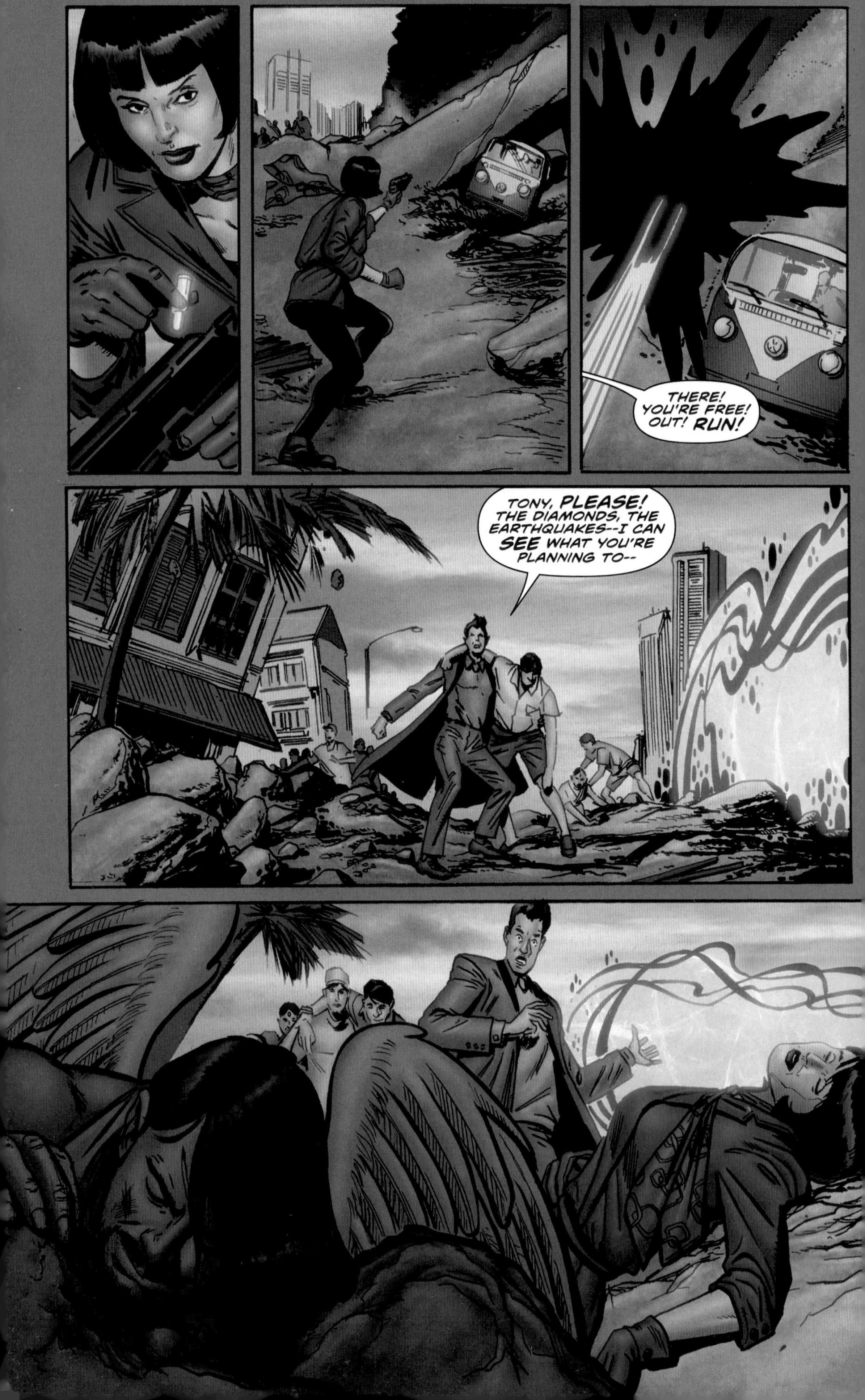
THERE! YOU'RE FREE! OUT! RUN!
TONY, PLEASE! THE DIAMONDS, THE EARTHQUAKES--I CAN SEE WHAT YOU'RE PLANNING TO--

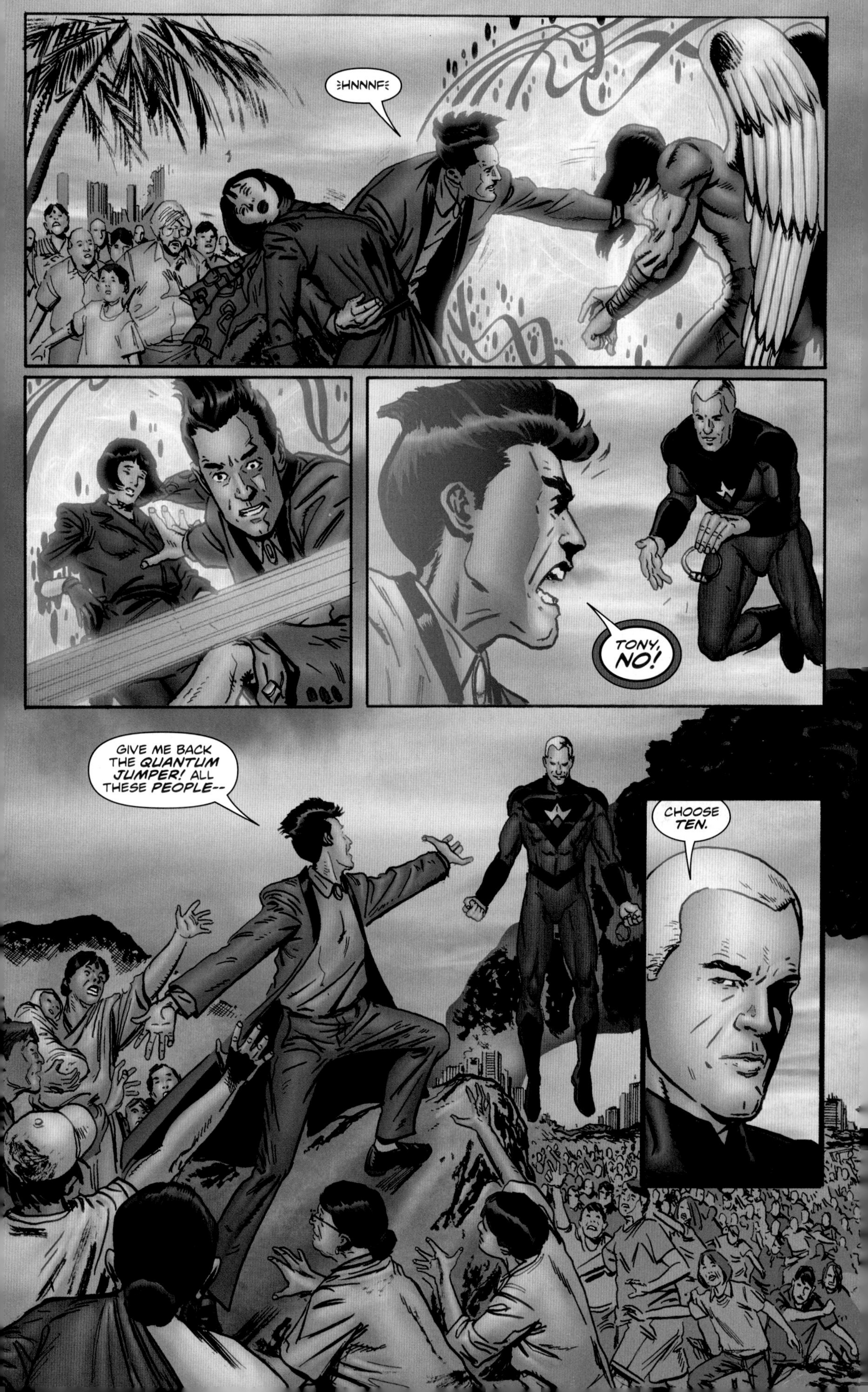
HNNNF
TONY, NO!
GIVE ME BACK THE QUANTUM JUMPER! ALL THESE PEOPLE--
CHOOSE TEN.

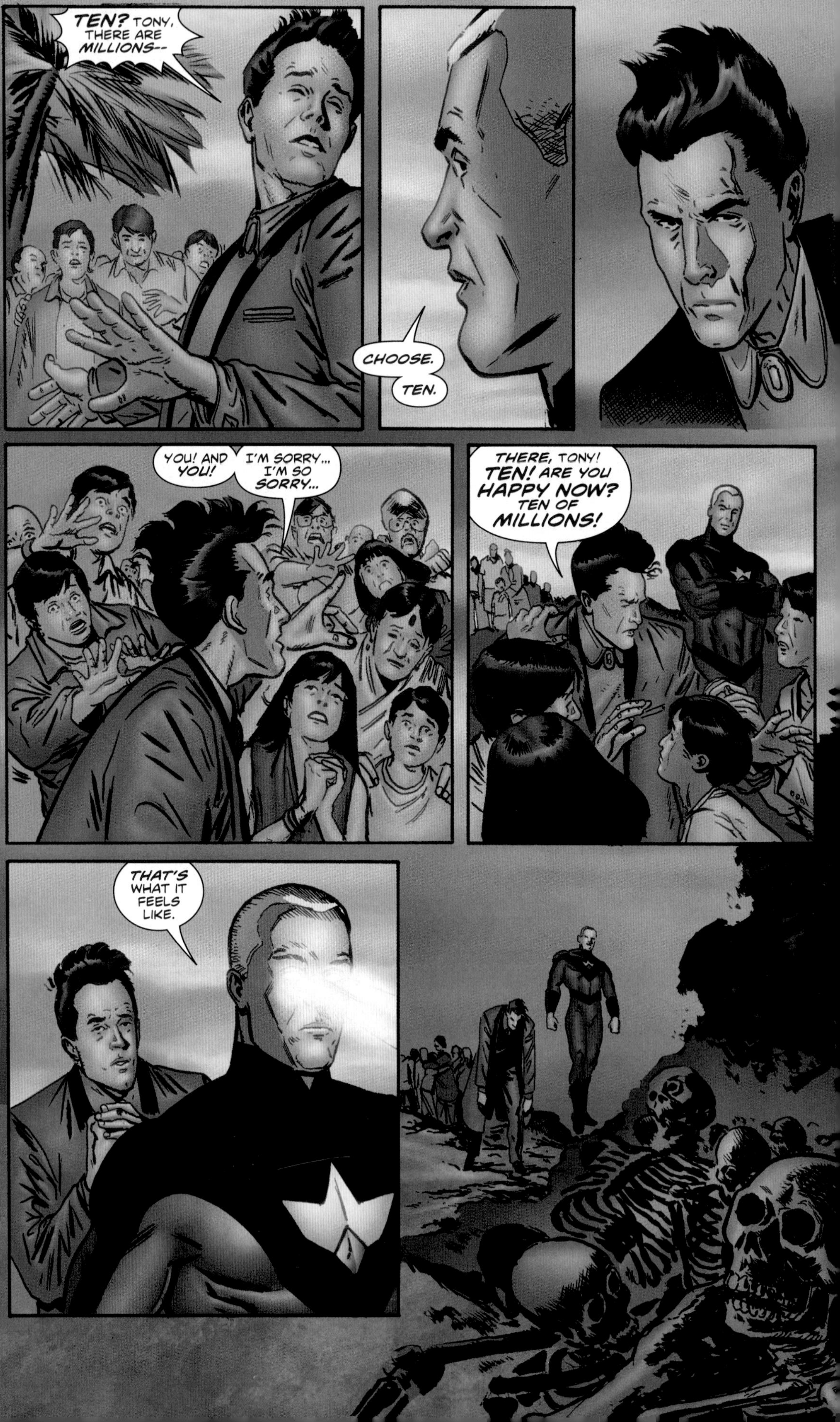
TEN? TONY, THERE ARE MILLIONS--
CHOOSE.
TEN.
YOU! AND YOU!
I'M SORRY... I'M SO SORRY...
THERE, TONY! TEN! ARE YOU HAPPY NOW? TEN OF MILLIONS!
THAT'S WHAT IT FEELS LIKE.

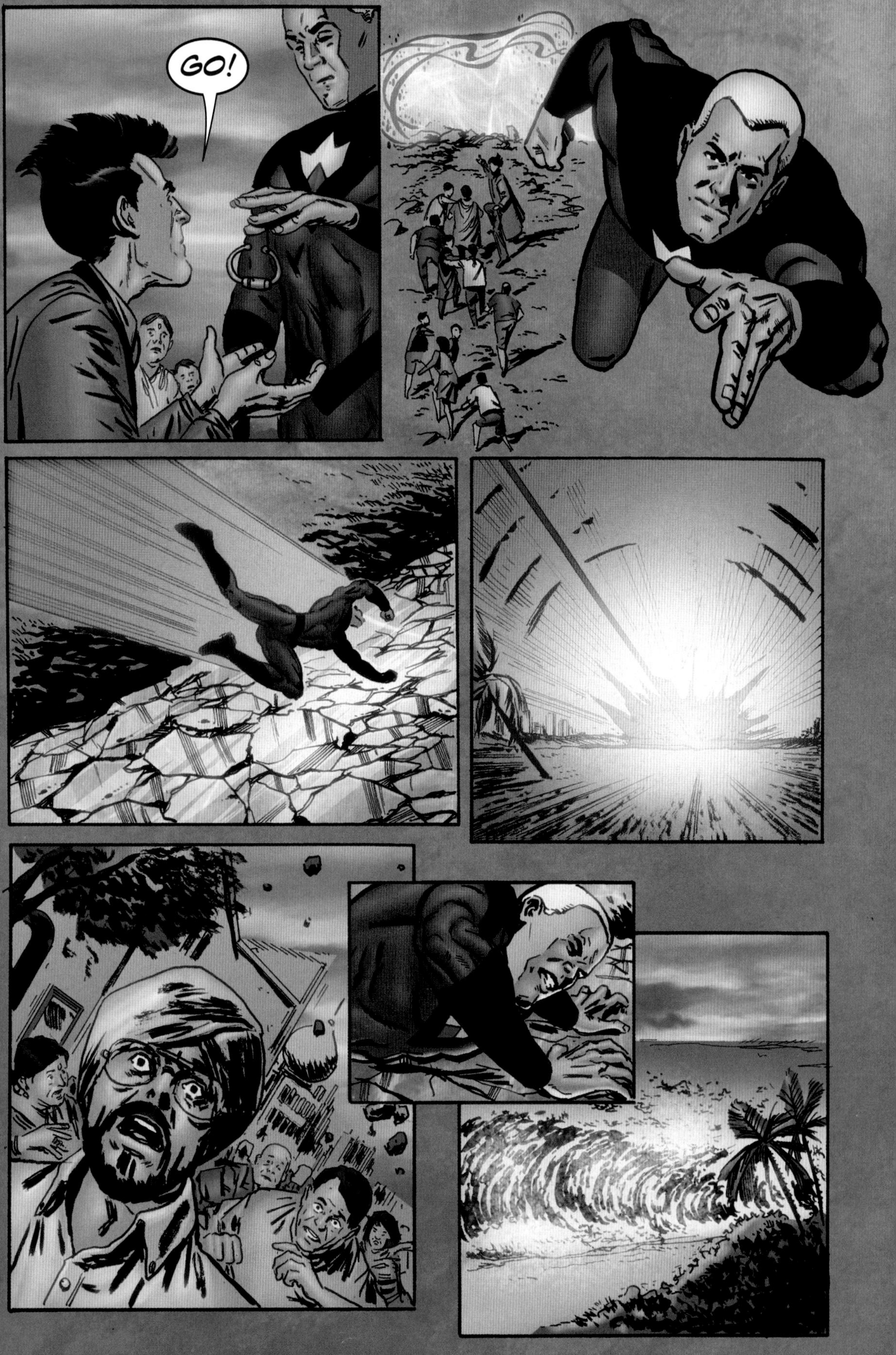
GO!

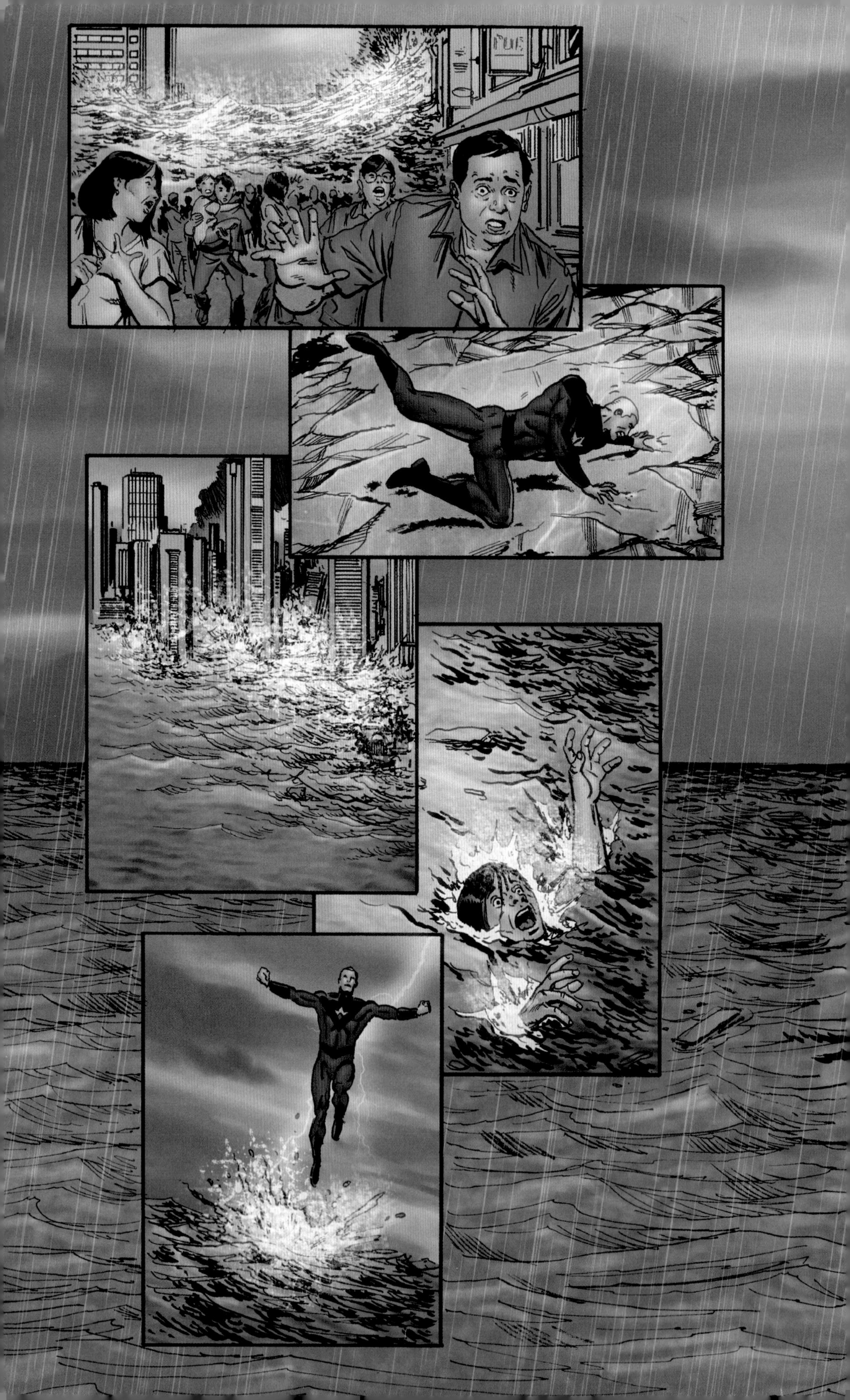

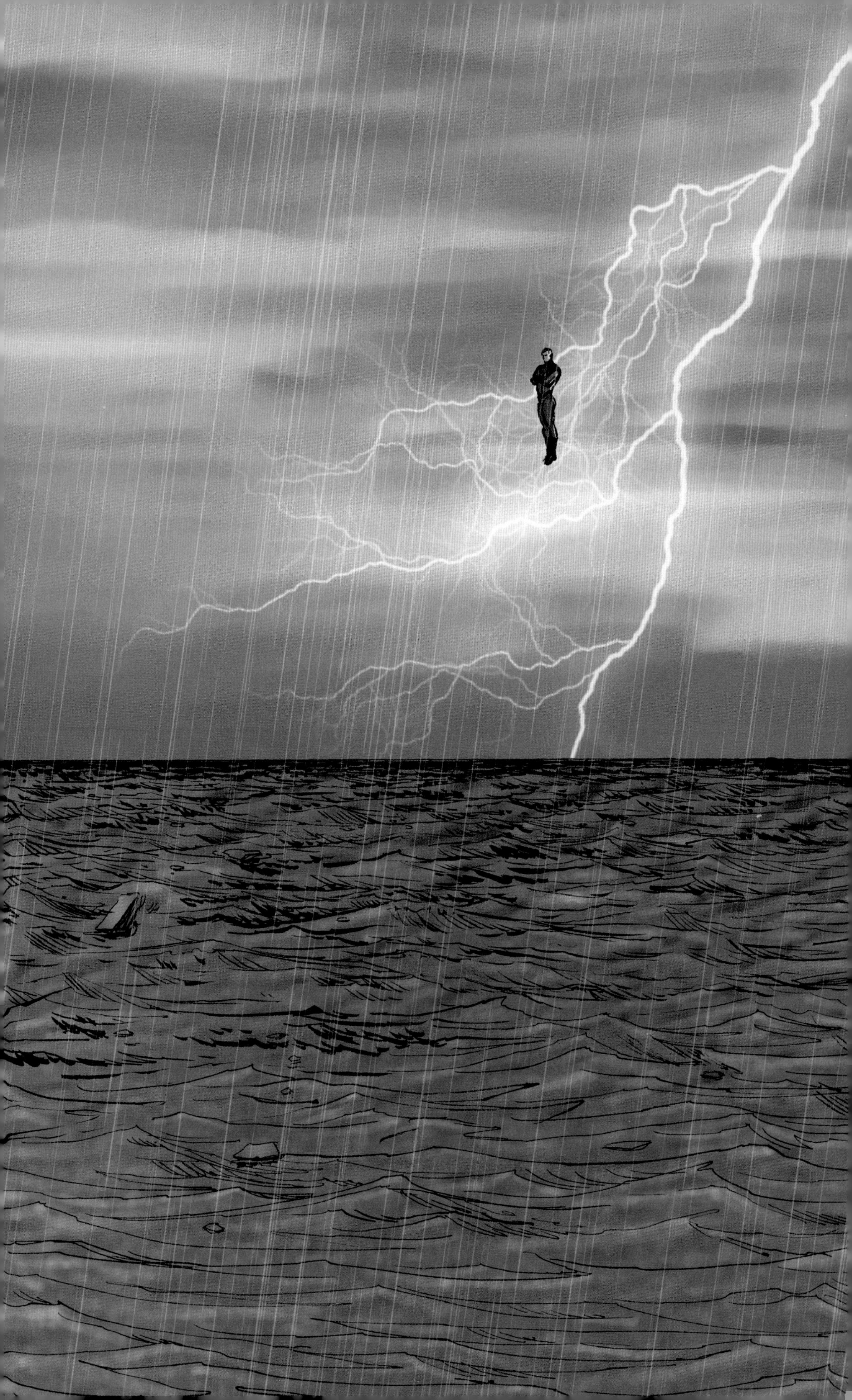

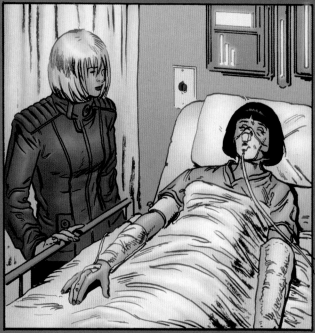

THAT'S IT, DAMN IT. THAT'S *IT.* I'VE GIVEN YOU ALL THE TIME WE CAN AFFORD.

ANSWER THE QUESTION YOU WERE BUILT TO *ANSWER!*

MODEUS... *WHERE ARE YOU?*

To be continued...

MARK WAID · PETER KRAUSE

IRREDEEMABLE
VOLUME 1

CREATED & WRITTEN BY: **MARK WAID**
ARTIST: **PETER KRAUSE**

COLORIST: **ANDREW DALHOUSE**
LETTERER: **ED DUKESHIRE**
EDITOR: **MATT GAGNON**

Afterword

In a recent e-mail to Mark Waid, I found myself grumping and moaning about this concept of "patterning" and how ill-served by it all I, personally, was feeling that day. We'd both read the same, somewhat disheartening article in **New Scientist** magazine, wherein it was explained that once a given group has categorized you under one convenient heading or another, it becomes pretty much impossible to shake the tag, even by acting differently.

For me, this simply confirmed a horrible suspicion that no matter how watertight I might try to make my plots, no matter how well-structured my narratives became, no matter how conventionally I organized my ideas, I would always be regarded in comics fan circles as the madcap purveyor of free-form gibberish. I saw future generations scratching their heads over the wording on my overgrown tombstone, declaring "incomprehensible" the simple name of the simple soul below.

As for Mark Waid, the specter—or "category," as we scientists like to call it—that haunted his career was conjured up from a mouldering grave no less confining.

For some reason, towards the end of the last decade, Mark Waid was saddled with an inexplicable reputation as the Sterling Sentinel of Silver Age Nostalgia comics. Curiously misrepresented as the defender of Kennedy-era values, the exemplar of the devoted fan-turned-pro, Waid became the go-to geek as the vogue in funnybooks turned briefly to unironically old-fashioned, Julius Schwartz-style sci-fi dad-fests. When an aging readership cried out with one ravenous beak for a return to the days of Ollie, Barry, Hal, or Larry, Sally, Ray, Rita, Jack, Bobby, Sue, John, Paul, George and Ringo too, Mark Waid was the first guy on the editorial speed dial. Waid, it was decided, would bring the necessary gee-whiz, "If I wasn't doing this for money, I'd do it for free!" mixture of wide-eyed wonder and bug-eyed delusion the task of refreshing these pop icons of yesteryear required.

And yet, this was the writer of **The Flash**. How could that run of streamlined, electric stories, those comics so super-charged with the raw voltage of modernity that they thrummed and kicked in the readers' hands, ever give any indication that Mark Waid favored the traditional and the comfortable? How could the writer of **Kingdom Come**'s state-of the-art farewell to the old guard find himself declared the representative and advocate of an "Age" that he himself had cleverly and carefully closed the door on?

Even now, against all evidence to the contrary, and even after his creation of "Wicker Sue," that ultimate, unforgettably abnormal symbol of hopeless loss and love become horror and madness, there are still people who insist on imagining Mark Waid as some faithful, owlish archivist, alphabetically arranging the 4-color debris of his youth.

So it was in consideration of all this that I composed my disgruntled e-mail, blaming patterning and flip categorization for everything that was, is and will be wrong with the world. Sometimes, especially when it's cold and dark and wet and miserable, which is nine-tenths of the year here, living in Scotland can inspire a kind of genuine, no-bull, soul-gloom and **New Scientist** had done nothing but stoke the black furnace.

Writing from yet another radiant, sunlit night in Los Angeles, however, Waid dismissed the findings of **New Scientist** by reminding me of the famous Elvis '68 TV special, when the all-but-neutered, out-of-touch King of Rock 'n' Roll reinvented himself as a relaxed and human God in Leathers. The rest being history.

To be honest, as willing as I was at the time to concede how expertly Waid had refuted patterning by invoking this example of Elvis Presley, the more I was sure of a fundamental flaw in the argument. Before I could figure out what it was, however, a far more convincing proof arrived in the form of electronic mail from...Mark Waid! I opened two files entitled "Irredeemable 1 FINAL" and "Irredeemable 2 FINAL," and as I read through the scripts contained within, the concept of patterning was reduced to a parcel of half-baked, pseudo-scientific confetti before my grateful eyes.

It's not that I haven't been watching him hone his skills across a number of recent projects. Look through the last few years of Mark's work and you can see him trying out new tricks, absorbing new influences, saving what works, and re-interpreting and refining it all through his own rigorous filtration system. His recent work on corporate icon characters has been pitch-perfect while his own new creations and concepts have displayed a growing range, power and clarity. It's clear he's been working towards something big.

And so, **Irredeemable**.

Those **New Scientist** conversations developed out of a brief discussion on the corrosive effects of relentless Internet criticism on human self-esteem. Waid had jokingly referred to the Internet as the "Zone-O-Phone" and it seemed to me a chillingly-apt comparison. The Zone-O-Phone was Superman's window onto the Phantom Zone, a twilight world of bodiless murderers, serial killers, war criminals and madmen, where the greatest criminals of the planet Krypton endured permanent exile in a disembodied hell. The Zone-O-Phone was Superman's hot line to a jeering crowd of phantoms with nothing better to do than to insult, taunt and threaten the Man of Steel for all eternity.

In **Irredeemable**, Mark imagines a superman who has spent a few too many hours at the Zone-O-Phone screen. The Plutonian is a character whose heart has been poisoned, whose belief in the essential goodness of human nature has been rotted to thread by a steady drip, drip of insinuation, scorn and criticism. What happens to a superhero who can't stop overhearing just how much he's hated and mocked by the people around him? And what would be the result if all the antipathy, jealousy and lies finally just killed his soul?

It's a simple, elegant and terrifying concept and better yet, it's in the hands of someone who knows exactly how to make the most of it. This is the comic only Mark Waid, who loves Superman more than anyone living or dead, could write. On first read, it feels like being caught in the jet of a high-powered hose filled with hydrochloric acid. The energy of the storytelling is immense but it's harnessed to a laser-eye vision and executed with a grasp of plot dynamics that is simply awe-inspiring.

If you ever find yourself lying on a sterile bed with your internal organs glistening under the overheads, you'll be praying for a surgeon who can cut and edit with this kind of thrilling bravura. From the opening sequence of narrative detonations through the massive turns and reveals in every single scene, this is 'what happens next ???...' storytelling evolved into a super-predator. This is blindfold open-heart surgery with a samurai sword. This is any number of metaphors I could invoke to hint at the simple, devastating work of a master telling a comic book story, just so. Just like that. And that. The sweeping confidence in the construction of this beautiful machine makes me grin with sheer delight every time I read it, and bear in mind I haven't seen any of this with art. I've seen the naked skeleton and the programming language, the precise, written instructions that the artist renders up into comic book form. I've only seen the Terminator under the skin of this book so far, and what I've seen is all precision-engineered whirring gears, glistening chrome and diamond-etched circuitry. As a technical and structural achievement, it's a 'How to...' handbook for every other writer in the field. As a super-adventure story for the 21st century, it's a page-turning monster of a read.

Irredeemable is brilliant, hard-edged, progressive super-hero comics. There's no trace of nostalgia, no backing down from the horrors it summons onto the page.

It's big and resonant and it rides the zeitgeist like Roy Rogers rode Trigger. Clever, dark and frightening, it dares to look directly into the demonic churn of recrimination, fear, entitlement and rage that drives our media discourse. It spits venom across the you're-too-thin, too-fat, too-clever, too-stupid, too-old, too-young, too-flawed, too-human black hole of self-loathing judgement that spins at the centre of our culture and threatens to devour us all.

Irredeemable dares to show us what might happen when the best in us is finally brought low by the worst in us. And, more frighteningly, it shows what happens next.

This story has real fuel in its tank, its urgent roar tells us that this is Mark Waid's darkest nightmare and his best revenge all at once, served cold and bitter. I can't wait to read more.

This then, is the proof I needed, the proof that the Elvis '68 special could not entirely provide; if you thought you knew what Mark Waid was capable of, think again. That glorious, apocalyptic noise you hear is the sound of categories shattering.

Grant Morrison
Glasgow, Scotland
March 2009

COVER
GALLERY

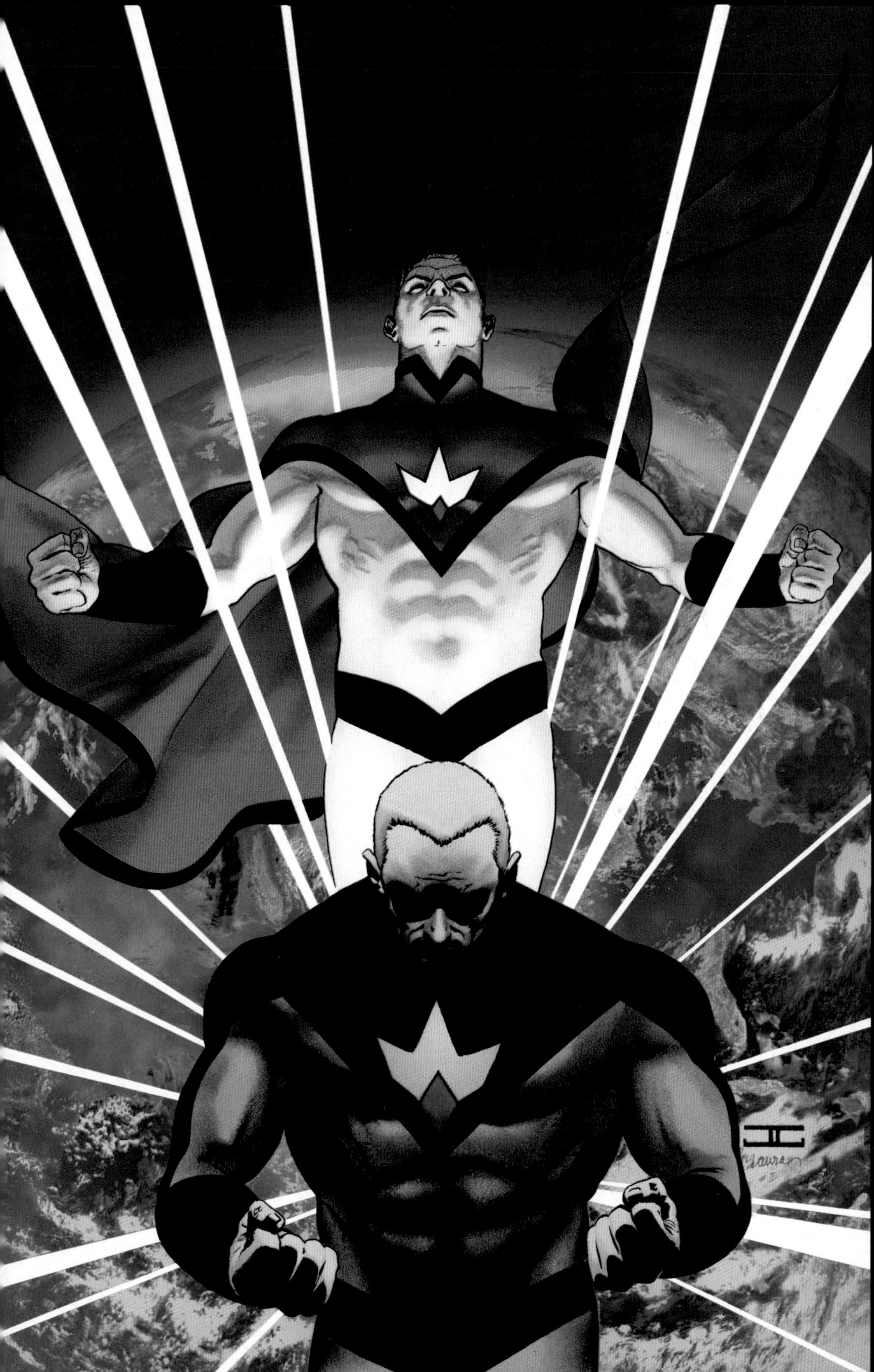

COVER 1A
JOHN CASSADAY / COLORS BY LAURA MARTIN

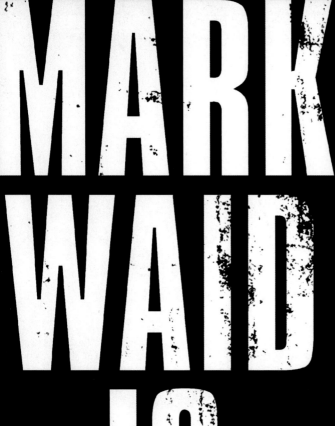

MARK WAID IS EVIL

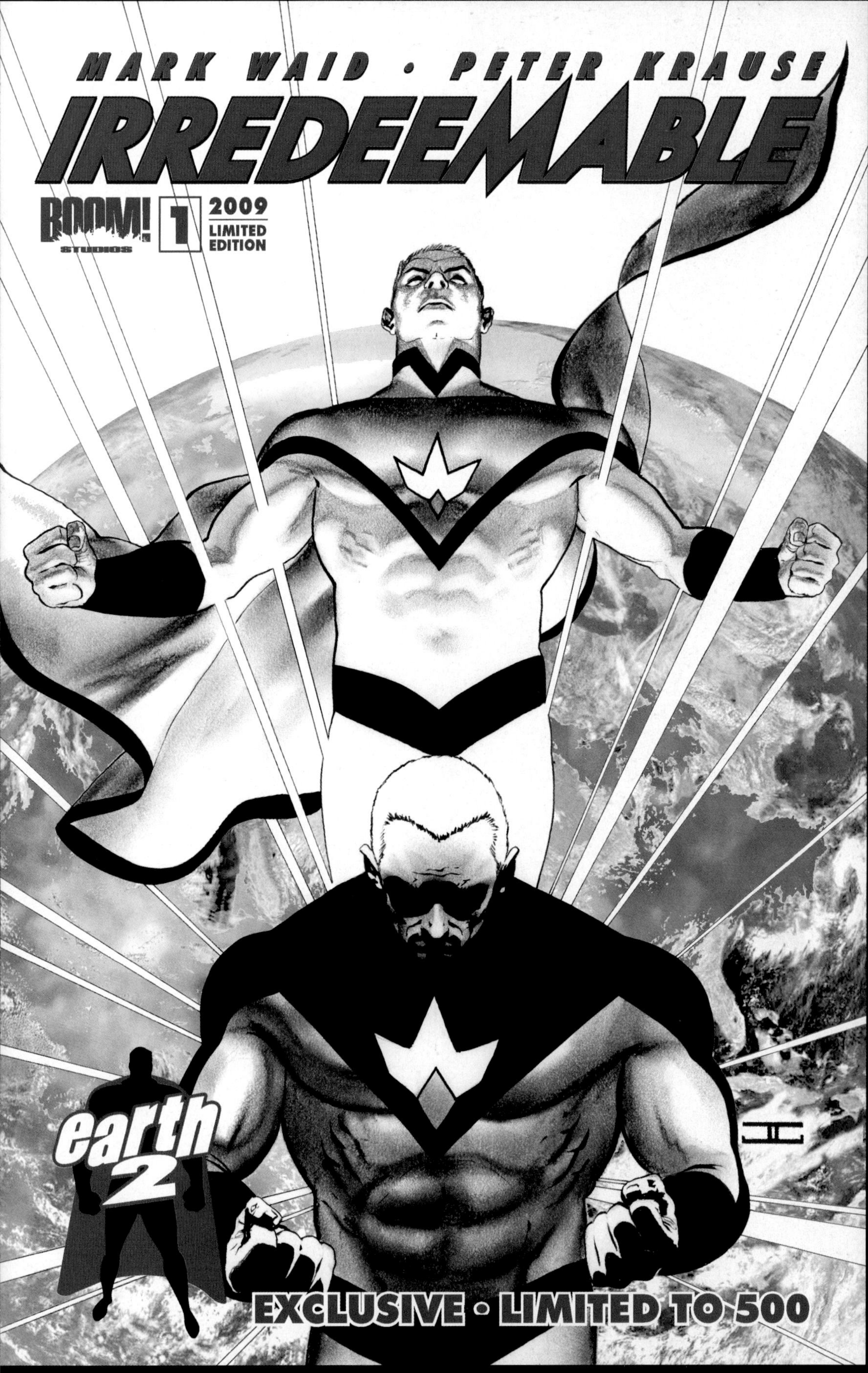
MARK WAID · PETER KRAUSE
IRREDEEMABLE
BOOM! STUDIOS
1
2009
LIMITED EDITION
earth 2
EXCLUSIVE · LIMITED TO 500

EARTH 2 EXCLUSIVE
JOHN CASSADAY

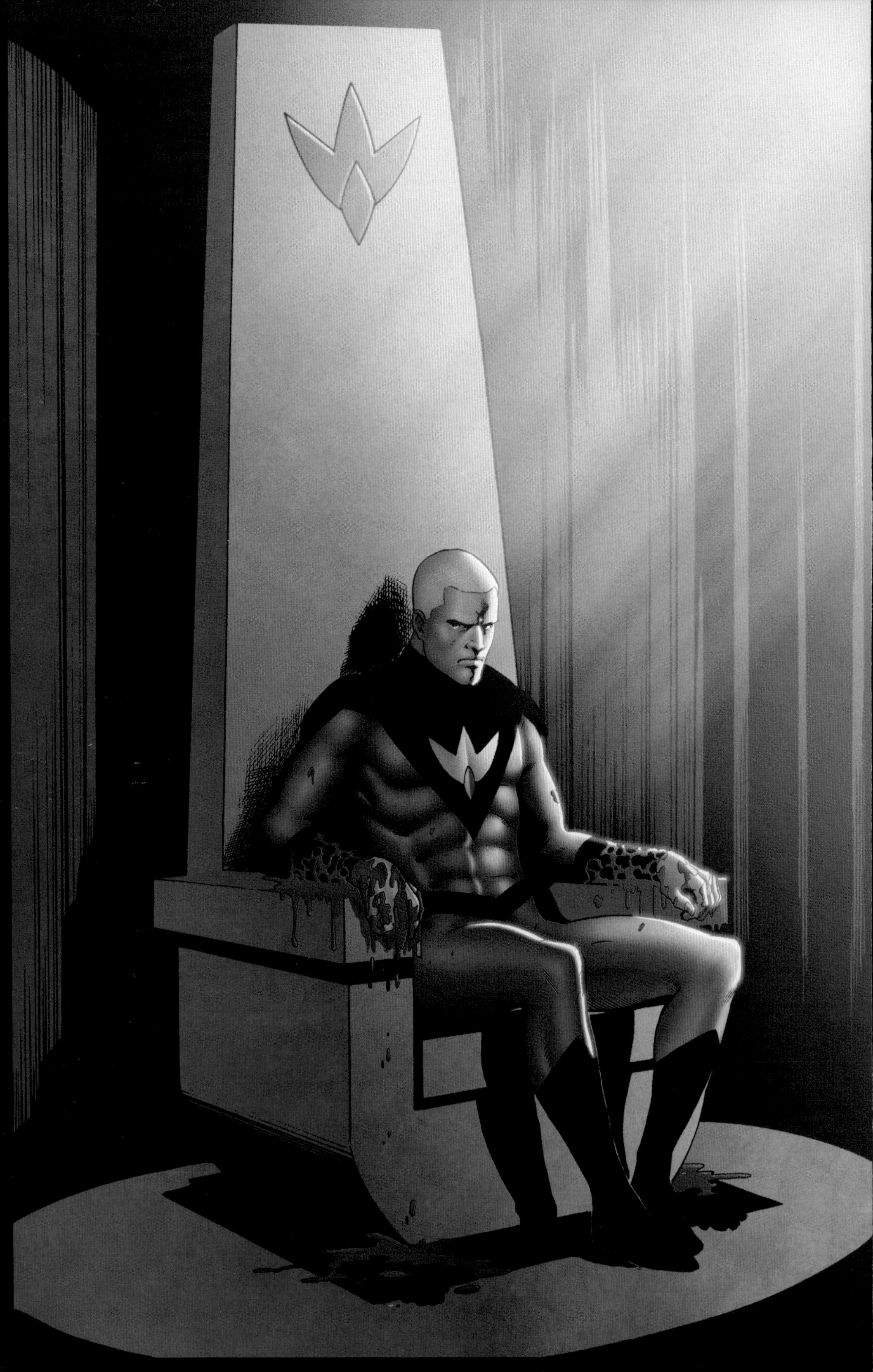

COVER 1B
BARRY KITSON / COLORS BY ANDREW DALHOUSE

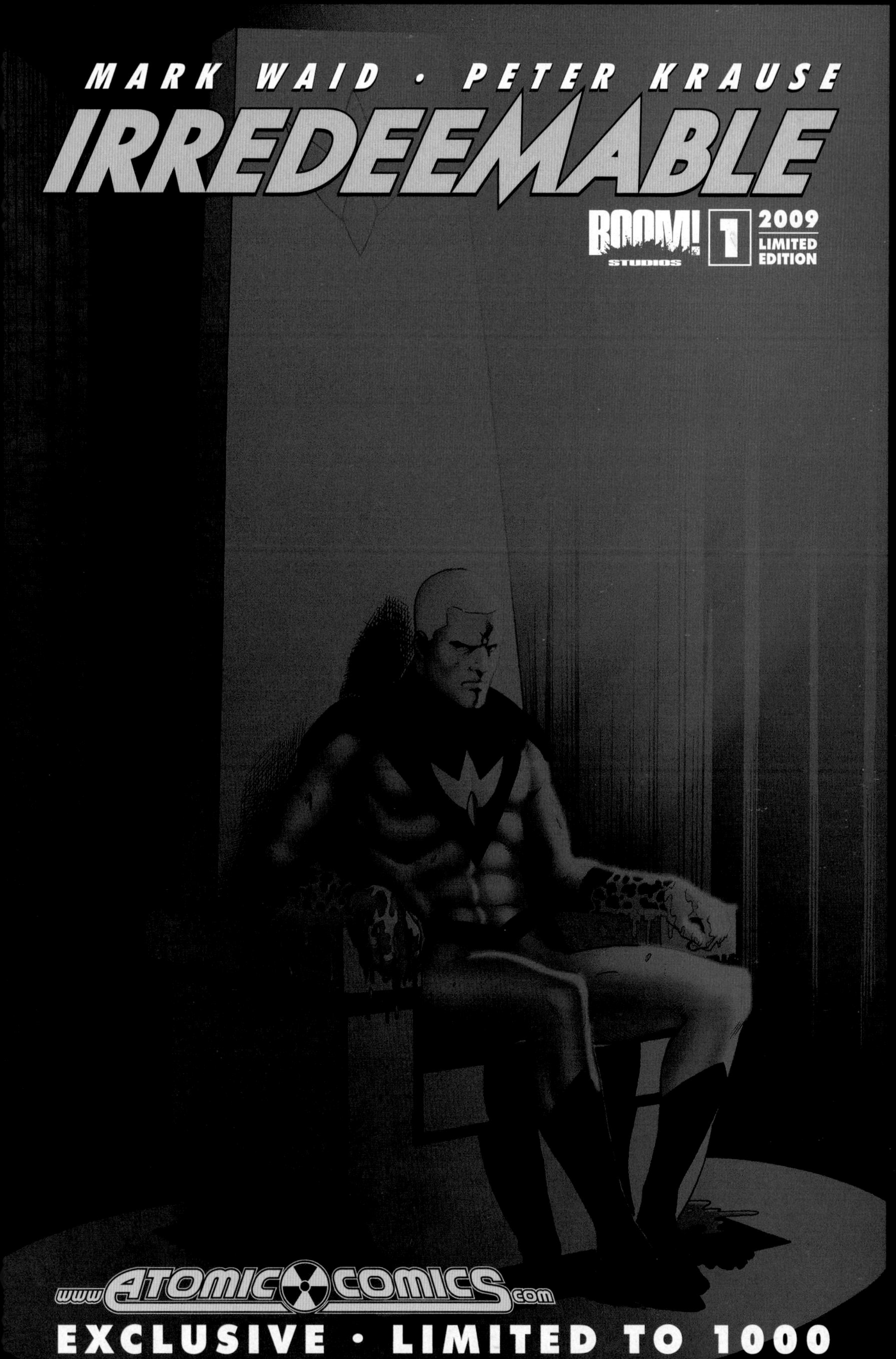
MARK WAID · PETER KRAUSE
IRREDEEMABLE
BOOM! STUDIOS
1
2009
LIMITED EDITION
www ATOMIC COMICS .com
EXCLUSIVE · LIMITED TO 1000

ATOMIC COMICS EXCLUSIVE
BARRY KITSON

BY JEFFREY SPOKES

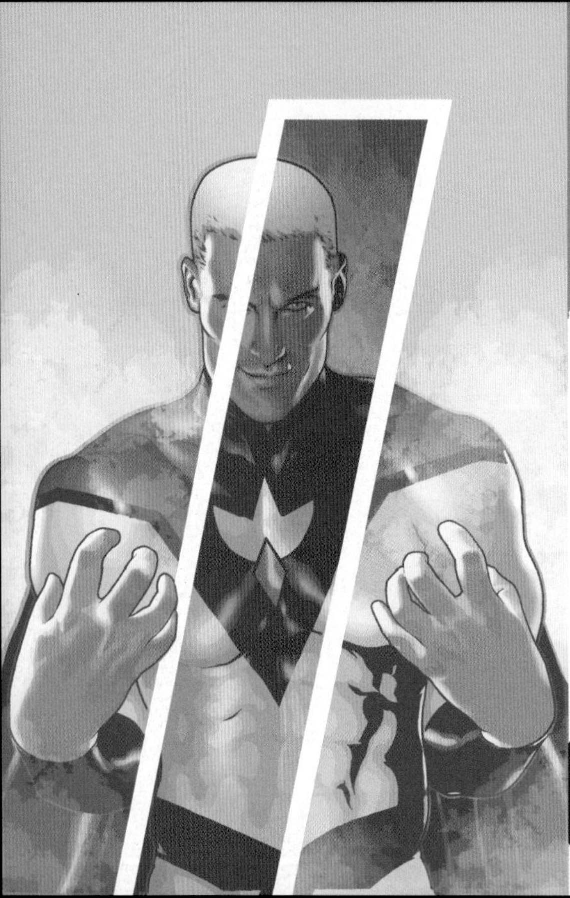

1 IN 50

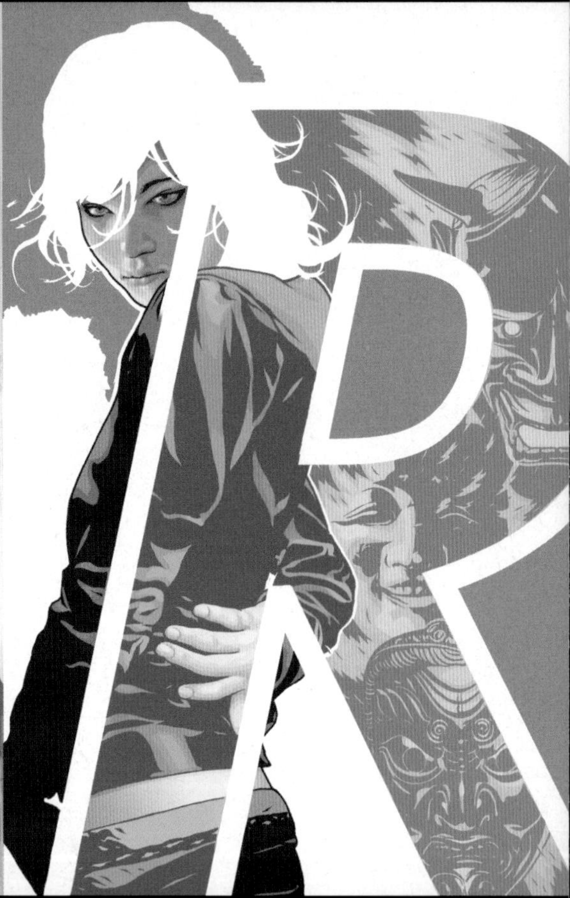

1 IN 25

COVERS 1C-4C

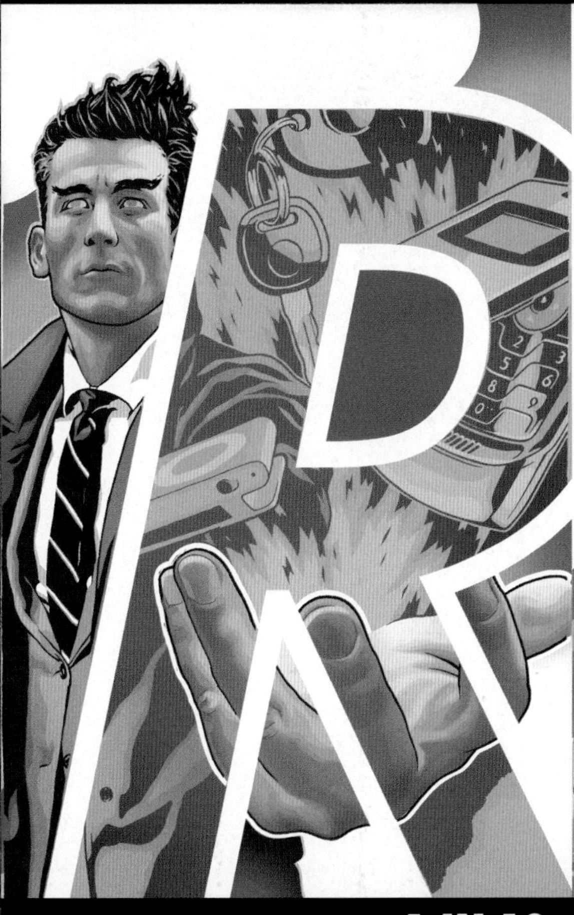

1 IN 10

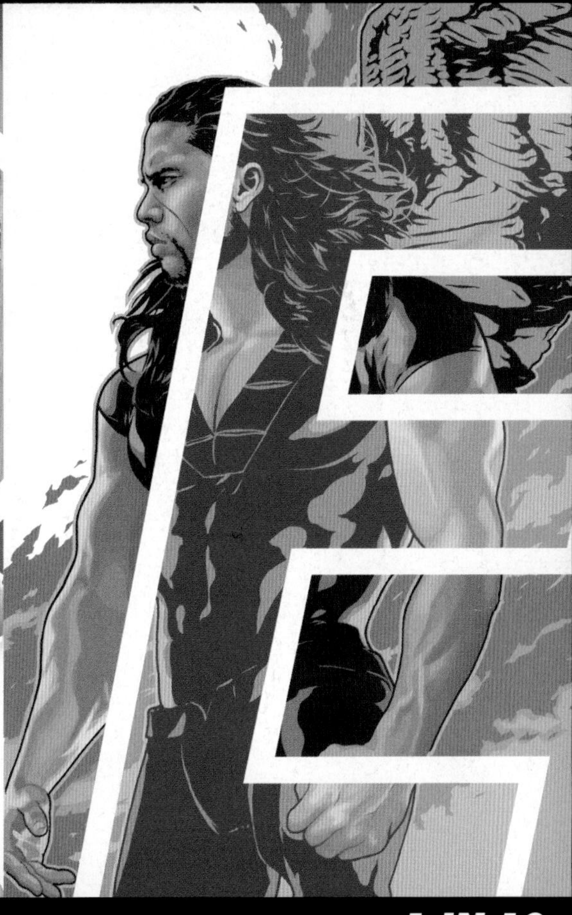

1 IN 10

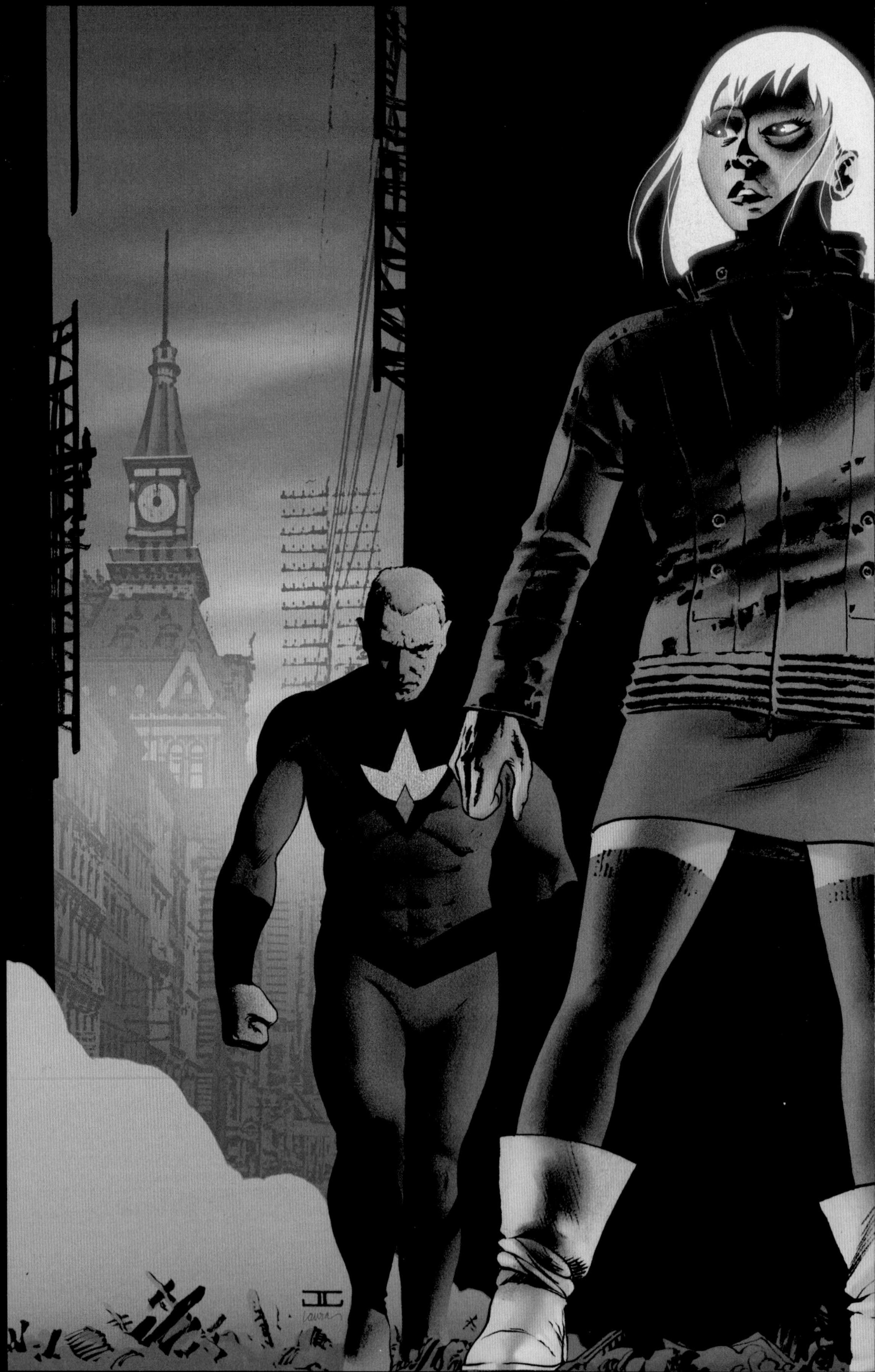

COVER 2A
JOHN CASSADAY / COLORS BY LAURA MARTIN

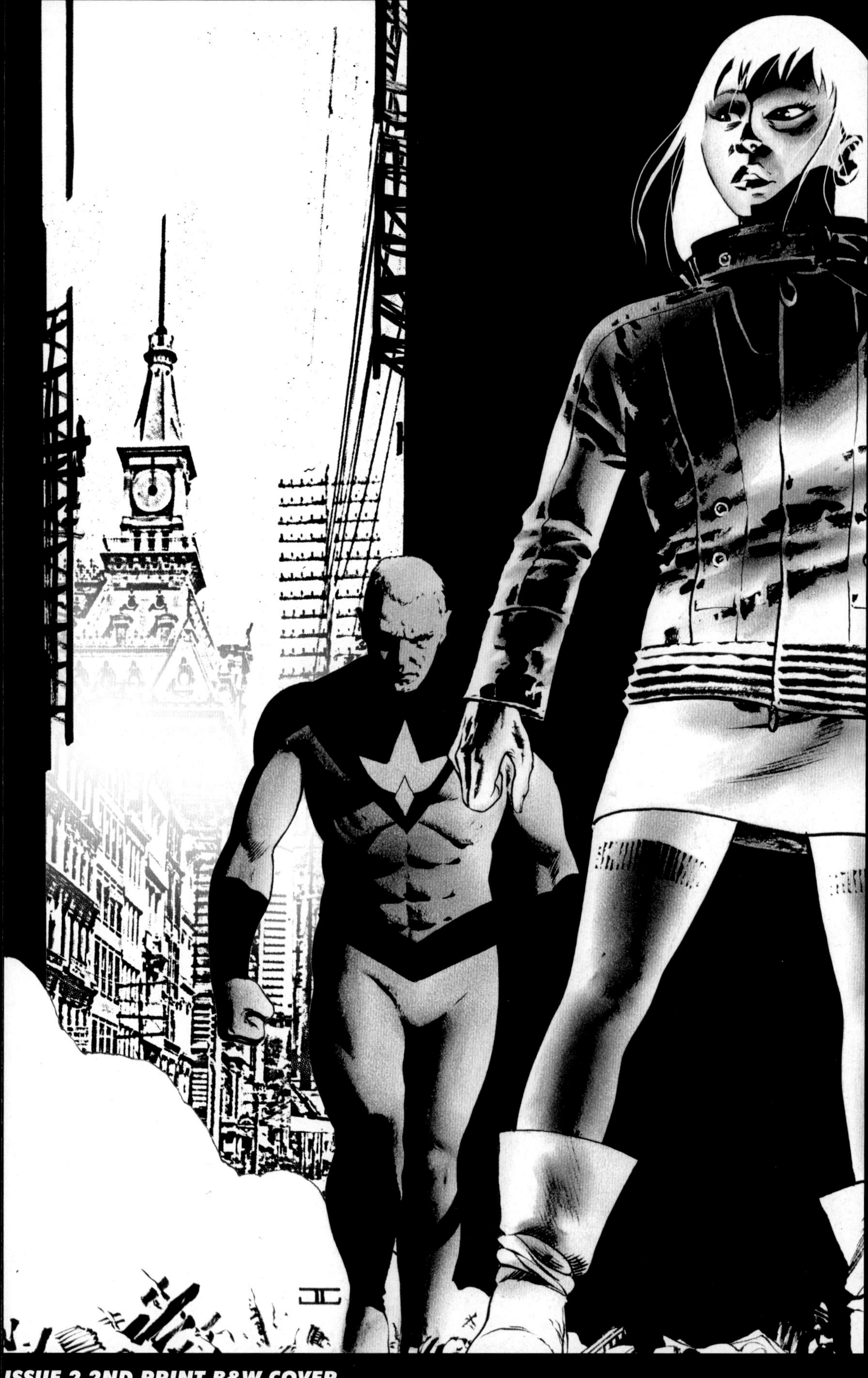

ISSUE 2 2ND PRINT B&W COVER
JOHN CASSADAY

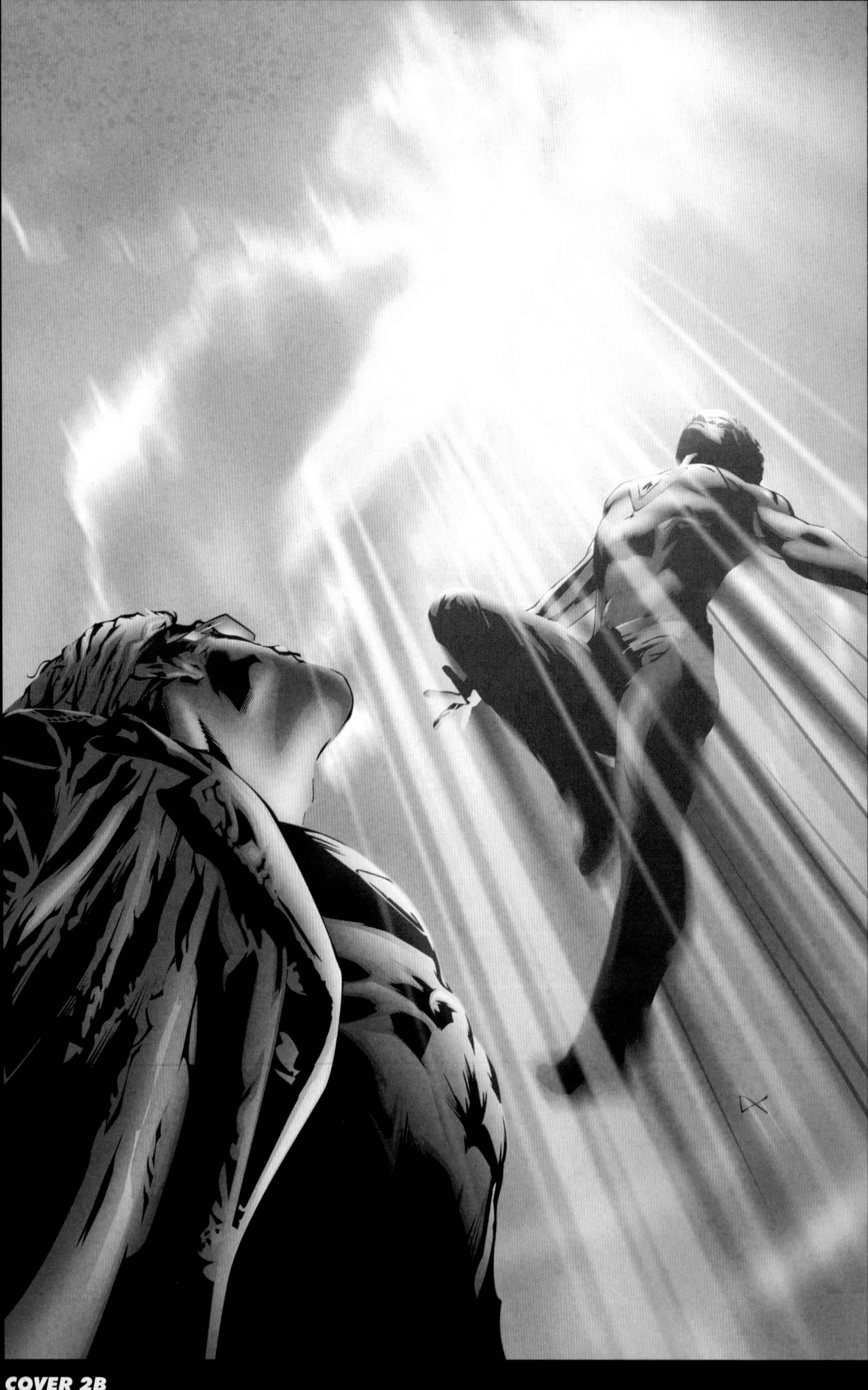

COVER 2B
DENNIS CALERO

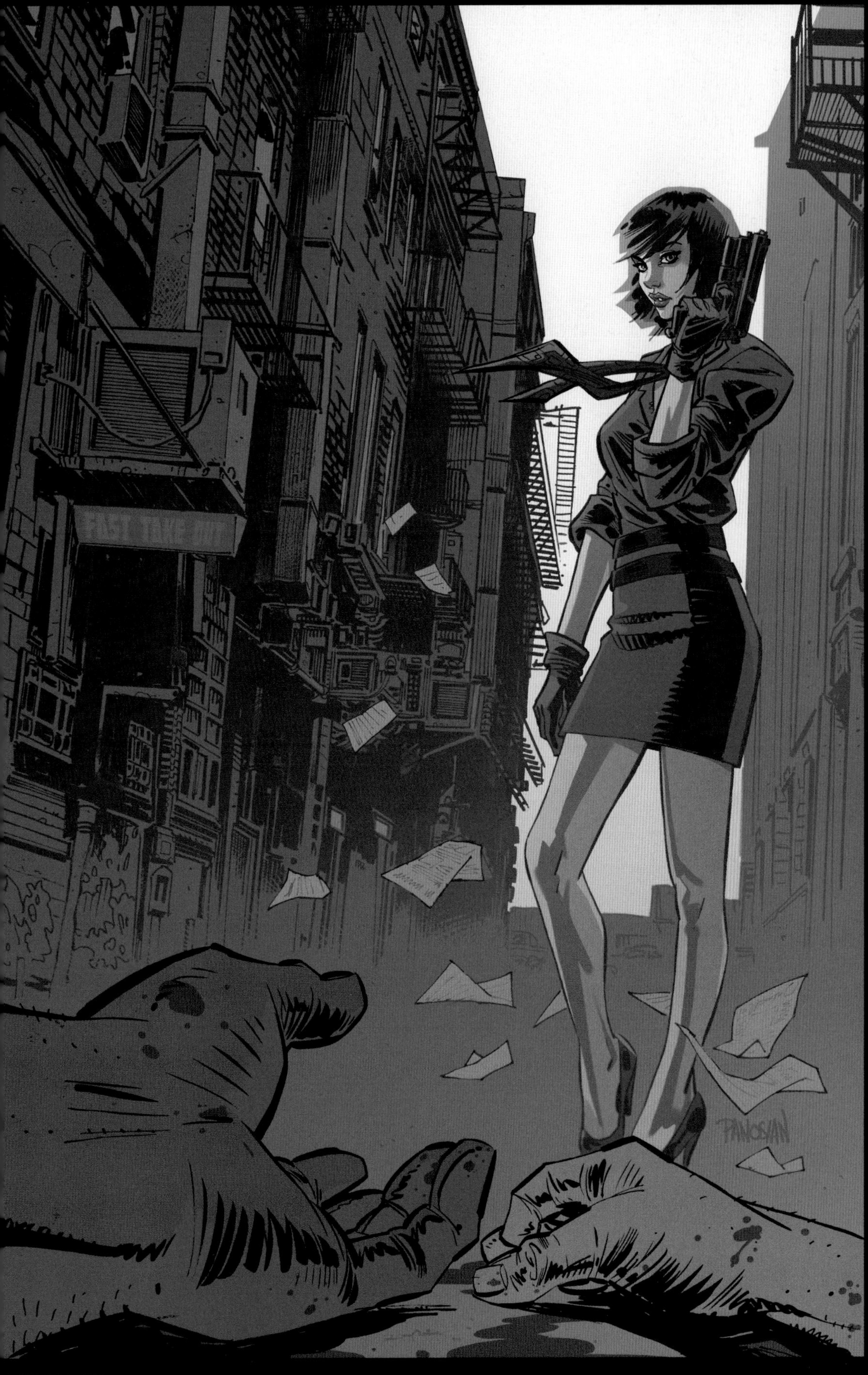
FAST TAKE OUT
PANOSIAN

COVER 3B
DAN PANOSIAN

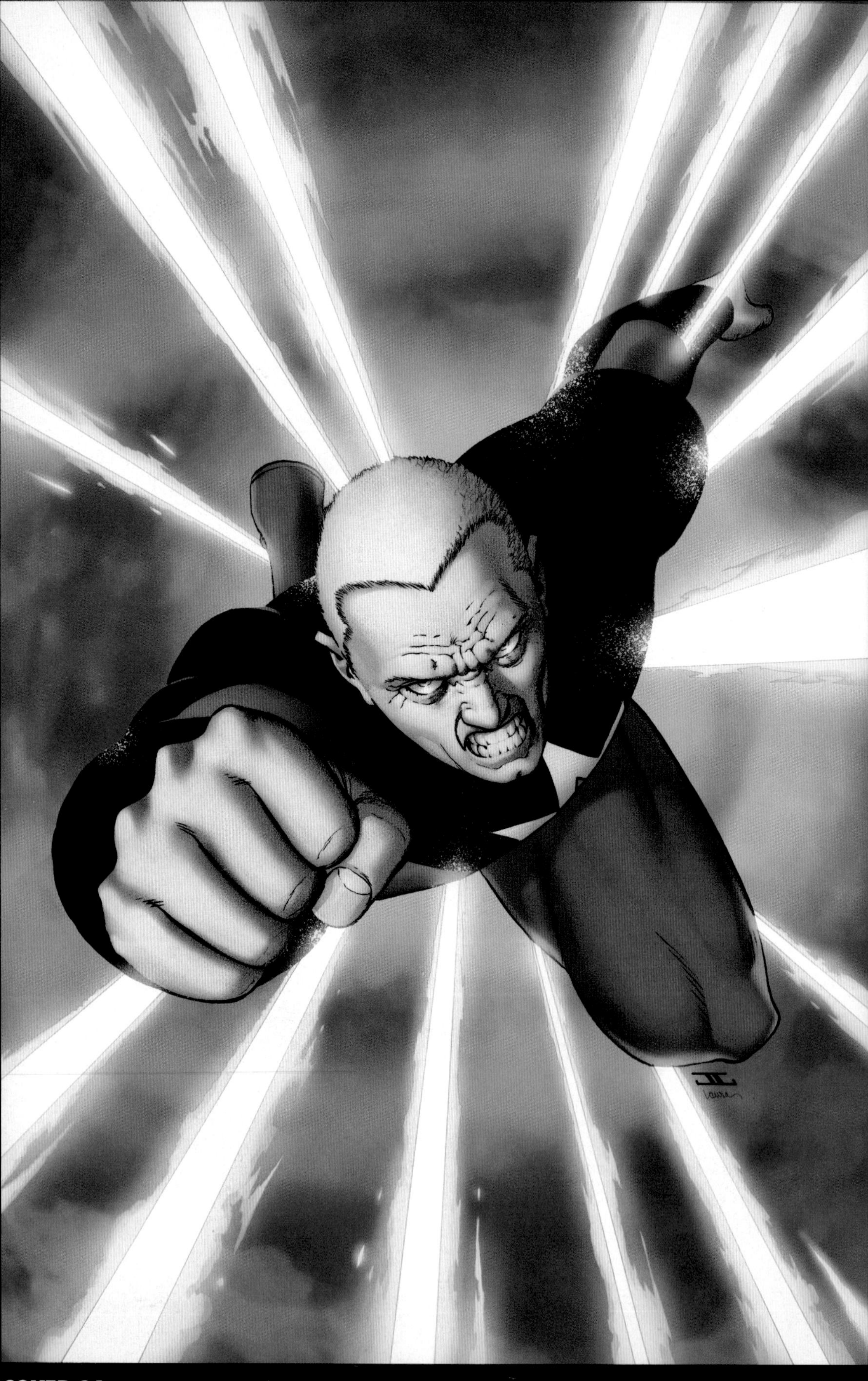

COVER 3A
JOHN CASSADAY / COLORS BY LAURA MARTIN

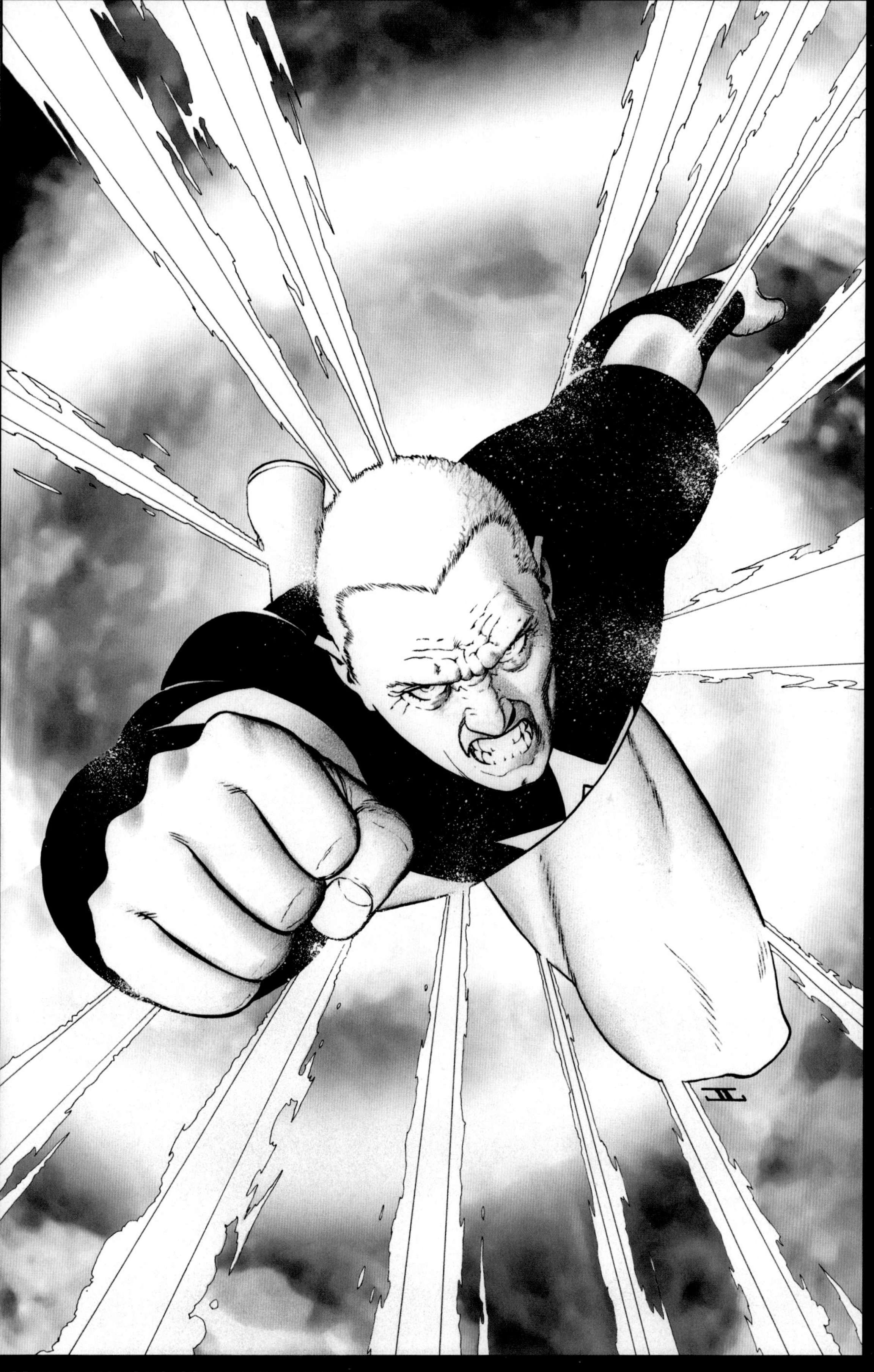

ISSUE 3 HEROES CON EXCLUSIVE
JOHN CASSADAY

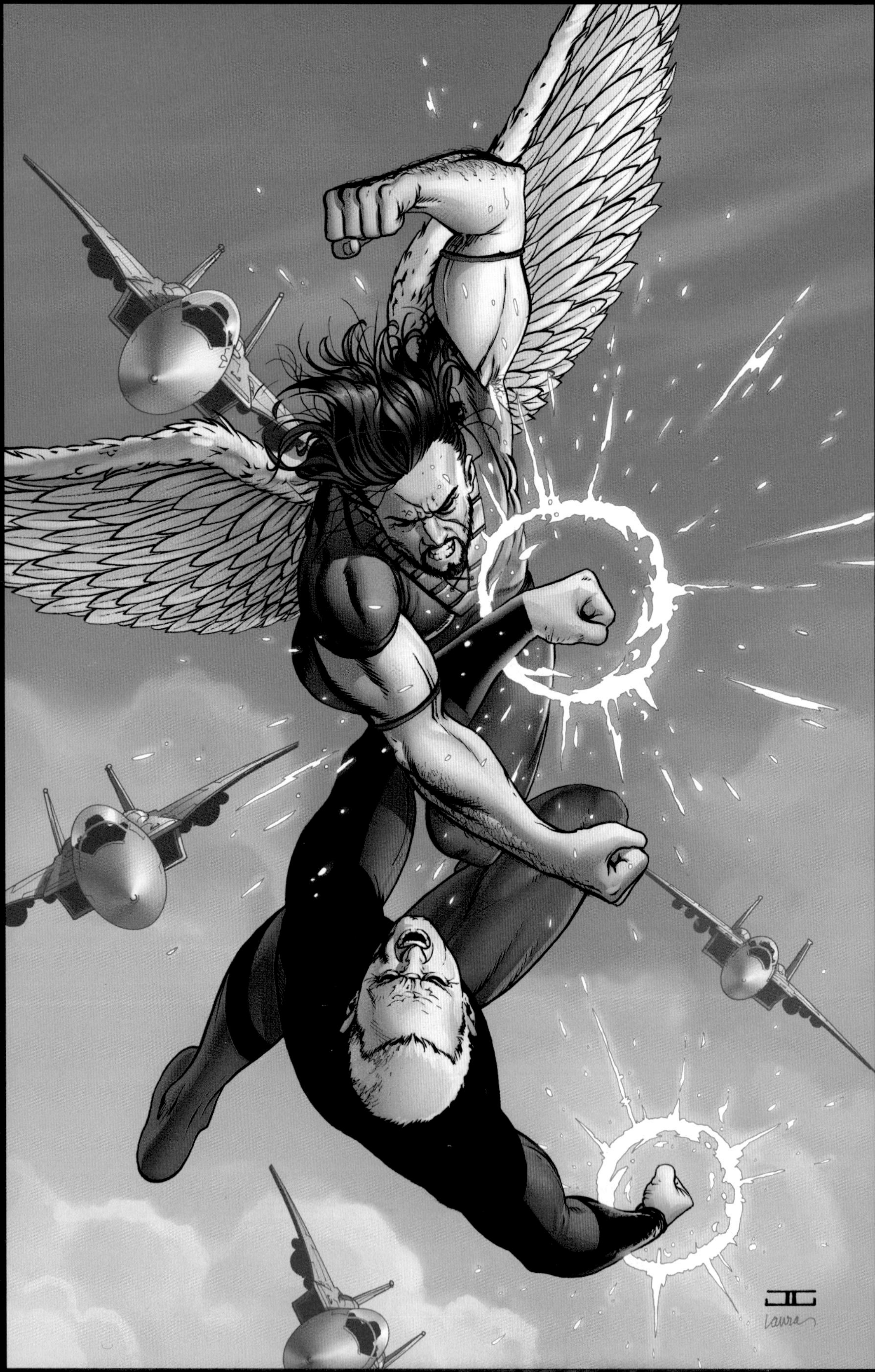

COVER 4A
JOHN CASSADAY / COLORS BY LAURA MARTIN

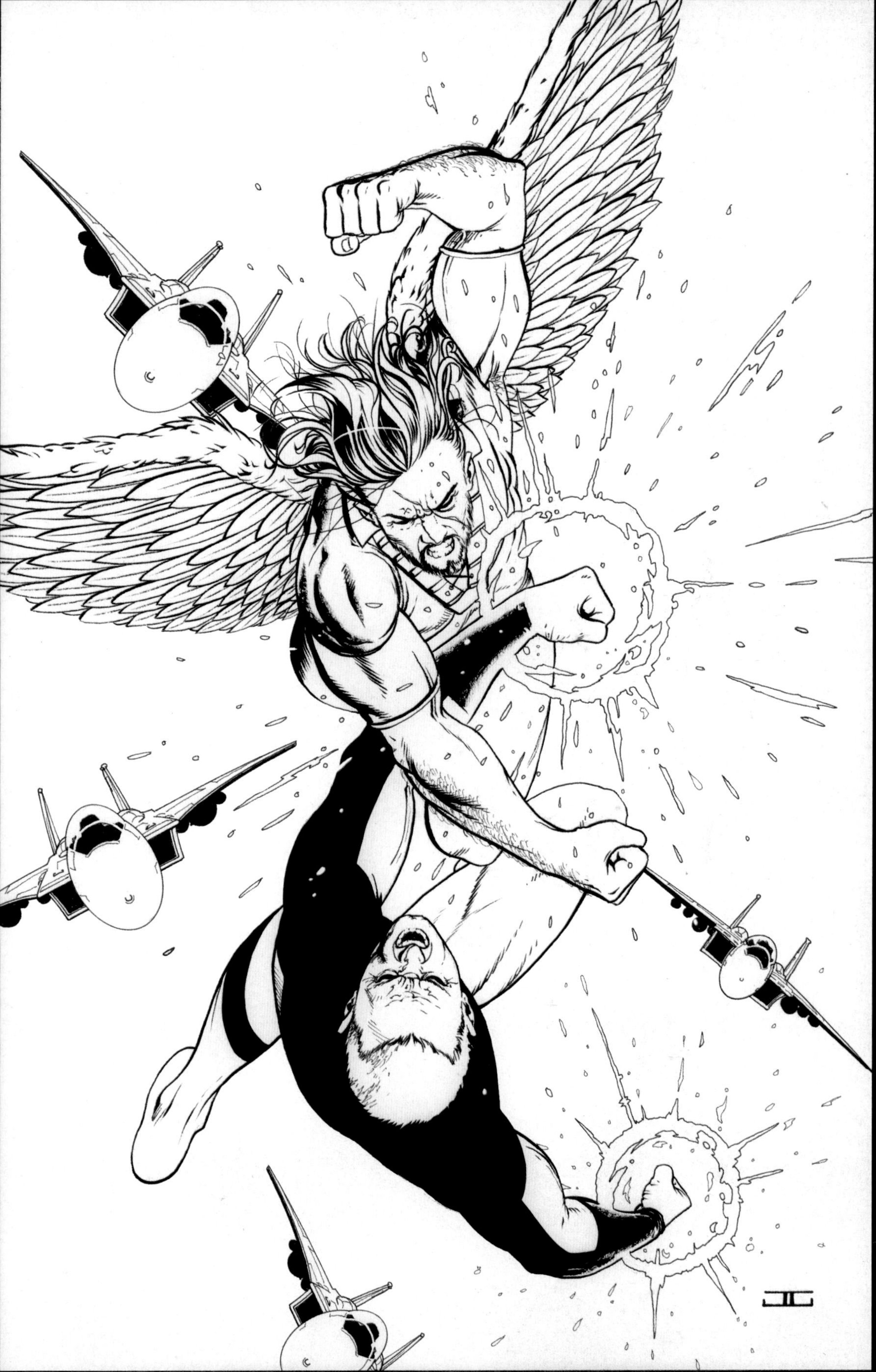

ISSUE 4 SDCC EXCLUSIVE
JOHN CASSADAY

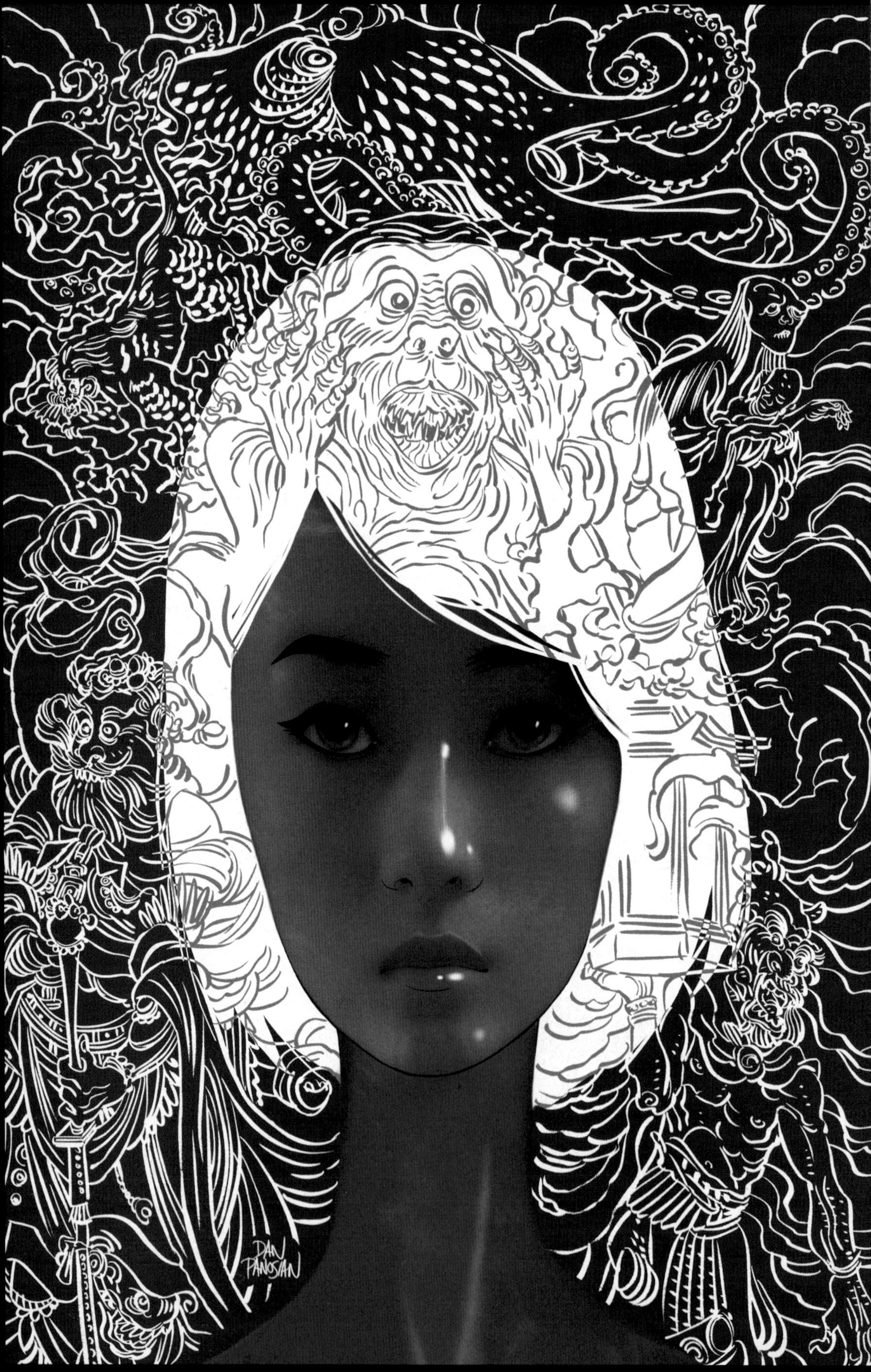
DAN
PANOSIAN

COVER 4B
DAN PANOSIAN

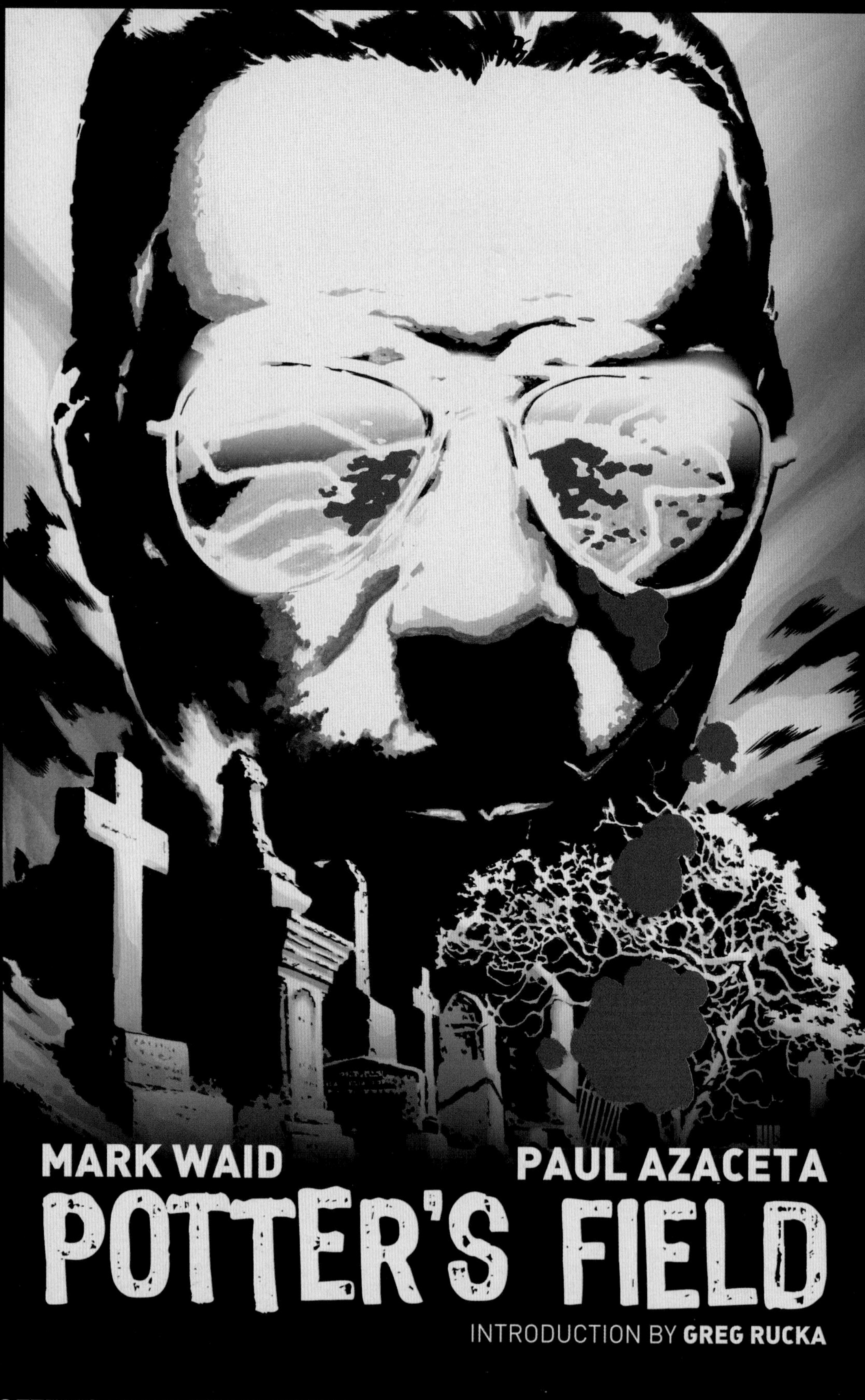
MARK WAID
PAUL AZACETA
POTTER'S FIELD
INTRODUCTION BY GREG RUCKA

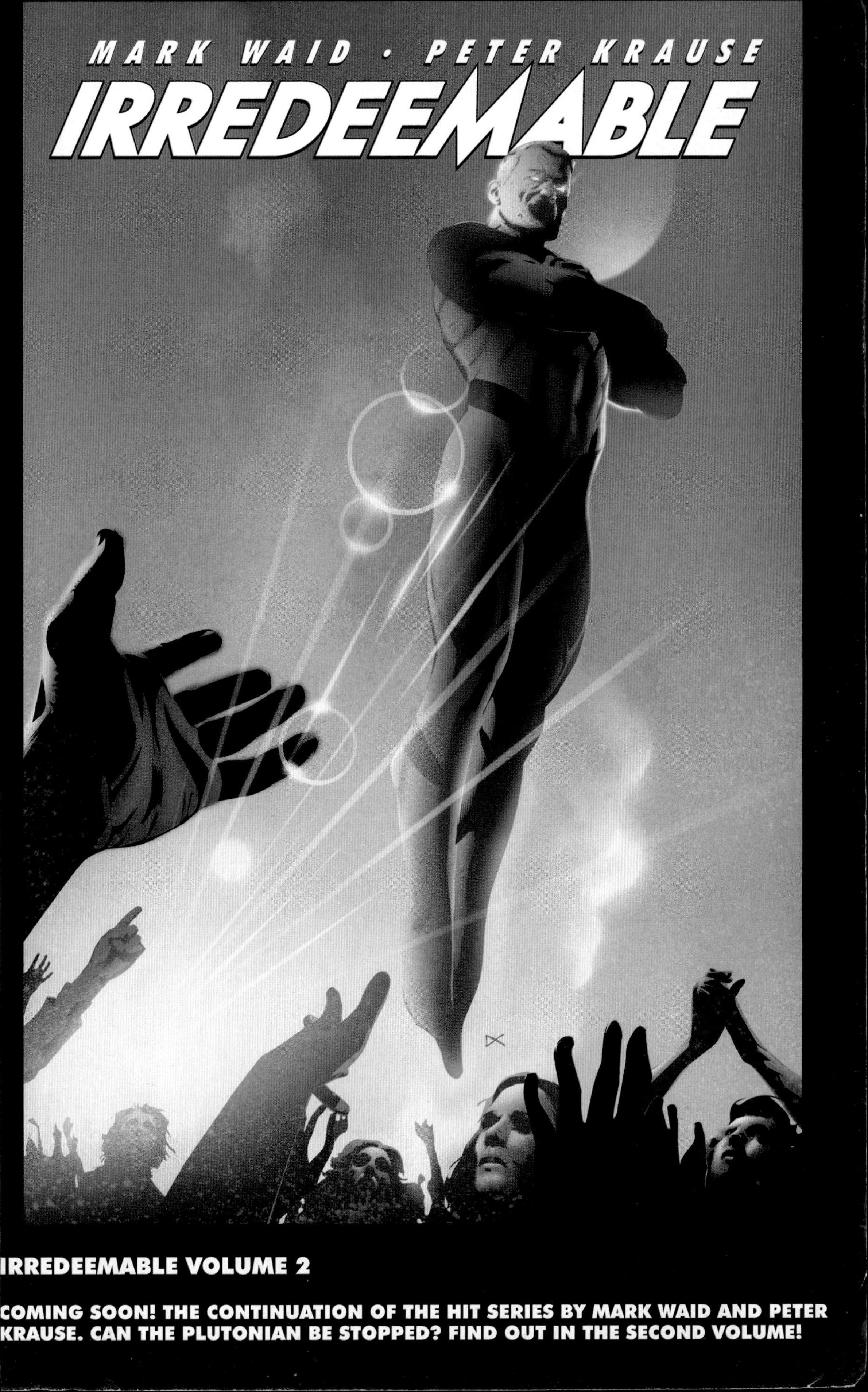
MARK WAID · PETER KRAUSE
IRREDEEMABLE

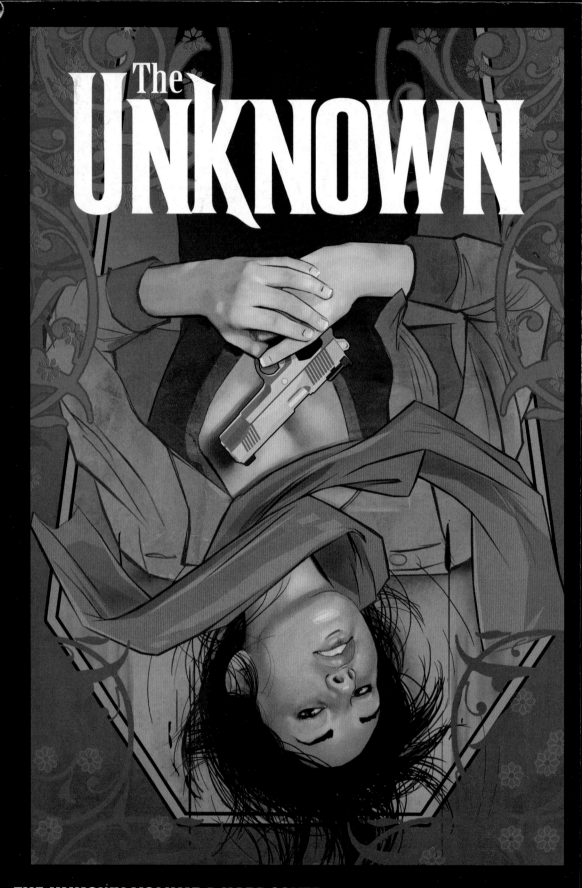

The UNKNOWN

THE UNKOWN VOLUME 1 HARDCOVER

SHE HAS SOLVED EVERY MYSTERY KNOWN TO MAN. BUT THERE IS ONE MYSTERY
THAT REMAINS... UNKNOWN! A NEW GRAPHIC NOVEL FROM WRITER MARK WAID
WITH ART BY INTERNATIONAL SUPERSTAR MINCK OOSTERVEER.

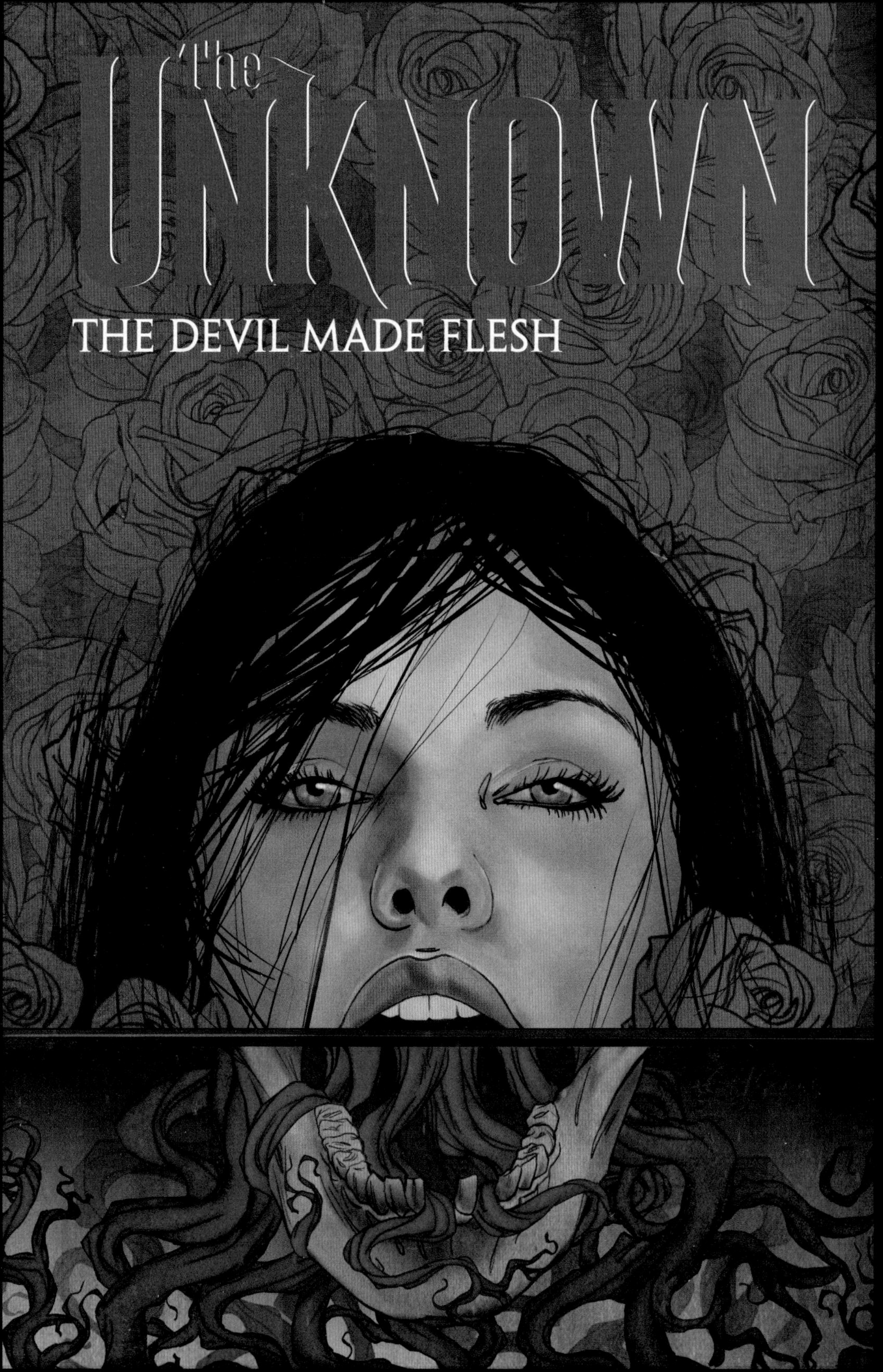
The
UNKNOWN
THE DEVIL MADE FLESH

THE UNKOWN: THE DEVIL MADE FLESH

THE SAGA CONTINUES! CATHERINE ALLINGHAM IS THE WORLD'S MOST FAMOUS PRIVATE INVESTIGATOR. FOLLOW HER ADVENTURES AS SHE SETS OUT TO SOLVE THE ONE MYSTERY SHE'S NEVER BEEN ABLE TO CRACK — DEATH!